SOCIAL
WELFARE
POLICY

SOCIAL WELFARE POLICY

Analysis and Formulation

Charles S. Prigmore

Charles R. Atherton

University of Alabama

D. C. HEATH AND COMPANY

Lexington, Massachusetts   Toronto

For Shirley and Zoe

Photo Credits
page 3   Paul S. Conklin
page 23   Ginger Chih
page 41   Sybil Shelton/Monkmeyer Press
page 63   Paula Rhodes/The Picture Cube
page 89   Bobbi Carrey/The Picture Cube
page 115 Paul S. Conklin
page 143 Marion Bernstein
page 165 Marion Bernstein
page 191 Paul S. Conklin
page 207 Marion Bernstein
page 221 Peter Southwick/Stock, Boston
page 241 Sam Sweezy

Published simultaneously in Canada.

Printed in the United States of America.

International Standard Book Number: 0-669-01425-7

Library of Congress Catalog Card Number: 78-57165

Preface

Our central task in *Social Welfare Policy* is the presentation of a rational set of criteria to guide social welfare policy analysis and formulation. It is our belief that social workers can and should be more involved in the policy process. Therefore, we have tried to provide an approach that will assist both instructor and student (as well as the general social work reader) in building a base for the analysis and formulation of alternatives to present social policies.

This text is intended for use in undergraduate and graduate courses in social welfare policy analysis. It is assumed that the student has some knowledge of the history and philosophy of social welfare. We have deliberately taken some controversial positions. In some chapters, our position may sound quite radical; in others it is more conservative. The purpose of this is not to develop a "party line," but to offer the student and instructor a place to start in their own interactions. It is not important that the reader agree with our stand. It is our belief that we will have succeeded if the reader is provoked into thinking through his or her own position. This we find to be a sound educational approach.

The first three chapters lay the groundwork. In these chapters we explain our own viewpoint toward the importance of social welfare policy, discuss the relationship of social and professional values to policy analysis and formulation, and present our approach to policy analysis. The next five chapters look at specific policy areas: income maintenance, poverty, health and mental health care, housing and neighborhood living space, and the general problems of service delivery. We analyze the current policies that guide programs in these areas and suggest alternative policies for discussion. The last three chapters introduce the student to social action, social planning, and administration. These chapters are intended to act as a bridge from social welfare policy analysis and formulation to the implementation of policy. Each chapter is only a primer, since these are complex subjects. We assume that students in schools of social work will take courses in these subjects later in their professional curriculum. Readers who are not in formal educational settings may find these chapters useful as a general road map that will suggest directions for independent study.

Each chapter has a set of questions for discussion. While some of the questions are aimed at reviewing and focusing material from the chapter, many of them lead beyond the material in the book. We think that the questions will give leads for term paper topics, panel discussions, or debates. In addition to the questions, projects are suggested at the end of each chapter that can be used to enrich and extend the student's knowledge. No instructor will want to assign all the projects, but it should be possible to select one or two from each chapter that will supplement the student's classroom experience. There is an annotated bibliography with each chapter with readings that amplify and extend the points made in the chapter and which we think will be useful additions to the instructor's reading list.

In short, we think of the book as an outline. The questions, projects, and readings are intended to be of assistance to the instructor in guiding the student through the rich and sometimes confusing content in the welfare policy field.

We are indebted to Len Altamura, Jerry Griffin, Richard Crow, and Charles Odewahn for their contributions to this volume. Chapter 6 was written by Len Altamura; Chapter 10 by Jerry Griffin; and Chapter 11 was a joint effort by Richard Crow and Charles Odewahn.

C.S.P.

C.R.A.

Contents

PART II
Challenges to Policy Analysis and Formulation: Five Examples **61**

Introduction

Social welfare policy is an exciting and complex subject. Unfortunately, some students and some educators are less interested in policy than they ought to be. For them, direct service is more immediate in its challenges because results can be more quickly seen. Policy seems ethereal and remote. Some of our own students have argued that there is little that they can do to affect policy decisions unless and until they reach positions of influence. They have argued that most policy decisions are reached in the state capitol or in Washington, rather than on the firing line. We argue that policy is influenced at all levels.

First of all, while final policy decisions are made by legislators, administrators, or judges, they are not made arbitrarily. Decision makers are political animals. Because the decision maker wants to go on making decisions, he or she must be sensitive to influence. While social workers are not the most powerful influence group in the world, they can affect some policy some of the time through joint action with other interest groups. In the past, social workers have, in fact, participated in successful policy changes with respect to children's programs, the handicapped, and the mentally ill. While social workers do not win every battle, they have made important contributions to social welfare policy decisions.

Second, not all policy is made in the capitols. Most agencies make some allowance for input from line personnel in the decision-making process. In the agencies that we know most about, staff serve on task forces and committees that have something to say about what the agency does. While other decision makers may set ground rules governing the structure and services of a given agency, much of the actual operative patterns and service delivery elements will be worked out within the agency. Therefore, line social workers can influence how the agency will actually operate.

Third, the direct service social worker is, in a sense, in the most important of policy positions. He or she is the one who has direct contact with the clientele. Whether or not clients get services and the kind of services they actually get are both determined by the social worker's application of agency policy. In effect, what the social worker does is the real policy of the agency. Social workers, then, can and do affect social welfare policy. They can do more.

Certainly more help is needed by policy decision makers, for the policy arena is a confusing place. Ten years ago the late Richard Titmuss pointed out that "concepts and models of social policy are as diverse as contemporary concepts of poverty." Little has happened to alter the truth of his remark. There is still no dominant picture or model of what "good" social welfare policy ought to look like. There remain a number of conflicting value positions. Early consensus is unlikely.

Many important needs continue to go unmet, and the country's efforts continue to be misshapen and fragmented. Clearly, time is being lost in the constant war that must be fought against poverty, injustice, and the meaninglessness that characterizes so much of so many people's lives.

Why has policy development been so fragmentary and confused? Ronald Dear has leveled three criticisms at the process of policy development in the United States.* First, the United States has waited too long to recognize problems or has made no response at all. The United States was the last industrial nation to develop a social security program. We still have no coherent population policy. Second, when policies have been formed and implemented, they are often in conflict with each other. Third, in the United States, welfare policy makers tend to oversimplify complex problems and look for simplistic solutions.

Beyond these problems, there are others. Proposals are often suggested without regard to political feasibility. When Senator George McGovern embraced the proposal of a guaranteed family income of $6,500 for a family of four during the 1972 campaign, he encountered a great deal of opposition. He wisely withdrew his proposal, but not before it had been milked dry for the benefit of his opposition.

Those who propose policy do not always relate their proposals to research findings. While it is true that research in the social sciences is seldom conclusive, it makes no sense to disregard it on those occasions when there is consistency. A good example is the research on the rehabilitation of prisoners. Some who should be knowledgeable continue to argue for the expansion of traditional treatment services despite repeated findings

* Ronald Dear, "The Current Crisis in Social Welfare," in *Social Work in Transition* (Seattle, Wash.: School of Social Work, University of Washington, 1974), pp. 24-26.

that such services are ineffective. Clearly, something has to be done about the American penal system. It is equally clear that more of the same is not the answer.

Too often decision makers have not thought enough about the criteria by which alternatives can be measured. There is a current tendency toward embracing some version of cost-benefit analysis as the sole criterion of a policy's worth. This leaves out consideration of other values.

Finally, some changes are selected for their cosmetic effect, and do not reflect any actual improvement.

Despite the difficulties in the social welfare policy field, we think that it is important for social workers to devote more of their professional energies to the policy process. We have no quick and easy solutions. The central question that we address is: How does one analyze and formulate social welfare policy? The answer that this book provides focuses on what we think has to be done when considering policy issues.

Part I
The Basis for Social Welfare Policy and an Approach to Policy Analysis and Formulation

The first three chapters lay the groundwork that we believe is necessary to an understanding of our approach to policy analysis and the formulation of alternatives. In the first chapter we present our view of the importance of social welfare in human affairs and the historical and philosophical approach upon which our approach rests. The second chapter discusses the crucial question of values and choices in social welfare policy. It is our contention that the kind of social welfare policy that a society has depends ultimately on convictions and beliefs, of which rationality and science are only two values among many.

Chapter 3 presents our outline for policy analysis. We believe that we have included in this schema the essential factors that must be considered if the social worker is to successfully analyze current policies and to suggest useful alternatives.

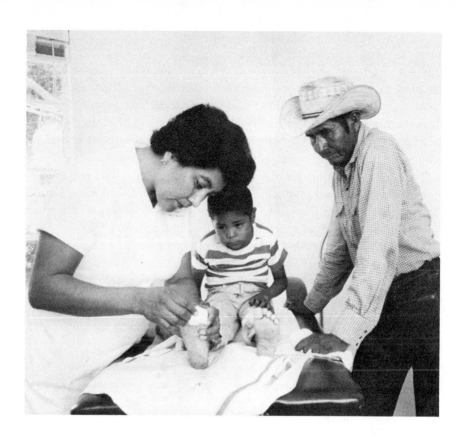

I *The Context of Social Welfare Policy Analysis*

Social welfare policy is always related to the social, political, economic, and cultural context in which it exists. To provide a background for what we have to say about analyzing and formulating social welfare policy, we will describe our understanding of that context in this chapter. We think that it will help if the reader has some idea of our philosophical outlook. The chapter will also reveal some of our biases!

To begin, let us look briefly at the status of social welfare in the modern world. Societies today are expected to provide for the delivery of a secure level of basic life supports (consumer goods, food, housing, health care, and various kinds of counseling and protective services) as benefits of membership in the society. Alfred Kahn has observed: "Social services appear everywhere in the modern world. They continue to exist and even expand as productivity increases and as average standards of living are raised. Indeed, they are seen as part of the improved standards."[1] Some societies provide a wider range of programs and services than others. There is great variation in the mix between government sponsored and privately sponsored delivery systems. While some societies' services are viewed more enthusiastically than others, virtually all societies accept the principle that society ought to provide resources against problematic social situations, economic cycles, health crises, and unfavorable living conditions.

The idea of providing social services is not a new one. The provision of supportive services and programs has its roots in a very old idea in human society—that cooperation rather than competition is necessary for group survival in the face of an uncertain and often hostile world.

The anthropologists tell us that the basic historical unit of society was the tribe or clan. The earliest people lived in a nomadic existence, surviving primarily by food gathering and hunting. Survival was possible only through cooperation. Stewart Easton, a historian, offers an important insight:

> It used to be thought that man in a state of nature was forced to compete with all other human beings for his very subsistence, or, in the famous words of Thomas Hobbes, that his life was "solitary, poor, nasty, brutish, and short." We have no record of such a way of life, either in early times, or among present-day "primitive" men. And it no longer seems as probable to us as it did in the nineteenth century, under the influence of the biological ideas of Darwin, that human survival was a matter of success in the constant struggle for existence, if this struggle is conceived of as a struggle between human beings. It now seems much more probable that survival has always been due to successful cooperation between human beings to resist the always dangerous forces of nature.[2]

Mutual aid, then, is a key characteristic of human society. Examples can be found far back in the history of human affairs.

The Functions of Social Conflict

Some years ago Lewis Coser explored the adaptive function of social conflict as a basic human process.[3] At first glance, the ideas of Coser and other conflict theorists seem to suggest that human social organization is formed and even held together through the clash of cultures and personalities. We do not think that conflict theories are necessarily out of harmony with our point of view. In the seminal work of Robert E. Park and Ernest W. Burgess, the groundwork was laid for the notion that there are four basic processes in the interaction of social groups: competition, conflict, accommodation, and assimilation. These processes form a rough continuum of the development of human social organization. Briefly, the notion is that humans begin by *competing* for scarce resources. This competition is carried on without necessarily involving social contact as in the simple example of two tribes who inhabit the same geographical space, hunting the same animals, but avoiding each other. At the point when the tribes identify each other and engage in a struggle for scarce resources, they move to a situation of *conflict*. It is possible for one tribe to survive by killing off the other. However, if this happens, it is obvious that survival comes only at the expense of the nonsurvival of another group. There are examples of this in human history, but this is not usually the case. What usually happens (and this must be true, or we would all be Huns or Mongols) is that the two tribes eventually realize that conflict is expensive, wearisome, and, in the long run, counterproductive. At this point they seek to *accommodate* to each other and begin to work out adjustments that will permit the survival of both groups. Ultimately, accommodation leads to *assimilation*.

> Accommodation has been described as a process of adjustment, that is, an organization of social relations and attitudes to prevent or to reduce conflict, to control competition, and to maintain a basis of security in the social order for persons and groups of divergent interests and types to carry on together their varied life activities. *Accommodation in the sense of the composition* (resolution) *of conflict is invariably the goal of the political process.*
>
> Assimilation is a process of interpenetration and fusion in which persons and groups acquire the memories, sentiments, and attitudes of other persons or groups, and, by sharing their experience and history, are incorporated with them in a common cultural life. *Insofar as assimilation denotes this sharing of tradition, this intimate participation in common experiences, assimilation is central in the historical and cultural processes.*[4] (Emphasis added)

Conflict, then, is an important stage in the process of the development of human society. Coser says:

> In loosely structured groups and open societies, conflict, which aims at a resolution of tension between antagonists, is likely to have stabilizing and integrative functions for the relationship. By permitting immediate and direct expression of rival claims, such social systems are able to readjust their structures by eliminating the sources of dissatisfaction. The multiple conflicts which they experience may serve to eliminate the causes for dissociation and to re-establish unity.[5]

It is important to notice that conflict is not viewed as an end in itself, but as a means of bringing about unity.

We can see vividly the working out of these social processes in two contemporary examples. There is a long history of conflict in the relationship of Israel and the Arab world. Both sides have clearly expressed rival claims. In 1977 we saw the beginnings of the accommodation process in the statesmanship of Premier Begin of Israel and President Sadat of Egypt. It is too soon to tell if the conflict phase is really over. Many Arab leaders are mistrustful and angry, and many Israelis are watchful and uncertain. However, from a sociological point of view, the meetings between Egyptian and Israeli leaders that began in 1977 contain the elements of the accommodative process. Even if accommodation is eventually reached, assimilation is still a very long distance down the road.

Parenthetically, we need to point out that assimilation does not mean the elimination of all cultural, religious, or political differences. As Park and Burgess point out, assimilation involves a sharing of tradition and an intimate participation in common experiences. This can occur as a social process without forcing people to give up important identifications and traditions.

Another example can be found in the relationship of blacks and whites in the United States. The history of conflict is a very lengthy one. Only a few years ago the National Advisory Commission on Civil Disorders went so far as to say that the country was moving toward two nations, one black and one white. Since then we have been able to see movement toward accommodation. Like the Arab-Israeli example, genuine assimilation is still far off.

Conflict, then, is an important stage in the development of human social life, but only a stage. People cannot survive in a constant state of conflict; they must either find ways of avoiding contact or move to some kind of accommodation. It is our bias that social welfare concerns must be based on something that points toward mutuality and accommodation. Survival becomes hollow if it can be achieved only at the expense of others.

To most of us "survival" may not seem to be a relevant concept. Most of us in the industrialized countries manage to do quite well. However, the ecological movement has raised our consciousness of the delicate balance of human life and the fragility of our security. We think that welfare planning must deemphasize the "we-they" kind of relationship that has characterized much of our past. Catastrophic illness, economic turmoil, emotional problems, and meaninglessness in life are not just things that "they" face. We must learn to seek mutual goals, because threats to a fulfilling life are threats to us all. We are slowly becoming aware of the interrelatedness of life on this planet. Dust from atomic explosions in the People's Republic of China falls on the United States. Our consumption of energy means that there will be less for the rest of the world. In the hard world of international relations, old fashioned "jingoism" has declined. We have learned to trade with the Russians, and we have cultural exchanges with the People's Republic of China. We have at last come to the realization that we are interrelated and failure to get along can result in a holocaust that all would prefer to avoid. Unquestionably, survival is the name of the game.

The Need for Social Welfare

Social welfare programs and services are important answers to many of the personal and social perils that threaten human life. Modern human beings need socially provided support systems—just as our ancestors needed mutual support—or life would indeed be, as Thomas Hobbes described it, "solitary, poor, nasty, brutish, and short." Religion and humanitarianism have given social welfare as we know it a distinctive coloration and shape, but the need for mutual aid and the facts of human interdependence are not limited to Western civilization. Non-Western peoples have a number of similar religious and philosophical systems that emphasize the mutuality of human needs. It is our conviction that no human society anywhere can survive for very long without some awareness of the necessity for mutual support systems. The rationales and the values may differ throughout the world but the awareness is there. It is customarily expressed through increasingly larger and more complicated public and private social welfare systems. Mutual aid in the modern world is more complex than helping to rebuild a neighbor's barn when it burns or sharing a pot of chicken soup with a sick friend, although these simple acts of kindness are still important. Before we explore this complexity, we need to define our terms.

What is social welfare?

We recognize that "social welfare" is defined in many ways and that no one definition is entirely satisfactory to everyone. We have chosen to use Friedlander and Apte's statement:

> Social welfare is a system of laws, programs, benefits and services which strengthen or assure provisions for meeting social needs recognized as basic for the welfare of the population and for the functioning of social order.[6]

We like this definition because it leaves room for the inclusion of both public and voluntary programs and services and recognizes that certain needs are basic for the welfare of people. We also like this definition because it is consistent with our belief that social welfare is an essential part of organized social life. We interpret it to mean that a society that does not recognize and plan for meeting basic needs is not really a functional society.

We recognize that there are elements of social control or, to use Talcott Parsons' phrase, "boundary maintenance" in most definitions of social welfare. We have deliberately chosen to minimize the role of social welfare as social control in this chapter, since we are arguing that welfare ought to be based on mutual needs. This bias in favor of seeing welfare as mutuality-

based will become apparent in later chapters when we criticize work requirements and needs tests.

What is social welfare policy?

We are going to use a very simple definition: Social welfare policy is a
generic term for the guidelines used for decision-making on social welfare
programs and issues. This is a simplification of Kahn's position:

> a policy is a "standing plan," a "guide to future decision making," or a "con-
> tinuing line of decisions. . . ." It is the implicit or explicit core of principle
> that underlies specific programs, legislation, priorities.[7]

Kahn emphasizes the idea that social welfare policy has to do with the
principles on which specific social welfare programs and service delivery
systems are based over time. Good (in the sense of effective and appropriate) social welfare policy is not just a knee-jerk response to a problem, but
a reasonably well thought out long-range plan. There is a subtle warning in
Kahn's definition. He notes that policies may be implicit. A good part of
accurate policy analysis, as we shall see in Chapter 3, depends upon one's
ability to recognize implicit factors and make them explicit.

In this book we will limit our discussion to "social welfare policy" in order to focus on our major concerns. Other policies, such as economic policy
or population policy, are also social policies, but we will not discuss examples from these fields. We do think, however, that our approach could
be used with other social policies.

We also need to point out that we have tried to avoid confusing social
welfare policy as a generic thing with any specific viewpoint. Richard Titmuss seems to have used the term "social policy" as synonymous with economic redistribution. Actually, in a given nation, social welfare policy
might very well be quite conservative and not at all the same thing as
redistribution. The mixing of policy-as-a-thing and policy-as-a-specific-
meaning is confusing.

Just as we have avoided relating our use of "social welfare policy" with
any political coloring, we also do not identify one set of values that is permanently related to social welfare. What we do want to share with the
reader is an approach that we think will help practicing social workers to
find answers that will be of use as they are needed.

It is important to repeat that social welfare policy (or any other type
of social policy for that matter) is formed in a context. To forget that there
are connections between social welfare concerns and the rest of the social
system is disastrous. Quite often it seems as if those who are interested in
social welfare set priorities for action as if there were no other interests to be

considered. This naiveté is surely related to the failure of many humane proposals.

Accordingly, as we discuss the context in which to think about social welfare policy, we will be interested in a number of elements that bear on the decision-making process.

Social Welfare and Humanitarianism

But is it all this complicated? Isn't it enough to recognize that social welfare is based on humanitarian concerns? Is not social welfare policy merely a matter of making decisions on the basis of what is right and humane? Let us examine the case for humanitarian philosophy (putting to one side the problem that we may not all agree on what is right and humane) as the only important variable.

It can be argued that the appearance of social services everywhere is indicative of a growing sense of the love of humanity. Certainly, social welfare and social work have deep roots in religion and humanitarianism. The structures that we have today have been described as the institutionalization of the philanthropic impulse and love of mankind:

> Social work as an identifiable profession had its point of origin in the final decade of the nineteenth century. The feeling of charity toward one's fellow man and actions based on that feeling, however, had their origins in antiquity. The philanthropic impulse, the love of mankind that is manifested in beneficent deeds has, it appears, always been a part of human nature—an essential ingredient of the mixture of emotions and beliefs that makes man human. As the motivation has persisted in human nature, so has the movement toward institutionalization, that is, the organizing of formal structures or agencies and laws designed to regulate social behavior, has taken place as social relationships have increased in complexity. The performance of charitable acts has been carried out under the aegis of voluntary and governmental organizations throughout history; the need for giving help and the acceptance of responsibility to do so has been a constant in human society.[8]

In many cases welfare programs and services have come about because of people's compassion. Much about social welfare reflects genuine unselfishness. Using the charitable impulse as the *sole* basis for social welfare, however, leads in the direction of trusting to human nature to do charitable acts. But even social welfare must be pragmatic. Consider these words of Orville Brim in his presidential address to the American Orthopsychiatric Association:

> How much more than the price of a lunch will it cost society over the long term in lost productivity, and in the need for institutionalization, of children

damaged by nutritional deficiencies? This is a cold-blooded way to make the case for the care of children in our society, but I say again that the competition for goods and services in the American economy is economic and political, and we can no longer rely solely on good will and individual acts of charity and kindness to provide for children in this country.[9]

We share Brim's cynicism to a degree. Over the years it has not been enough to appeal to legislatures, public administrators, contributors, and taxpayers to provide social welfare programs and services out of humane motives. It is often necessary to resort to lawsuits, political pressure, and citizen action to compel society to live up to "the feeling of charity." Therefore, we think the case for social welfare rests on more than the philanthropic impulse, although that may be an important value in certain parts of the world. However, social welfare provisions exist in places where Western philanthropy is not a prominent part of the cultural tradition, e.g., the People's Republic of China and Japan.

The Shift from Informal to Formal Welfare Systems

In the pages ahead we will argue that social welfare institutions as we now know them have deeper historical roots that we ordinarily think about. A crucial question was raised some years ago by Wilensky and Lebeaux. The problem that they were addressing was whether social welfare was a matter of giving aid to people in emergency situations or providing services as a normal, ordinary function of society. They put it this way:

> Two conceptions of social welfare seem to be dominant in the United States today; the *residual* and the *institutional*. The first holds that social welfare institutions should come into play only when the normal structures of supply, the family and the market, break down. The second, in contrast, sees the welfare services as normal, "first line" functions of modern industrial society.[10]

We think that Wilensky and Lebeaux may have missed an important point. They looked at the formation of *formal organizations* as the beginning of social welfare. Since most agencies as we know them had their start in industrial times, it may seem logical to assume that social welfare as an institution had its beginnings at that time. It is true that orphanages, poorhouses, and hospitals are products of industrialized societies. But an institution (in the sociological sense of the word) is more than a formal organization. As defined by Arnold Rose, an institution is "a number of culturally defined and evaluated behavior patterns, closely related to each other logically and culturally, which are transmitted continuously to individuals who come into an expected social role for what the institution is relevant." [11]

If an institution is a set of behavior patterns, then welfare as an institution existed long before the orphanages, poorhouses, and hospitals. What seems to have happened is that functions which had been lodged (institutionalized) in the family, clan, or tribe gradually shifted into organizations outside the family as the nature of society changed during industrialization. If the institutional view (as Wilensky and Lebeaux define it) is that social welfare should be thought of as a pattern of behaviors which continues over time, then social welfare as an institution has been around for a long time. What is different is that during the Industrial Revolution the *structure* in which welfare programs and services was nested changed, but the *function* had been institutionalized all along.

Consider the example of the mentally ill. Nonindustrial societies all have an institutionalized (patterned) way of dealing with those whose behavior is different. Some societies have a very harsh policy (which, like it or not, is still an institutionalized "service"), but there are other societies that venerate the mentally ill and create special roles for them. If the society industrializes, these special roles tend to disappear. The mentally ill are left without supports. They wander about to live as best they can. At some point, these people become an annoying problem that must be dealt with. The first solutions (some of our early mental hospitals, for example) were hardly better than a policy of killing them off. These services, crude as they were, were clearly residual. They were used when normal (traditional) structures failed. Over time, because the problem of the mentally ill remains with us, more effective and efficient solutions are generated. These more sophisticated solutions may be devised because they are more humane, or because the state has a moral obligation to its citizens, or simply because people are too valuable to allow to go to waste. Whatever the motive behind the policy, the new provision for the mentally ill becomes institutionalized very quickly and becomes a "first line function" to which people turn because of its sophistication.

It was Wilensky and Lebeaux' belief that, as industrialization continued, the institutional view would prevail over the residual. Our analysis leads us to concur. We think that the institutional approach is historically the one that prevailed (in a different format, of course) prior to industrialization. Now that industrialization has advanced to the point it has, we think that welfare has *returned* to its institutional status—even though there are changes due to specialization, bureaucratization, and the urban character of modern society. To put it as simply as we can, it could be said that humans ordinarily recognize their interdependence, lose sight of it during the transitional period to an industrial society, and regain it when industrialization has taken hold. Therefore, after a brief (as history goes) hiatus of two hundred or so years, we humans in the Western world seem to be regaining an understanding of the need to reach out to each other and to find ways to be supportive in a very fragile world.

A Brief History of Mutual Aid

We will trace the idea of mutual aid in Western society in order to point out that a concern for human welfare was a part (in some degree) of the historical and cultural situation and cannot be understood apart from that situation.

When early humans discovered the use of tools, it enabled them to have alternatives to hunting and food gathering. Eventually society took on a more formal and geographically permanent structure:

> At the next stage of development, called the Neolithic Revolution, man ceased to be totally dependent upon nature and began in some degree to control it. He learned to breed and to tend animals, so that they were always available to him for food when he needed them, and he taught them to work for him and supplement his own labor. He learned to plant crops and harvest them, laying down seeds in some spot cleared for the purpose and in which such plants did not grow by nature. He learned to build himself a home where none had been provided by nature, and he even discovered how to grow special crops such as flax from which he could make himself clothing.[12]

Generally, the core institution in this early agricultural society was the extended family. Planned cultivation, which replaced food gathering, allowed the family to provide its members with more goods and services as well as relatively consistent social statuses and roles. Human beings could stay in one place long enough to begin to develop a more complex culture than was possible before. One was protected from the hazards of the old life (as well as could be, given the state of technology) by the resources of the family. Villages and tribes composed of several families could now acquire a more or less permanent home and a distinctive social shape. Unemployment was not a societal or personal problem except for those who had no family. Those without a family as a resource usually turned to begging or stealing. A member of an extended family had certain welfarelike provisions as a right. When a person was ill, the family provided care. Children whose parents died would be cared for by another relative as a matter of course. There was no need for a formally organized welfare system for most members of this kind of society. The informal system worked for most of the people most of the time.

A clear example of this built-in mutual aid provision can be seen in Scottish Highland society. The clans of Scotland are largely ceremonial today, but historically the Highlanders were held together by common bonds of kinship and territoriality. Tribal organizations in other cultures may have had a farming or fishing base, but the Scots' society was organized around fighting. As a consequence of the felt need to wage frequent war, the clans were mutual aid societies. In theory at least, no clan member starved so long as the chief had resources in land or food. Work, either in the form of maintenance of the land or as warfare, was available. There were risks of disease and risks of injury, but one was protected against them as far as resources allowed. The clans protected their members because it was necessary for survival. The chief, of course, was an autocrat, hence his or her protection was paternalistic.[13] But each member of the clan was important, a member of an "honorable community," and could claim clan support as a right.

While other tribal organizations differed from that of the Highland clan, they shared the principle of mutual aid. Support from one's society or clan as a matter of right was supplemented by the actions of organized religion up through the end of the Roman Empire. It is important to repeat that receiving assistance from one's extended family was a right firmly enmeshed in the web of custom. It was a first line function of the tribe, clan, or community and not just a residual service offered when one's family felt like it. This firmly institutionalized system of mutual aid worked well enough through the Middle Ages until the beginnings of industrialization. It continues to work to some extent today in rural communities and among closely knit ethnic groups.

Welfare and the Medieval World

With the decline of Rome, a great source of unity and universality disappeared from the Western world. Without the empire, life was much more uncertain. Roads, the major means of travel and communication, were no longer safe. People became much more localized, and as a result new economic and political systems evolved that were appropriate for the day.

"Feudalism" is properly used to describe the political system of the Middle Ages. Theoretically, in feudalism the king dispensed land to the aristocracy in return for loyalty. In actuality, no neat arrangement was possible. No medieval king, not even the first in a given location, was ever in a position to parcel out the entire land to his followers. Medieval kings had to depend on their own personal family land and retainers for power and wealth, and none could enforce their will much beyond the immediate area that they controlled. In reality, each small landholding was a kingdom unto itself.

The economic system that supported feudalism is usually referred to as "manorialism." Each aristocratic lord held a piece of land "in fief" from the king. These lands ranged from a few acres to great estates of thousands of acres. The poor knight on a few acres was barely able to make enough to pay for a horse and armor. The rich lord might have a fairly large retinue of relatives on horses and a group of foot soldiers. Peasants worked the land. The peasant was not a slave but rather like a sharecropper—except that he could not leave the land but had to stay on it and till it. The typical manor also had a mill, a blacksmith shop, and a church. The manor was, for all practical purposes, a self-supporting economic unit.

Medieval men and women had certain rights under this system. The peasant was not permitted to leave the land, but he could not be made to leave it either. He had a right to a certain amount of land for his own use. If he died, his widow and children had certain rights. These rights were among the few feudal laws that were observed to some degree throughout Europe. Although there were some notably bad masters, most were reasonably faithful to their obligations.

Descriptions of the medieval peasant's life indicate that the peasant led a filthy, almost animal-like existence, but the master was not much better off. Most concepts of the medieval noble are romanticized, as in the tales of Sir Walter Scott, and do not show how little social distance there was between master and serf. Knight and peasant drank out of the same well, and the fever killed them both with great equality. Privileges were somewhat unequal, of course, but at least those "below the salt" had a secure place at the table that was generally acknowledged to be legally enforceable.

Town life was different from that of the manor. Here freemen, merchants, and craftsmen worked out their own unique social system. Most relevant to our discussion were the welfarelike arrangements made by the gilds for their members. The gilds were associations of skilled craftsmen. As independent entrepreneurs, the craftsmen regulated the market by setting wages and prices. They also regulated entry into the trades. Each gild had a kind of social insurance scheme that provided for members unable to work and for the families of deceased members. These benefits were limited to gild members and were far from universal, but they represent an attempt to provide a basic kind of economic and social protection against economic insecurity on a mutual aid basis.

The Role of Religion and Philanthropy

What has been described so far represents only a rough attempt at social justice. Early humans aided and protected each other because they had to in order to survive in a hostile environment. In the medieval period, the rights of the peasantry were protected only up to a point. This protection was only a minimal kind of guarantee of resources and little in the way of anything that would be recognized as a social service. The gilds did provide some resources for their members, but they had nothing to do with the urban poor or the small tradesmen.

Large numbers of people were not part of a network in which they could benefit from a system of mutual aid. The treatment of the emotionally ill, the care of children who had no close family, and the survival of large numbers of people who had no secure place in the system was uncertain. It was the existence of these large numbers of "outsiders" that prompted the social consciousness of organized religion to respond with humanitarian programs and services.

Others have traced the history of the contribution of organized religion and philanthropic societies. For our purposes it is important to see how these contributions relate to the development of the concept of social welfare as a social necessity. It was religion that gave social welfare its humanitarian flavor in the Western world.

The Jews have a long tradition of concern for the poor and homeless. The Christian church developed a similar concern, although hampered at times by a certain moralistic puritanism.

> Among the peoples of antiquity, the Jews made the care of dependent children a special duty under the law. Their practice of placing orphans in selected family homes was carried over into the early Christian Church where the necessity to care for many children made dependent by the persecutions of emperors led the Church to begin boarding children with "worthy widows," paying for a child's care by collections taken in the various congregations.[14]

For centuries, this concern was somewhat parochial. The church took care of its own. It is important to note that the development of human services on a large scale for those outside one's own religious group did not come about until the Industrial Revolution forcibly brought to public attention the enormity of the problems faced by many human beings. As problematic situations became visible, both Judaism and Christianity broadened their concerns and provided (and still provide) many needed direct services to the community in general. Religion and its secular cousin humanitarianism responded to the needs directly but also acted as a motivating force for governments to provide for the social welfare. It is our contention that religion was forced to recognize the social implications of its theology by the tremendous needs that were growing apparent as the character of social life changed. The obligation of mutual aid for all humanity was always there as a theological imperative. It was not acted upon beyond one's own group until the societal needs became compelling. Let us examine the impact of industrialization with this in mind.

The Modern World

It is not accurate to describe the medieval era as the "Dark Ages." Learning, trade, and manufacture continued to advance in this period. The only thing needed for development was better communication between social units. This difficulty was overcome when the Italian merchant princes swept the pirates from the Mediterranean and reopened trade routes that had been closed for years. The reopening of international trade unleashed, ultimately, several forces that transformed the Western world. One area changed was the nature of social welfare.

As trade and manufacturing increased, a merchant class gained ascendancy over the traditional nobility. The bankers, merchants, traders, and manufacturers challenged the traditions of aristocratic society, and eventually this challenge brought about a revolution in life that eclipsed the changes of the neolithic revolution. Increased trading opportunities brought about an increase in demand. This increase in demand prompted the invention of machinery. Machinery meant factories and the general transfer of population from rural areas to urban centers.

The rising middle class's attack on the landed aristocracy involved more than the transformation of the economy from an agricultural to a manufacturing base. Business does better in a politically stable climate. The middle class initially tended to support strong kings, and the kings therefore tended to favor the middle class. The cooperation between kings and merchants involved no political magic. They were simply two parties whose ambitions happened to coincide. Kings expanded their power to national boundaries, pacifying the countryside as their influence increased. Business people responded by willingly paying taxes to the central authority. The trade routes became safe and secure. The monarchies became far more stable than they had ever been in the medieval era. True, kings still were deposed and assassinated on occasion, but the institution of strong central monarchy, and later a strong central legislature, came about because it was good for business.

An important factor involved in the rise of the middle class was the development of liberalism as a political philosophy. It must be emphasized that eighteenth- and nineteenth-century liberalism is not the same thing as contemporary liberalism.

Liberalism has always been hard to pin down in any version. This is not the place to try to offer a comprehensive definition. However, there are certain common elements in Classical Liberalism that are important for this discussion. Basically, Classical Liberals believed firmly in the rights of the individual, the protection of private property, representative government, a free press, and laissez-faire economics.[15]

The Classical Liberal's belief in "individual rights" is not the same thing as today's call for social justice. To the Classical Liberal, "freedom" meant "freedom for the middle class" as opposed to privileges for the aristocracy. The middle class wanted representation in constitutional assemblies as opposed to the concentration of power in the nobility. The call for a free press meant a press that could be owned by the merchant class free from interference by the aristocracy. The economic notions of the free market and the desire to have national protection for property have to be seen as a desire to be free in business affairs instead of participating in a governmentally controlled economy.

In short, the industrial middle class was no more democratic than were the aristocrats. In place of an absolute monarch, they eventually substituted themselves as the source of decision-making, when they had used the monarch as far as they could. For the traditional support of the medieval world, the middle class substituted the vagaries of the free market and the factory system. We would argue that with the rise of Classical Liberalism the sense of mutuality diminished, individualism was untempered by a sense of community, and welfare became charitable instead of a matter of mutual aid. Charity has tended to deteriorate into self-righteousness, creating a gulf between "us" and "them."

The Factory System

The industrial world was a wholly different situation when compared with its predecessor. The basis of European life in the Middle Ages had been agriculture, and the relative abundance of low-cost labor (except during exceptional times of war and famine) may have retarded the development of machinery. The manufacturing that was done usually took place in the home or in small "cottage" industries. However, as demands for goods increased due to trading opportunities, there was a concurrent demand for new machines and procedures that would increase production. The new means of production were more efficient than hand labor and more profitable because of the high volume of goods that could be produced.

There has been much historical disagreement about the effects of industrialism. Wilensky and Lebeaux have reviewed the arguments.[16] They conclude that industrialism and its cousins, urbanism and bureaucratization, are not as intrinsically evil as some writers at the turn of the century believed. In a book written in 1925, M. Dorothy George, after a careful review of historical records, made the same point for industrial London in the late eighteenth century:

> London had become healthier; the dangers and uncertainties of life had been lessened, partly by a change of manners, greater cleanliness, less drinking, partly by a better police and by the reform of some gross abuses in poor law administration. Crimes of violence were fewer and different in kind, and

there have been a great reduction in the number of prisoners for debt. The traditional violence and brutality of the London populace was gradually diminishing. At the end of the Century it is no longer a subject of comment by foreign visitors.[17]

While most contemporary writers no longer consider industrialism and urbanism as automatic evils, no one denies that they have had an effect on human behavior and social organization. Rosalind Mitchison, in a highly readable history of Scotland, notes that

> the movement of the population and the big scale of the towns broke the bonds that hold a man into society, his local community, the widespread kinship, the religious congregation, even the band of regulars at an alehouse, and it was only slowly that these would be reformed.[18]

It is probably true, then, that when industry moves from the cottage to the factory, from generalization and specialization, from country to city, something happens to make human life different for at least a transitional period. The old Highland clan became ceremonial at the point where it was no longer practiced as a system geared to survival. When the jobs were no longer available in local warfare and the care of the chief's land, the character of traditional life simply had to change.

This effect is not limited to past history. Modern emerging nations in Africa, for example, are going through some of the transitory dislocations of industrialization and urbanism. Traditional tribal relationships have broken down to the extent that it has been necessary in the last few years to organize a child welfare service in Nigeria, for example, to contend with the problems of homeless urban children. It is possible that the dislocations are temporary and limited in their effect. However, one could expect that services will continue in new forms appropriate to industrial and postindustrial societies if these nations continue to develop modern institutions.

The United States and Mutual Aid

The case can be made that the United States is moving toward the practical realization of the provision of welfare programs and services on the basis of mutual aid. Ronald Dear points out that

> an ever-increasing share of our GNP is devoted to public social welfare. Less than 3% was spent by government for all types of welfare in 1890, today over 17% is spent for public social welfare. This rate of increase is accelerating each year until now one dollar in four is funnelled into public and private welfare. Examination of such data tells us something about the values and priorities of our country. We also get the notion that social welfare is the principal job of government and that welfare is the biggest of big business.[19]

On the other hand, Dear goes on to say that despite the vast sums of money devoted to social welfare and social problems, such as poverty, hunger, lack of quality education, and inadequate medical resources and services, conditions continue to get worse.

So, while there is movement, there are signs that we have not yet arrived at a genuine realization that our earliest ancestors recognized easily—that social welfare is not simply a matter of humane concern and charity, but a matter of *necessity* because of human interdependence. In modern societies, we cannot do without welfare services any more than we could do without fire or police services. Welfare reform continues to be a popular topic, but no one seriously suggests that social welfare be discontinued. The crucial question, then, is not whether or not there should be some kind of welfare system. The question that is really before us is, What should the welfare enterprise do and how should these tasks be done? The answer to this question can only be given by persons who can analyze and formulate constructive social policy. We have to make the best choices that we can. The choices that we make are obviously dependent upon the values and knowledge that we use as the basis for decision-making. We shall look more closely at the role of values in social welfare policy in the next chapter.

REFERENCES

1. Alfred J. Kahn, *Social Policy and Social Services* (New York: Random House, 1973), p. 14.
2. Stewart C. Easton, *The Heritage of the Past* (New York: Holt, Rinehart and Winston, 1964), p. 4.
3. Lewis A. Coser, *The Functions of Social Conflict* (Glencoe, Ill.: The Free Press of Glencoe, 1956).
4. Robert E. Park and Ernest W. Burgess, *Introduction to the Science of Sociology*, 2nd ed. (Chicago: The University of Chicago Press, 1924), pp. 735–736.
5. Coser, *op. cit.*, p. 154.
6. Walter A. Friedlander and Robert Z. Apte, *Introduction to Social Welfare* (Englewood Cliffs, N.J.: Prentice-Hall, 1974), p. 4.
7. Kahn, *op. cit.*, p. 69.
8. Russell E. Smith and Dorothy Zietz, *American Social Welfare Institutions* (New York: John Wiley, 1974), p. 3.
9. Orville G. Brim, Jr., "Macro-Structural Influences on Child Development and the Need for Childhood Social Indicators," *American Journal of Orthopsychiatry*, Vol. 45, No. 4 (July 1975), pp. 518–519.
10. Harold L. Wilensky and Charles N. Lebeaux, *Industrial Society and Social Welfare* (New York: The Free Press, 1965), p. 138.

11. Arnold Rose, *Sociology* (New York: Alfred A. Knopf, 1965), p. 727.

12. Easton, *op. cit.*, p. 3.

13. Chiefs were often women, since it was the general rule for land and leadership to descend to the oldest child, not just to the oldest male. Some clans were exceptions, but most followed this practice. If a man married a chief who was a woman, he took her family name (if she intended to retain the chiefship) and became a member of her family. Historically, a woman who was chief performed the same duties as a man even to active participation in warfare including command in the field. See, Sir Thomas Innes of Learney, Lord Lyon King of Arms, *The Tartans of the Clans and Families of Scotland*, 6th ed (Edinburgh: W. & A. K. Johnson and G. W. Bacon, Ltd.), 1958.

14. Lela B. Costin, *Child Welfare: Policies and Practice* (New York: McGraw-Hill, 1972), p. 323.

15. For one of the most durable and provocative treatments of the rise and change of liberalism, see Harry K. Girvetz, *The Evolution of Liberalism* (New York: Collier Books, 1963).

16. Wilensky and Lebeaux, *op. cit.*, Chs. 3, 4, and 5, pp. 49–133.

17. Dorothy George, *London Life in the Eighteenth Century* (New York: Harper & Row, A Harper Torchbook, 1964), p. 3.

18. Rosalind Mitchison, *A History of Scotland* (London: Methuen and Company, 1970), p. 381.

19. Ronald B. Dear, "The Current Crisis in Social Welfare," in *Social Work in Transition* (Seattle: The School of Social Work, University of Washington, October 1974), p. 16.

QUESTIONS FOR DISCUSSION

1. Critically examine the viewpoint taken toward social welfare in this chapter. What would you add or subtract from the concept that is used?

2. Take the position that social welfare services and programs are optional and should rightly depend only on the level of goodwill in society. What kind of services would you see growing out of this position and what kind of policies do you think that they would follow?

3. This chapter argues that formal social welfare programs and services are products of forces that exist only in modern industrial societies. Why do the authors think this is so? Why could not, for example, the ancient Babylonian empire have the same kind of social welfare programs and services that we have today?

4. What would be the difference in social welfare policy if a given program was defined as "residual" as opposed to "institutional"?

5. Discuss the limits of social welfare. What areas should be included? What should be left in the hands of other types of public policy?

6. The authors take the position that social welfare is a necessary institution in modern industrial societies. Evaluate that argument. Isn't voluntary humanism enough?

7. The authors argue that mutual aid is a functional necessity for individuals and their society. Why couldn't a society simply be organized to operate solely on behalf of the powerful without regard for justice? Certainly some societies in the past have seemed to be organized on just that principle. Why would the authors think that this would no longer be a possible way to organize a society?

8. Do you agree with the authors' statement that there was relatively little social distance between master and serf in the Middle Ages? Is there a greater social distance today between social classes in the United States? If so, what implications does this have for social welfare policy?

9. What difficulties do you see in considering social welfare policy as an equal partner to social work treatment? Has there been any movement in this direction in your opinion?

SUGGESTED PROJECTS

1. Describe in a short paper a present-day example of mutual aid in action. How do the mutual aid provisions operate to enable the members of the group or neighborhood to get on with satisfactory living?

2. As an exercise, study some previous period of European or American history. Select a problem area. Given the constraints that exist at the time you have selected, try your hand at devising a social welfare policy that you think may have worked better than the one apparently followed. Keep your example simple and your policy solution as neat as is possible. Share your proposal with the class and discuss the adequacy of your policy.

FOR FURTHER READING

Edward P. Cheyney. *The Dawn of a New Era.* New York: Harper & Row, A Harper Torchbook, 1962. First volume of the "Rise of Modern Europe" series. Excellent general survey of the transition from the medieval world to the modern era.

Nathan E. Cohen. *Social Work in the American Tradition.* New York: The Dryden Press, 1958. Traces social work and social welfare in the framework of humanitarianism and American democracy. Cohen relates the development of social work and social welfare to important social, economic, and political developments in U.S. history. Unfortunately, the book ends with the Eisenhower years and has never been revised, but it is still well worth reading.

Stewart C. Easton. *The Heritage of the Past*, 2nd ed. New York: Holt, Rinehart and Winston, 1964. A most readable and scholarly general world history Goes from prehistory to the beginning of the modern world. Outstanding for his insights into the development of social, economic, and political factors in history. A real joy to read.

Harry K. Girvetz. *The Evolution of Liberalism*. New York: Collier Books, 1963. An extremely scholarly, yet provocative view of the development of liberalism as political and social thought.

Roy Lubove. *The Professional Altruist*. Cambridge, Mass.: Harvard University Press, 1965. A highly readable and detailed history of the emergence of social work as a profession. Discusses the emergence of specialization, the occupational subculture, and the bureaucratization of volunteerism as social work moved from "cause to function."

Harold L. Wilensky and Charles N. Lebeaux. *Industrial Society and Social Welfare*. New York: The Free Press, 1965. An extremely influential book outlining the relation of the development of social welfare programs and services to industrialism. The paperback edition contains Wilensky's views on the prospects for the welfare state. Some aspects of the book are dated, but it is still worth reading for its analytical merit.

2 *Values and Choices in Contemporary Social Welfare Policy*

In this chapter we will discuss some beliefs that affect social welfare policy decisions in the United States. Decision-making of any kind is ultimately a matter of choosing among various alternatives. The choice hinges upon a person's *values*. A value, as defined by Milton Rokeach, is "an enduring belief that a specific mode of conduct or end-state of existence is personally or socially preferable to an opposite or converse mode of conduct or end state of existence." [1] These "enduring beliefs" about the preferability of certain means or ends over others are the bases for deciding whether a given alternative is "good" or "bad."

One theorist, Gil, makes the point that choices in social welfare policy are heavily influenced by the dominant beliefs, values, ideologies, customs, and traditions of the "cultural and political elites recruited mainly from among the more powerful and privileged strata."[2] Although the social welfare planner may be operating from a more liberated position than that of the powerful and privileged, he or she must be aware of the durability and influence of some major traditional values. The social welfare policy maker needs to recognize that a number of these values conflict with others. Some will be easy to share with the culture whereas others will act as constraints on policy formulation and implementation.

The Relationship of Values and Knowledge

Many social workers who have shared their opinions with us believe that we have overemphasized the role of values and suggest that knowledge is an equally important input to policy choices. Pincus and Minahan discuss the relationship of values and knowledge to social work practice. By implication, the same distinction applies to social welfare policy. They define values as "beliefs, preferences, or assumptions about what is desirable or good for man."[3] Knowledge consists of "observations about the world and man which have been verified or are capable of verification."[4]

The problem is that the policy formulation process is not as rational as one would like. Knowledge is itself a value, after all, based on a set of beliefs about what constitutes truth. Readers with a background in philosophy will recognize that Pincus and Minahan's distinction between values and knowledge only holds so long as one is an empiricist, and that empiricism is only one way of looking at truth.

There are others who take a cynical view of rationality in decision-making:

> Those who look to evaluation to take the politics out of decision making are bound to be disappointed. Within every organization, decisions are reached through negotiation and accommodation, through politics. . . . Evaluative facts have an impact on collective decisions only to the extent that program effectiveness—inevitably and justifiably—competes for influence on decisions with considerations of acceptability, feasibility, and ideology.[5]

Decisions can only be based on knowledge when all participants in the decision agree on what is true. Thus, one person's "tested knowledge" is another's wrong-headed opinion.

At the heart of the problem is the question of whose values (or whose knowledge) are to be used in making decisions. A number of interested publics are involved in social welfare policy decisions. Politicians, business people, farmers, members of the professions, and client groups all have a stake in social welfare policy. Everyone seems to have a set of beliefs about what should be done and how it should be done. All believe that they are guided by facts. Few suspect that they are really operating in the realm of beliefs. The decision-making process is further complicated because some of the people interested in the decisions have more influence than others.

Social workers—who we think have not been a major factor in social welfare policy decisions—can play a larger role in the decision-making process if they are aware of the values in the process.

Central Values in the United States

Although the United States may not have achieved a mature pluralism in all areas of social and political life, there is certainly a pluralism in the realm of social and personal values. We have seen the country move from what seemed a fairly unified and perhaps simplistic set of middle-class values into an incredible diversity of viewpoints. Each of the social, ethnic, religious, and cultural movements has added something to the richness of life in the United States. These movements, particularly those of blacks, youth, and the feminists, have had an impact on American values, but the decision-making process has not yet been revolutionized. Much of the core of the traditional value system remains intact and continues to receive support from the powerful and privileged.

A number of traditional value orientations are commonly held in the United States. They are not respected by all people, and some are clearly in conflict with others. We do not claim that social welfare policy must be governed by all of them, but they must be recognized and taken into account. Some can be supportive, but others will clearly need to be challenged. These major social values were identified by Robin Williams.[6] We have summarized his comments but have also added what we see as the implications for social welfare policy.

Achievement and Success

The American culture values the accumulation of money in the operation of one's business or profession. Despite some renewed awareness of the virtues of a simple life-style exemplified by the commune, most Americans have a strong tendency to hold money and position as symbols of success and personal worth. Part of the discontent with public welfare stems from the notion that it is something for the nonachiever and the unsuccessful. People still generally equate public welfare with incorrect interpretations of the word "charity." We do not wish to digress into a long technical discussion here, but "charity" (from the Latin *caritas*) originally meant esteem or high regard for one's fellow human beings.[7] Charity has come to mean something that "we" do for "them." Obviously, if welfare services are to be seen as a "first line" service or a social utility, social welfare policy needs to focus on the mutuality of the human condition and avoid the "us-them" trap related to strong achievement and success-oriented norms. One of the reasons (but not the only one) that the Retirement, Survivor's, Disability, and Health Insurance provisions of the Social Security Act have been successful is that these programs take into account the American beliefs about achievement and success. One appears to "earn" benefits that are universal to the work force, and the recipient can identify his or her eligibility as something that is deserved. Retirement allows one, so the myth goes, to live on the benefits of a successful life.

Activity and Work

There is general agreement that the United States is a busy place. Visitors from other countries sometimes have difficulty understanding the continual noise and bustle of American cities. Williams suggests that this American characteristic came about because our population was largely recruited from the working classes of Europe. The accent on work was intensified with the struggle for survival on the frontier. In welfare programs the high value that Americans put on work has usually surfaced in making work requirement provisions a condition for eligibility for public welfare. Some social workers have argued that requiring work is punitive and should not be a feature of welfare policy, but it is doubtful that Americans would accept a program that does not acknowledge the importance of work in some way. It is important to note that the poor, when they are asked, generally state a preference for work over "going on welfare." In Chapter 5 we will return to this theme.

Value Orientation

Americans tend to see the world from a moral perspective. Although there is great individual and group diversity in values in the United States, virtually all Americans believe that their view of events is morally responsible. Few publicly espouse an amoral or totally hedonistic way of life. This strong sense of morality has led to a number of value conflicts, some with considerable violence.

Despite the diversity in personal values, there is a kind of "public morality" that pervades the culture. True, there is a certain amount of ritualism, hypocrisy, and cynicism in public morals, but there are some fairly wide areas of agreement. Currently, for example, there seems to be general agreement that honesty in public office is an important moral value. We are not surprised, because of our cynicism, that there are dishonest officials, but we do not like it. If the violation is flagrant enough, the official will be removed.

Unfortunately, one of the more widely shared beliefs in this country is a kind of warmed-over seventeenth-century puritanism that is directed toward the poor, the unemployed, and other client groups. This attitude has a powerful effect on social welfare policy, as we shall see later.

It is unlikely that social welfare policy analysis can be formulated without some attention to moral values. However, the puritanistic tendency might be countered by stressing strong positive values, such as the protection of children or the self-development of people.

Humanitarian Mores

Although Americans generally take a harsh attitude toward the chronically poor and unsuccessful, they are often generous toward the victims of natural disasters and temporary distress. There is a certain philosophical conflict between the willingness to contribute to private philanthropy through the United Way or a service club and the punitive approach to the handling of public assistance. To most Americans, humanitarianism means private support for those who are in trouble "through no fault of their own." Public assistance, by the same logic, is not humanitarian but a governmental dole for those who are in trouble *through* faults of their own. Humanitarianism in the popular mind does not seem to extend to mass governmental programs. Thus, while humanitarianism is an important virtue to social workers and other humanistically oriented people, it has little appeal to the ordinary taxpayer. An effective welfare policy cannot rest solely on humanitarianism for its justification, since this value is not strong enough in the public mind to override other important values. Perhaps if public assistance were not seen as a dole and the short-term nature of most assistance were emphasized, it would be easier to gain public support for more humane policies.

Efficiency and Practicality

The stress on technology, expedience, novelty, and getting things done has led to the glorification of technology in the United States. Technical efficiency tends to become valued for its own sake, rather than for what it serves to accomplish. Williams observes that such a concentration on practicality tends to deemphasize intellectual, contemplative, ascetic, or mystical concerns. In order to have appeal to Americans, social welfare policy probably ought to address practical concerns and should emphasize efficiency, particularly in administration. Social workers may have made a serious tactical error in not responding to the taxpayer's concern for an efficient use of funds. We recognize that the public is getting a bargain in social welfare services. The point is that the public does not realize it.

Progress

The belief that things will improve and that we can fashion the best of all possible worlds is a central belief to many Americans. This belief is threatened on occasion, but it remains a sturdy part of the American creed. It is this value that leads to faddishness in social welfare as in other things. Part of the hostility that is shown toward social welfare may be related to the public's inability to see progress. While we do not advocate pandering to those who have expectations of automatic progress, we do think that social welfare personnel have not been sensitive to the public's desire to see things get better. Welfare gets bigger and bigger, but few equate this with change for the better.

Material Comfort

The wealth and resources of the United States have led to a high standard of living. Americans seem to work to satisfy their material desires. A few decades ago, automobiles, television, and dishwashers were luxuries enjoyed by a few. They have now become necessities. Increased leisure time has accelerated the drive for material comfort. For example, one can no longer jog without wearing the appropriate clothing!

Few Americans, however, see material comfort as a major value affecting social welfare policy. They do not believe that material comfort should be provided for those who do not work or are not moral. Thus, it is difficult to convince state legislatures and the Congress that benefits ought to be at least adequate.

Equality

The United States has abandoned formal social stratification like that still found to a degree in Europe. Americans have both a formal and informal commitment to political freedom and equality before the law. There is an obvious strain between freedom and equality in the real world. In the United States in the nineteenth century, freedom amounted to license, and a "manufacturing aristocracy" developed which endangered the concept of political equality. The resolution of this tension has historically been that "equality" has come to mean an equality of interpersonal relations, equality of formal rights and obligations, and equality of opportunity for social and economic rewards.[8] Williams emphasizes the notion that inequalities resulting from achievement have not been seen as violations of the American concept of political equality. For many years, rewards not resulting from achievement, such as those related to sex or race, were considered the natural order of things. Now, because of the social action of blacks, feminists, and other activist groups, rewards not related to achievement have become much less acceptable. It is interesting to note that with a very few exceptions, activists have not wanted to disturb the basic opportunity and achievement structure. Their efforts have concentrated on opening it, but not eliminating the notion that rewards should be related to achievement. Equality before the law is palatable to Americans, but social policies that stress economic equality have not gained much of a foothold in the United States. There have been periodic flare-ups of socialistic sentiment in this country (in the 1920s and among some of the youth of the sixties), but these movements have been more rhetorical than effective. There are a number of people connected to social welfare who have socialistic sentiments, but it is unlikely that this point of view will be popular in the present political climate. Although most supporters of social welfare favor some economic redistribution, social workers who espouse radical economic policies run the considerable risk of becoming an embattled minority with little impact on public policy.

Freedom

The American concept of freedom finds its expression in "a tendency to think of rights rather than duties, suspicion of established (especially personal) authority, a distrust of central government, a deep aversion to acceptance of obviously coercive restraint through visible social organization." [9] American citizens characteristically demand rights to privacy, engage in various forms of civil disobedience, and flaunt unpopular laws. Whereas Americans appear to accept diffuse control over their behavior (as in the case of impersonal markets), they object to concrete control through law and regulation. Personal autonomy is of high value and a certain amount of variant behavior is tolerated unless it is perceived as publicly threatening.

All Americans from the John Birch Society to the Socialist Workers' Alliance prize freedom, though their views differ on what it is. It is this strong tradition of personal freedom that has chiefly hindered the development of social welfare programs and services in the United States. Each new program is perceived by someone as an inhibition of freedom. This, we believe, is an unfortunate misunderstanding of the motives of social welfare planners. Most personnel in social welfare believe that they are enhancing freedom by increasing the life chances of the clientele for whom they are working. The social welfare enterprise needs to clarify its goals and be more conscious of the public's need to know them. The aims of social welfare policy do not deprive Americans of personal freedom but should provide supports that open up decisions and choices. The aim is to increase the availability of jobs, housing, and services to enable the clientele to have maximum life choices.

External Conformity

There is a strong tendency for Americans to conform, at least in external ways, to their contemporaries. This tendency toward conformity is not necessarily an evil, but there is a problem because the clientele of social welfare programs are usually seen as deviants or abnormals. Social welfare policy makers should, for this reason, stress that clients are the same as other people with the same needs and problems that are faced by all human beings. Emphasizing differences tends to widen the distance between client groups—whether they be mental patients or the poor—and the rest of society.

Science and Secular Rationality

Williams discusses the concern with "order, control and calculability" characteristic of an engineering society. This interest in order and predictability is closely related to the values of progress, equality, and practicality. Science is believed to be rational and disciplined. It has become a "secular religion" aimed toward control of an ordered world. The scientist is seen as one preoccupied with efficiency, technology, pragmatism, and expediency. To the extent that rationality is important, it is clearly in the interest of social welfare policy makers to support a more efficient system. It should not be expected, however, that social welfare be totally dehumanized in the interests of order and control.

Nationalism-Patriotism

Williams discusses a "means-ends" distinction between two types of nationalistic values in the United States. In the one, the nation becomes the end, and criticism of any feature of American life may be considered treasonous. In the other, the nation is regarded highly because of its identification with such values as democracy and freedom. In this latter case, the nation becomes a means to higher aspirations and values.

The two points of view clash periodically. Examples can be seen in the diverse and changing attitudes toward immigration, the McCarthyism of the fifties, and draft evaders in the Vietnam conflict. Wars have had a particularly polarizing effect on nationalism as a value orientation, with some people favoring and others opposing the expansion of military power and federal bureaucracy. Those who see the nation as the end perceive the need and inevitability of growth in military power and the controls of the federal government. Those who see the nation as the means protest any compromise with the ultimate values of freedom, equality, individualism, and democracy that might flow from increased military and civil power. Nationalism-patriotism might impinge on social welfare policy only if a policy stressed its similarity to a European practice. It is disastrous to try to sell a policy to Americans on the basis of how well it works in Europe. Americans are more likely to accept "American" policies.

Democracy

Williams lists major themes in the democratic creed as including "equality of certain formal rights and formal equality of opportunity, a faith in the rule of impersonal law, optimistic rationalism, and ethical individualism." [10] Many of these themes relate to other American value orientations, but they are uniquely tied together as part of the democratic value system. Underlying all these themes is "agreement upon procedure in the distribution of power and in the settling of conflicts," and agreement on the chief aim of government as maximizing individual self-direction as a means of ensuring worth, dignity, and the creative capacity for individual human beings.[11] Generally, this is an important value to stress in social welfare policy. It usually will not be confused with economic equality.

Individual Personality

Americans are taught from birth that the individual personality is of high intrinsic worth. The individual is viewed as a responsible, independent, decision-making unit. Although at times this value orientation may clash with other values, such as the achievement-success orientation that militates toward profit-making to the occasional detriment of individuals, it remains a deeply embedded value in our culture. The length to which our society goes to protect the individual can be seen, according to Williams, in our firm legal stance that an individual is not free to take his own life, since he would thereby be destroying an individual personality. Since this value conflicts with conformity, social welfare policy makers who set policy goals of supporting the growth of individuals should maintain that these individuals are very much like everyone else.

Racism and Related Group Superiority Themes

The values of equality, humanitarianism, democracy, and the worth of the individual are in a recurring conflict with pervasive patterns of racism, agism, and other group superiority notions. No American social policy should be based on notions of group superiority. Policy makers, however, must be aware of these themes in American society. They must be prepared to deal with opposition to policies that seem to have a significant payoff for cultural and ethnic minorities. In this area the principle of mutuality receives its strongest test since many social interactions are still at the conflict level.

Social Work Values

If one takes the position that social work is a major profession in the welfare enterprise, then social work values should become important factors in social welfare policy choices. We have noted elsewhere that this has not always been the case for a variety of reasons. We can now add another reason: There is no single consistent value position with which all social workers agree. Charles Levy, who has probably studied this problem more than anyone else, has observed that social work values are not simply a mirror of the values of society, but that there are some values that are shared, at least in part.[12] Levy suggests that what is shared includes the idea that human beings are changeable, self-actualizing, and equal in opportunity and that they deserve equal treatment, support, opportunities for participation in their own government, and nonjudgmental acceptance. This listing roughly compares to Williams' values of humanitarianism, equality, freedom, democracy, and the worth of the individual.

Martin Rein takes a much more complex and certainly less sanguine view.[13] He argues that there are many creeds and belief systems among social workers. He identifies four major ones.

1. *The traditional casework view.* The aim of the traditional caseworker is to enable people to meet the standards of society by learning to conform to traditional behavioral norms.

2. *Radical casework.* The radical social worker rejects traditional standards as normative and challenges hurtful norms through appeals to alternative standards and by challenging institutions to humanize.

3. *Community sociotherapy.* Those who follow this belief system encourage self-help among community groups on the principle that as people become involved in activity they displace their hostility and learn to become conformists.

4. *Radical social policy.* This is a reformist creed which focuses on the notion that changing political, economic, and social institutions is a precondition for individual change.

Other value positions can be added. There are social workers who see their activity and the purpose of social welfare as extensions of the ministry of a given religious body. Some social workers clearly see their mission in terms of protecting society against the deviant. Others see social welfare as a personal activity that expresses their own creativity. It does seem to us that Rein's point is quite valid. Levy's position is an idealistic one, and attractive as a goal. It does not, however, reflect present reality.

Pincus and Minahan point out that the social worker is caught in value dilemmas and complex, ambiguous situations. They identify a number of them. Examples include the issue of self-determination versus manipulation of the client and the problem of planned change in an atmosphere where the client perceives the world in fatalistic terms.[14] Their best counsel is to maintain a balance between flexibility and integrity and to develop self-awareness, technical expertise, and a tolerance for ambiguity.[15]

We have no resolution for the diversity of values in social work and social welfare. In the next chapter, the reader will note that social work values are one of a number of criteria for evaluating social welfare policy. In the absence of a clear and universally accepted set of social work values, we will suggest that the only practical approach that can be taken, pending some resolution of the problem, is to keep abreast of the positions taken by the National Association of Social Workers. These positions represent a good faith attempt to reach consensus within the profession, and they are periodically reviewed for their relevancy. This is, of course, a less than satisfactory solution, but it will have to do until social workers can come to a general agreement about professional values.

Values and the Problems Addressed by Social Welfare Policy

The nature of social welfare policy has something to do with the way in which problems are defined. The sociologists Robert K. Merton and Robert Nisbet have defined social problems as "the substantial, unwanted discrepancies between what is in a society and what a functionally significant collectivity within that society seriously . . . desires to be in it." [16] In other words, a social problem is defined when people who have enough influence to be heard realize that there is a discrepancy between what a society values and life conditions in the society. As can readily be seen, American social problems are closely related to American social values. For instance, since a high value is placed on work, achievement, and money, it follows that when the unemployment rate is considered high and poverty becomes visible, they will be seen to be problematical by a significant segment of the American public. If a significant segment of the public does not see the discrepancy as a problem, it will remain, in the public mind, only a personal problem to those who are afflicted.

This point may need some defense. To many social workers, social problems are not considered matters of opinion. They are definite conditions whose seriousness is obvious. How can there be any doubt? Social workers must remember that their view of certain conditions as problematic stems from their espousal of the beliefs that they hold about what is valuable. Those who are not social workers either do not share the same values, or they have a conflict between values that the social worker does not have.

Like it or not then, a social problem is whatever people with enough influence say that it is. Sometimes many people are in agreement. Almost everybody would join in saying that crime is a social problem—except for those for whom crime is a business. Sometimes something can be defined as a social problem by a relatively few people. In the 1920s an extremely well-organized group defined alcohol consumption as a major social problem, even though it became apparent that this was a minority definition.

To complicate things, it is also true that the size and importance of the group who define problems changes over time. In the middle 1960s a very large number of people who had influence saw poverty as a major problem in our society. Poverty is no longer central as a major social problem. If we are to believe the major opinion polls, it has been replaced by inflation and unemployment. In the public view, these two problems are more pervasive and threatening to more people.

Generally, then, social welfare policy is devised in response to a problem that has been identified by society or some segment of society. There have been attempts to suggest that social work, as a major service delivery profession within social welfare, should deal with prevention. The whole "institutional" focus of social welfare as a first line resource suggests that social welfare programs and services should be anticipatory and available whenever needed. Some fields, notably public health, have taken prevention as their guiding principle. We agree with this view in substance, but the reality is that we cannot readily anticipate many of the social welfare problems that we will need to deal with in the future. Further, society as a whole has not seen fit to finance preventive social welfare planning.

Social Problems, Social Policy, and Social Work

The kinds of things that a society considers problematic, then, depend very much on the values identified by that society. The nonindustrial nation *might* define its problems as hunger, lack of pure water, and disease. Because these problems are such a clear threat to survival, they would seem to claim the center of attention. Such a society *might* place the highest value on an effective means of producing food, finding a clean spring, and a good set of folk medicines. However, it is important to point out that values important to the Western world may have nothing to do with either problem definition or a policy for problem solution in the nonindustrial society. Instead, another set of values might govern the whole problem-definition-solution process. In some societies a significant number may decide that the people are hungry because they had failed to plant at the proper time to please the sun god. Therefore, the central problem would appear to be the anger of a god in a society where the most esteemed value is a good relationship to the sun. Hunger is (in such a framework) a secondary problem.

Defining any behavior, condition, or circumstance as a social problem is ultimately, then, a value judgment. For example, the United States before 1914 perceived drug abuse and addiction as a medical matter. In an era of widespread concern about "moral decay," or more accurately social institutional change, the nation redefined that condition during the period from 1910 to 1930 as a social problem. The goal became one of curtailing the use of dangerous drugs, and a policy of law enforcement emerged. Unfortunately, the law enforcement policy has led to a number of new social problems, including widespread crime in urban areas and intergenerational conflict.

If the above analysis is a correct one, and the authors believe it is, the charge to social work and other helping professions may well be to focus on professional roles and skills in addition to those of the clinic: redefining problems, reformulating more appropriate policies, and fashioning new techniques for educating the public in problem definition and policy formulation. The social worker of the future will have to be educator, value changer, and social institutional change agent, as well as individual therapist.

Present approaches to policy analysis and formulation choose to focus heavily on the organization context. They start from these premises: (1) that many social agencies already exist; (2) that policies (new, old, or revised) are most likely to be realized and implemented through such agencies or organizations; (3) that agencies or organizations are characteristically hard to change; and, therefore, (4) that policies have to be developed in such a way as to be usable within organizational contexts.

We do not argue with the partial validity of these judgments *if the focus is only to be on existing agencies or organizations,* although even then there is a self-fulfilling prophecy in the often-proclaimed difficulty of changing agencies. (The truth is that agencies can be and are changed often—if one wants to change them, works hard at it, and develops appropriate skills.)

Our position dictates that we focus on the broadest range of possible policy alternatives to handle perceived social problems or conditions, regardless of existing agency or organizational contexts. The real challenge is to try to develop policies that have the best chance of really working efficiently and effectively to cope with social problems or conditions. Many of them may be outside existing organizations or, if they require organizational implementation, there may be a number of possible ways to change or convince organizations to adopt the policies. Some policies may not require social agency implementation at all. For example, it is a common social work judgment that the prevention, control, or management of juvenile delinquency requires policies concerned with changing or "treating" individuals, families, groups, or neighborhoods. Actually, there are indications here and there in the literature that what may be more useful are policies concerned with fiscal and monetary management aimed at employment markets or with policies aimed at educational management. Such policies would be in the province of economic or educational agencies, not traditional social agencies.

Can social workers learn to become advocates, brokers, activists, and enablers with economic and educational institutions? Why not, if social work skills are those of influencing, building, and utilizing relationships, perceiving interorganizational connections, and fashioning new bridges?

Conclusion

Let us pull together what we have discussed thus far:

1. Social problems are whatever societies and communities perceive them to be, in their stage of development and in their particular complex of wealth, resources, technology, perception or social justice, and view of concepts such as equality and opportunity.

2. Social workers can learn how to help societies and communities reformulate and redefine social problems. In short, social workers can become value change agents. Currently, several states are redefining drug abuse as a medical matter. The U.S. Supreme Court has redefined abortion, school truancy, running away from home, and other behaviors. Why should social workers not become more actively engaged in proposing and facilitating these redefinitions?

3. Problem redefinitions are, in addition to being value judgments, an example of policy formulation. One way of handling a problem is to redefine it into more manageable behaviors or components. Hence, in considering the broadest array of policy alternatives, certainly some should be problem redefinitions.

4. Social welfare policies are also based on configurations of values. Policies can be and should be formulated regardless of existing professional, public, and organizational biases if one has access to stronger expressions or statements of values, for example, the law. U.S. District Court Judge Frank M. Johnson, Jr. has reformulated state policies for handling the mentally ill, mentally retarded, and criminal offenders in Alabama, in spite of some extremely resistant agency personnel, politicians, press, and citizenry. In that state, institutions have been reduced markedly in size, staffing patterns changed, conditions improved,

commitment procedures drastically altered, and community-based treatment facilities mandated, all on the basis of a series of court orders backed by monitoring mechanisms. Is there any reason why social workers could not participate responsibly in these policy formulations?

5. At the deepest level of conceptualizations, not only are both social problems and social welfare policies essentially matters of choice, but problems and policies are so intimately intertwined and interrelated that they become almost indistinguishable. The policy to handle one social problem may itself create another social problem or several social problems, as we saw above in the case of drug abuse and addiction.

6. The challenge is to prepare social workers who can free themselves of professional and organizational biases, constraints, traditions, and instrumental values in order to conceptualize problems and to analyze and formulate policies through a process that is objective, value aware, pragmatic, cost conscious, reality oriented, but also creative and imaginative.

In our next chapter we offer a system of policy analysis that we think will help expand the social worker's competence in the policy arena. It is a pragmatic system and is not limited in its usefulness to any one ideological position.

REFERENCES

1. Milton Rokeach, *The Nature of Human Values* (New York: The Free Press, 1973), p. 5.
2. David G. Gil, *Unravelling Social Policy* (Cambridge, Mass.: Schenkman, 1973), pp. 27–28.
3. Allen Pincus and Anne Minahan, *Social Work Practice: Model and Method* (Itasca, Ill.: F. E. Peacock, 1973), p. 52.
4. *Ibid.*
5. Carol Weiss, *Evaluation Research* (Englewood Cliffs, N.J.: Prentice-Hall, 1972), p. 4.
6. Robin Williams, *American Society: A Sociological Interpretation*, 2nd ed. (New York: Alfred A. Knopf, 1967).
7. Melancthon W. Jacobus, Elbert C. Lane, and Andrew C. Zenos, eds., *A New Standard Bible Dictionary*, 3rd rev. ed. (New York: Funk and Wagnalls Company, 1936), pp. 126–127.
8. Williams, *op. cit.* pp. 440–442.
9. *Ibid.*, p. 446.
10. *Ibid.*, p. 461.
11. *Ibid.*, pp. 461–462.

12. Charles S. Levy, "The Value Base of Social Work," *Journal of Education for Social Work*, Vol. 9, No. 1 (Winter 1973).
13. Martin Rein, "Social Work in Search of a Radical Profession," *Social Work*, Vol. 15, No. 2 (April 1970).
14. Pincus and Minahan, *op. cit.*, pp. 42–52.
15. *Ibid.*, p. 52.
16. Robert K. Merton and Robert Nisbet, *Contemporary Social Problems*, 2nd ed. (New York: Harcourt, Brace and World, 1966), p. 799.

QUESTIONS FOR DISCUSSION

1. Why are there so few examples of decision-making, whether in school or job or family life, not involving explicit or implicit value judgments?
2. Select a social problem not specifically discussed in the chapter and explore the value judgments involved in its definition and in its management.
3. Why can an advanced or postindustrial society address itself to social problems such as marital incompatibility whereas developing societies are concerned with poverty and illiteracy?
4. Discuss other examples besides drug abuse in which a policy to cope with a social problem has led to new social problems or aggravation of existing social problems.
5. Try your hand at redefining a social problem so that it might be more manageable. Consider prostitution or gambling since they are highly value laden, legal in some places, and illegal in others.
6. Robin Williams outlined major value orientations in American society in 1960. What changes in American values do you think have occurred? Do you think that the changes that you have identified would affect Williams' list?
7. Discuss differences between societal values and social work values. Are there more similarities than differences?

SUGGESTED PROJECTS

1. Talk with a social worker about professional values that are most relevant to social work practice. How consonant does the social worker perceive social work values to be with societal values?
2. Discuss societal values with a sociologist or anthropologist. Does he or she agree with Robin Williams' formulation?

3. Ask a state legislator or a member of Congress (or a person on the staff of the latter) about societal values of most relevance to policy-making. Which of Robin Williams' values seem most relevant to the individual interviewed?

FOR FURTHER READING

Nathan E. Cohen. *Social Work and Social Problems*. New York: National Association of Social Workers, 1964. An early effort to develop a model for the analysis of social problems that was heavily oriented toward recognition of the role of societal and social work values in problem definition, etiology, current operations, and the view of what would constitute ideal operations.

Joseph P. Garbin. "Professional Values vs. Personal Beliefs in Drug Abuse," *Social Work*, Vol. 19, No. 3 (May 1974), pp. 333–337. A penetrating discussion of the conflicts that arise between the values of a professional social worker in the various roles of practitioner, expert, and intellectual. The conflict centers around such questions as "Does an individual have the right to decide for himself whether to take drugs (marijuana or heroin) regardless of the consequences to his health?"

Charles S. Levy. *Social Work Ethics*. New York: Human Service Press, 1976. A thoughtful and readable book by the most influential contemporary scholar of ethics in social work.

Charles S. Levy. "The Value Base of Social Work," *Journal of Education for Social Work*, Vol. 9, No. 1 (Winter 1973), pp. 34–42. A useful attempt to clarify the place of values in social work and to propose three basic dimensions of value orientations shared by social workers: preferred conceptions of people, preferred outcomes for people, and preferred instrumentalities for dealing with people.

Roy Lubove. *The Professional Altruist*. Cambridge, Mass.: Harvard University Press, 1965. A discussion of value considerations and value choices occurring throughout the history of social work practice, such as direct service versus social reform, agency versus profession, individual versus social structure.

Milton Rokeach. *The Nature of Human Values*. New York: The Free Press, 1973. Discussion by a long-time student of human values and value systems.

Brian Segal. "Policy Science and Social Policy: Implications for the Social Work Curriculum," *Journal of Education for Social Work*, Vol. 12, No. 2 (Spring 1976), pp. 36–42. An important article which suggests that the social work curriculum now has an overabundance of values and a dearth of technical substance. Policy science can bring more scientific methods of policy development to approaches to solving social problems.

George R. Sharwell. "Can Values Be Taught? A Study of Two Variables Related to Orientation of Social Work Graduate Students Toward Public Dependency," *Journal of Education for Social Work*, Vol. 10, No. 2 (1974), pp. 99–105. A review of the literature dealing with the impact of graduate education upon the values of social work students. Also discusses a research project aimed at evaluating change in values toward public dependency. The findings suggest that selective processes and graduate education combine to produce a social worker with a favorable attitude toward public dependency.

Robin M. Williams, Jr. *American Society: A Sociological Interpretation.* New York: Alfred A. Knopf, 1967. Chapter XI, "Values and Beliefs in American Society," is perhaps the most comprehensive and useful analysis of major value orientations in the United States.

3 The Systematic Process of Policy Analysis and Formulation

In this chapter we present a systematic way of analyzing social welfare policy. As we said in the last chapter, social welfare policy is closely related to the culture in which it is found and to the values and knowledge of that culture. There are, however, a number of other important factors that must be taken into account. The questions that we will discuss fall into four areas:

CONSIDERATIONS RELATED TO CULTURAL VALUES

Is the policy under consideration compatible with contemporary "style"?

Does the policy contribute to equity and justice?

Is the policy compatible with social work values?

Is the policy compatible with other important values in society?

41

DIMENSIONS OF INFLUENCE AND DECISION-MAKING
> *Is the policy politically acceptable?*
> *Is the policy legal?*
> *Does the policy satisfy relevant interest groups?*

KNOWLEDGE CONSIDERATIONS
> *Is the policy scientifically sound?*
> *Is the policy rational?*

ELEMENTS RELATED TO COST/BENEFITS
> *Is the policy economically feasible and economically superior to other*
> *alternatives?*
> *Is the policy workable?*
> *Is the policy efficient?*
> *Will the policy be likely to generate other social problems?*

We will discuss these questions in some detail later. It is evident that in addition to their usefulness in analyzing a current policy, they also serve as a basis for evaluating alternatives that may be proposed.

We think that the ideal social policy would produce a "yes" to each question. In the real world, however, few (if any) policies would satisfy all criteria. Some of these factors are obviously more important than others. We have tried to develop a meaningful weighting system that would have precision but have not yet succeeded. At this point our best judgment is that the closer a given policy fits this set of criteria, the more likely it will be effective in reaching its goals. Perhaps the chief use of this scheme is not the comparison of a given policy with an absolute standard but the comparison of one policy with an *alternative*. If one policy more nearly satisfies these criteria than another, we feel that it is more likely to be effective.

Necessity for Criteria for Evaluation

It is helpful to look at the way policies have been selected in the past. We would argue that the determination of which policy to select or support has not always been approached systematically. Braybrooke and Lindblom discuss two frequently used but primitive approaches to policy analysis and formulation.[1] In one, the "naive criteria" method, it is assumed that all one needs worry about are a few general values, such as "security" or "full employment." In this approach, if a policy to gain "full employment" is developed, then it must be right, since full employment is an important value. It is apparently not necessary to worry about the inflationary effect of full employment or whether or not everyone is prepared and able to work. Another example is the notion that the solution to the problem of fathers not supporting their children is to "lock the bastards up." This policy panders to a very naive criterion for problem solution. It should be obvious that a policy of this simplistic sort does not take into account a whole series of very complex issues.

The second primitive approach is the "naive priorities" method. This consists of merely ranking the priorities of one's own group and using them as a guide to policy determination. It is as if one operated in a vacuum in which no one else could have a conflicting set of priorities. Like it or not, we do have to make policy in a world in which other priorities exist—and we must take them into account.

In social welfare, these unsystematic approaches have kept us from improving policy-making through organized creativity and structured rationality. They have kept us from projecting new approaches to social problems. Yehezkel Dror has written on this topic; he describes the current situation:

> Misery, poverty, war, the gap between the haves and have-nots (individuals and countries alike), the utilization of limited space for increasing humanity, environmental issues, human and community relations, distribution of health services, individual and public safety, recreation, transportation, telecommunication, and so on and so forth—these are among the areas and issues for policymaking, all and each of which are filled with difficult problems that, at present, we are quite incapable of handling.[2]

What are the requirements of a more sophisticated and systematic process of policy analysis and formulation? First, it must employ rational method. The evidence should be derived from scientific research, and data should be collected from substantial sources. Second, the method should be clear and explicit. Any person using the same method and evidence should reach the same conclusions.[3] Third, the objective should reach the solution of maximum benefit for the least social cost. The ecologist Ian McHarg calls this "the solution of maximum social utility." [4] What is needed is to produce a new policy which avoids as many social costs as possible while creating or enhancing as many social values as possible. Fourth, one must be able to understand the ecology circumscribing the process of policy analysis and formulation. What is the range of potential impact on surrounding social problems, policies, and people? What, at an even higher level, is the possible impact on the total environment? The essential precondition of planning, according to McHarg, is the formulation of choices related to goals, as well as the criteria for assessing them and the means for their realization.[5] Fifth, good public policy should insofar as possible coincide with individual self-interest. If one is to establish the largest base of support as well as to ensure the greatest opportunity for individual benefit, this would seem to be a clear requirement. Sixth, if planning requires the posing of alternatives with the costs and benefits of each, it is necessary to be able to demonstrate the consequences of the status quo extended into the future.[6] The future of each alternative, including the status quo, needs to be predicted. Seventh, successful policy must be consistent with relevant social and personal values. Eighth, social welfare personnel must be more concerned with creating the environment in which people can function in self-fulfilling ways than with coping with social problems.[7] This last requirement is a fairly uncommon notion. Let us cite an example. In keeping with this requirement, efforts should be made to promote a condition of mental health, not to treat a condition of mental illness.

You may wonder why the requirements above are largely borrowed or adapted from the work of an ecologist. We have much to learn from ecology. A principle illustrated often is that "every time a decision is made, countless other decisions are simultaneously precluded."[8] The traditional social welfare policy and services sequence in schools of social work has been criticized for failing to observe this principle: "Our most fruitful guide for selecting materials from the past comes from ecology. Our need, I think, is to implant the idea of the complex interrelatedness of variables over time, space, and systems, to alert students to social change processes and the unique role of values in human decision-making."[9]

This ecological principle can help social work to launch a systematic, rational, and efficient way to analyze and formulate social policies.

Other Frameworks for Policy Analysis

Most writers on social welfare policy have traditionally taken some ideological position regarding broad or specific social problems, usually poverty, or have directed their attention toward some goal, such as income maintenance or health provision, and then devoted the discussion to interpreting and defending their position. More recently a growing number of writers have addressed the analysis of social welfare policy as a process without infusing it with a specific ideological stance.

The approach of breaking social welfare policy into a number of key areas of concern may be of more help in an analytical understanding of social policy as a phenomenon than in knowing how to formulate a policy. Neil Gilbert and Harry Specht look at social policy analysis in this way. Their framework follows:

> The four major dimensions of choice in this framework may be expressed in the form of the following questions:
>
> 1. What are the bases of social allocations?

2. What are the types of social provisions to be allocated?

3. What are the strategies for the delivery of these provisions?

4. What are the methods of financing these provisions? [10]

A framework like this helps to analyze existing policy and to visualize its components. It may be less helpful in evaluating alternatives to existing policy.

Perhaps consideration of alternatives is just as important. David Gil argues that "the development and study of alternative social policies is perhaps the most important aspect of policy analysis.[11] He suggests that to analyze policy alternatives, one must consider: (1) the way in which resources are developed and the priorities that are given to various goods and services; (2) the way societies allocate position, functions, and tasks to its members; and (3) the way privileges are distributed.[12]

Gilbert and Specht's work and Gil's book are important contributions to social work's maturity in the policy area. We differ from them primarily in the position that we assign to the role of values in the policy process. Indeed, we support Alfred Kahn's contention that "large social policy changes are made in value terms and political perspective, not through weighing of effectiveness." [13] Others agree. Perlman and Gurin comment that "decisions are based ultimately on commitments to certain values or value systems." They recognize that practitioners juggle three main considerations in reaching decisions (values, patterns of influence or power, and rationality), but the first consideration—values—seems to have the center of the stage.[14]

Needs, Goals, and Policies

We are now ready to present our approach to policy analysis and formulation. This chapter will just sketch out the outline. Later chapters will show its application both to existing policies and to problems that need coherent policy.

We think that one should start from a needs assessment in which as many relevant actors as possible participate. The needs assessment leads the social worker to set some goals. These goals are broad statements of desired outcomes. The goals can be long term or short term, but are more likely to be successful when they are reachable and immediate. It is perhaps workable to suggest that any policy formulator have long-term goals that act as a general guide to the future, but to set within the long-term goal or goals a series of short-term goals, which are compatible. Having set the goal, the next step is to consider the alternatives that are available for reaching them. It is imperative to point out that the social worker should not confine his or her planning to existing organizational frameworks. They may or may not be the best option. The point is that good policy formulation should not be constrained by what *is*. There are enough constraints to consider, as we shall point out.

A Framework for Policy Analysis and Formulation

The reader should note that each of the questions that we pose can be asked of a current policy as one attempts to analyze its effectiveness. The same questions should also be asked of any proposed alternative once a need has been identified and a goal has been set. The questions follow the same order as the brief list at the beginning of the chapter.

Is the policy compatible with contemporary "style"?

Political scientists have realized that communities and governments have "climates" or "styles" in public matters and that people expect things to be done accordingly. We were as a nation preoccupied for some years with the Kennedy "style," at times praising it as innovative and dynamic, or criticizing its "Camelot" mystique. The Nixon climate was one of fear, evasion, suspicion, and distrust. The Ford style seems to have been one of caution, lack of political sophistication, and indecisiveness. It would have been less than reasonable, for example, to offer a policy alternative calling for a sweeping revision of a large federal program and expect the Ford administration to buy it. In the Kennedy years, on the other hand, the appropriate question might have been: Is it dramatic, exciting, challenging, and sweeping enough to involve an appropriate degree of real change? The Carter administration seems to have the same characteristics as its predecessor.

At the local level, communities vary from arch-conservative to very progressive, and styles vary from a preference for the quiet and cautious to the stormy and aggressive policy, from the piecemeal approach to the total approach, from governmental control to private responsibility.

An assessment of style, then, becomes a criterion perhaps not as obviously determining as political feasibility but certainly influential and therefore a necessary aspect of a thorough analysis. It is hard to suggest a totally dependable way of ascertaining style since it is a highly subjective thing. One can only be sensitive to the statements and behavior of community, state, and national decision makers.

Does the policy contribute to equity and justice?

There are strong reasons why a policy or an alternative policy moves the society toward a condition of equity. The term "equity" here refers to justice, fairness, impartiality, and right. If a policy moves toward equity, it provides for a fairer distribution of privileges and opportunities before the law. As we noted in Chapter 2, most Americans want to identify with a moral position. Justice and fairness are important moral values that people try to honor. Policies that aim at fairness and impartiality are more acceptable than policies that create obvious privileges. Generally, one can tell if a policy is just and equitable if it fails to attract legal challenges based on the "due process" or "equal protection" principles of the law.

Is the policy compatible with social work values?

The entire issue of compatibility with societal values is complicated by the tension between these values on the one hand and professional values on the other. This problem is particularly acute in social work.[15] The social worker often finds it difficult to choose between professional values and broader social values, since they are often at variance.[16] Very often, the policy alternatives developed by social workers will be more compatible with professional values, or with the values of the social strata of their clients, than with societal values. Charles Frankel, the philosopher, considers it urgent that the profession of social work retain the tension between professional values and social values to avoid purely political solutions to technical problems.[17] It would be equally desirable, on the other hand, to avoid purely professional solutions to quasi-political problems, so that both societal values and professional values need to be considered.

Examples of the discontinuity between social work values and societal values are not hard to find. A frequent clash arises over the societal value of parental responsibility and rights, on the one hand, and the professional value of rights and needs of children, on the other. This particular tension has led social workers to distrust and suspect courts that tend to respond to the societal value of parental rights.[18] A desired long-range goal might be the fashioning of policies that will be compatible with both sets of values.

Since it is clear that social workers operate from a number of value positions, it is not a simple matter to solve this problem. Our best suggestion here is to look to the position taken by the National Association of Social Workers as presented in their frequent position papers. Even though all social workers may not agree, the professional association does represent the best attempt to bring people to some agreement on highly charged issues.

Is the policy compatible with other important values in society?

This is a question critical to the success of any policy. We recognize today that the decision-making process is inherently one of choosing between values, but we also recognize that the decision is itself shot through with values from beginning to end. There is no value-free activity indulged in by human beings, not even the scientific pursuits.

To be more specific: Precisely which societal values are we talking about? Which have higher priority and which lesser priority? Do values change, and if so, how can we know which stage of change is to be considered in examining a policy alternative?

In Chapter 2 we discussed a number of important and enduring American values. In considering policy alternatives, these value orientations can be used as a rough gauge to test the public acceptability of a policy alternative. Because values do change, this list may need to be revised in the future, although values certainly do not change as often as styles. In fact, De Tocqueville's discussion of American values over a century ago is still roughly accurate today in indicating the nature of traditional American values.[19]

Here the policy analyst is using an approach analogous to the clinician's assessment of a client's functioning. Reference to the values described in Chapter 2 provides at best a crude checklist. This is a risky exercise, but it will identify those areas where there is greatest conflict between a given policy and major social values. From this exercise one can see that any social welfare policy that radically challenges an important value would face a rough future.

Is the policy politically acceptable?

Many social workers and persons in leadership roles in social welfare have tended in the past several decades to be fearful, suspicious, and uncomfortable with politicians and the political process. This response, of course, was justified by the political scandals of the seventies, climaxed by Watergate. This distrust of the political process was not always the case. Many of the early social workers, Jane Addams for example, turned freely and often to political action. In the past several years it has become clear that political power can be used to achieve social welfare ends, that political interests are not necessarily opposed to professional interests, and that politicians and social workers can work effectively together.[20]

Social workers' willingness to move toward the political arena has been reinforced by recent research findings by political scientists, which tend to take politics out of the arena of manipulation and chicanery toward the possibility of planned and rational activity. For example, the political scientist James Q. Wilson has called attention to the impact on public policy of the characteristics of local government, the party arrangements animating local governments, and the values permeating local governments.[21] The concentration of political power in the hands of a strong mayor leads to quick and successful efforts to get federal antipoverty funds, but works against the opportunity for the poor to achieve maximum feasible participation in the program.[22] Or, to put it differently, reform cities more successfully distributed power in the War on Poverty whereas the machine cities were better at distributing material goods.[23] Moreover, centralized political systems are seen as more likely to act in enlightened ways to fluoridate water and integrate schools, as well as to get money for the poor, whereas decentralized systems were more apt to let the voters decide these issues by referendum, resulting in a loss of time and impairing the ability to act.[24]

Also, the political culture, or the common view of the scope and behavior of public institutions in regard to public matters, has a strong impact on public policy, including social welfare policy.[25] Underlying the dominant political culture of any community is a class-based conception of what government should do, and this culture may change from time to time.

It seems clear that social workers will need to understand political institutions and processes, if the policies they want to see adopted are to get any kind of favorable consideration. We will need to know a great deal about the timing of policy efforts, the legislative process, techniques of joining forces with other power groups (even though the price is some change in timing or in content of policy), and the techniques of influencing public opinion.[26]

But in terms of social policy analysis (as opposed to implementation) it is obvious that no policy alternative, however humane in its motivation, is apt to receive serious public consideration unless it is politically feasible. One needs to take the particular political pattern into consideration because the attitudes and ideology of political figures or groups are crucial factors.

Political feasibility involves an assessment of what is possible today, and what might need to be deferred until next year or ten years from now. We will need to be comfortable with and knowledgeable about conflict strategies, techniques for resolution of conflict, skills in working with power groups such as business and labor, and methods of dealing with politicians and their staffs.

Political feasibility may mean redistributing a share of power to the disadvantaged and powerless (suggestive of an earlier criterion of equity) in addition to the usual, more pragmatic meaning of political acceptability to existing power groups. So we would ask not only: Will the decision makers accept this policy, and can we get it adopted? We would also ask: Does it open up possibilities for some degree of power redistribution to the poor and powerless in an American society that is basically pluralistic? All groups in the society need to have access to decision-making bodies in order for a democratic process to operate well. It is in the interests of all groups in the society to see that the poor, the disadvantaged, and the powerless gain such access.

Assessing political feasibility must be done by appealing to strategically placed persons who are knowledgeable about current political trends. It is not necessary that these advisers be sympathetic. They do need to be accurate. It may even be good if they are opponents. Friends tend to be sympathetic and, in this instance, we need hard advice.

Examples of the importance of political feasibility abound in social welfare policy. Roosevelt succeeded in getting the Social Security Act of 1935 through the U.S. Congress. It was revolutionary in its acceptance of federal responsibility for social insurance and public assistance. The nation, desperate with a quarter of its citizens unemployed, could therefore accept as politically feasible a reversal of a centuries-old policy of local responsibility for the care of the poor. President Nixon, on the other hand, could not get welfare reform through the Congress in the seventies, because there was no similar feeling of imminent catastrophe and the nation had resumed its centuries-old suspicion of welfare cheating and a concern about damage to incentive from liberal welfare grants.

Is the policy legal?

The legality of a policy may seem to be such an obvious criterion that a discussion of it would seem unnecessary. At various times, some very workable policies have been proposed. However, they were illegal!

Costin notes the danger of unwarranted and illegal invasions of privacy that may occur when agencies providing protective services become overzealous in investigating child neglect or abuse.[27] Costin also points out the violations of legal rights that have occurred in juvenile courts, ultimately necessitating redress by the U.S. Supreme Court.[28] Social welfare policies should consider the legality of both present and alternative policies. There are a number of attorneys (some of whom are also professionally trained social workers) who can assist the social worker in this aspect of policy analysis and formulation.

Does the policy satisfy relevant interest groups?

This consideration is somewhat closely linked with political feasibility, but our earlier discussion was mainly in terms of political and legislative institutions. It is best to examine other interest groups under a separate heading. You may recall that a major assumption in this book is that a good test of policy is the amount of agreement about its value. It stands to reason that if a policy offers some benefit, service, or goods to an interest group, it will tend to look with favor on that policy. Of course, any interest group will want the policy that has the most to offer in advantages, services, or goods. Most interest groups, however, are smart enough to realize that no one gets everything they want, and they know the value in bargaining.

It could be argued that the delay in getting legislation through the U.S. Congress that would extend universal health insurance to other groups besides the aged is due to the lack of attention to this criterion. No universal health insurance law is apt to pass the Congress unless it is acceptable to the medical profession, business, insurance companies, labor, and other powerful groups. Medicare and Medicaid were finally passed only when changes were made that removed many of the objections of opposing interests and when the law clearly offered advantages to opposing groups.

Obviously, the only way one can analyze a policy along this dimension is to ask major interest groups for their judgments. Formulation and promotion of alternative policies will be enhanced if social workers build coalitions with relevant interest groups. Social workers run a considerable risk if they follow the "naive priorities" approach to social welfare policy. We would do better to acknowledge the priorities of other interest groups and try to build cooperative efforts whenever this is possible.

Is the policy scientifically sound?

The formulation of social welfare policy has not historically been closely related to scientific research for a number of reasons. Verifiable data in the social sciences is harder to acquire than in the natural sciences. We are inhibited from many kinds of experimental research. Value premises remain "non-concretized, vague and general" so that research inferences are drawn with one set of premises missing.[29] Social research involves attitudes and institutions that are complex and fluid, and that are themselves important in the causal relationship. Our own influence on research situations may cause events to change in one direction or the other.

Even more significantly, "Its [research] translation into action for the welfare of society is a . . . cumbersome process." [30] The discoveries and inventions of social scientists are not easily accepted by the groups and individuals with power at the national, state, and local levels. These groups and individuals have their own ideas and interests, and do not have as much regard for the findings of social scientists as they have for those of the physical scientists. Furthermore, social scientists have not come together on their ideas in a solid front, nor have they won over political support for their ideas from lay society. When we try to translate new ideas and knowledge into social reform, we face the extremely difficult problem of promoting change in people's institutionally anchored attitudes, and a planned and organized effort is required. It will take time and work to convince the vested interests that studies support the thesis that "well-planned social welfare policies are profitable for all classes." [31]

As we have seen in an earlier chapter, social welfare policies have been very closely tied to economic, political, and social development, as demonstrated by the shift in Western civilization from feudalism to industrialism. As welfare institutions changed in response to changing religious, social, and economic ideologies, the social welfare policies also tended to adapt to the changing circumstances. This observation was made in regard to welfare policy: "The evolution of economic security policy has been marked not so much by the abandonment of previous practices as by their incorporation within the changing pattern of welfare institutions." [32] So our welfare policies today are apt to include vestiges of earlier policies, regardless of contemporary need or contemporary research findings.

In spite of the dearth of hard data, there are indications that scientific research is increasingly being utilized in some social policy formulations. For example, Myrdal's research on American race problems is considered to have been influential as expert opinion in the Supreme Court's *Brown v. Topeka Board of Education* ruling of 1954. Eveline Burns has argued that social scientists including Keynes, Marx, Freud, Myrdal, Samuelson, Lazarsfeld, Parsons, Merton, Titmuss, and Galbraith have had a considerable impact on social policy.[33]

We can measure whether a social welfare policy is scientifically sound. We may not have perfect instruments, but evaluative research procedures, pilot projects, and genuine experimentation are increasingly being applied to social welfare programs and social treatment techniques. Within the limits of the state of the art of measurement, we can make informed judgments about whether or not things will work and how well.

Is the policy rational?

This criterion is very closely linked with the preceding one. Even though there is no scientific research at all on which to draw, there are instances when social policy formulation must take place. In these cases, one can at least ask that the policy be the result of a process of rational thinking and that it be a rational solution in the light of the goal or goals. Moreover, the policy should be judged better than other alternatives, from the standpoint of critical and rational thinking.

Is the policy economically feasible and economically superior to other alternatives?

There may be several alternatives with much to commend them. In choosing between two equally promising and acceptable alternatives, economy is certainly a sound criterion to use in making a final decision. Resources are always limited, and to commit resources in one direction is to take them away from another. Social workers have unfortunately not always seen it as part of their responsibility to assess the comparative costs of two or more alternatives. They will need to do this if their recommendations are to be heeded in the marketplace. Major American power groups, such as labor and industry, are accustomed to considering economy as a leading criterion for choosing between alternative policies, and we can only have a strong impact on national decision-making if we give close attention to economic costs. For this reason schools of social work have added evaluative research, which includes cost/benefit analysis to their curricula.

A clear-cut example of the failure of a social policy or set of policies due to lack of attention to economic considerations is the War on Poverty of the sixties. President Johnson found himself forced to choose between the War on Poverty and the War in Vietnam. He did not call off the War on Poverty, but it was fought as a rear guard action. Although there were other factors involved, the lack of funds played an important role in the shortcomings in the War on Poverty. Social workers know that there is never enough money. We are beginning to understand that there never *will be* enough, since needs always seem to be increasing. We will have to become more adept at getting the most out of our allocations.

Is the policy workable?

Workability can be looked at through various lenses. It can be assessed through rational means and through study and evaluative research. It can be assessed on quite another level in terms of acceptability to professional groups, power groups, and to the public. This acceptability factor is not necessarily reducible to the value criterion outlined above because professional and power groups may find an alternative acceptable under some circumstances in spite of dominant value positions. Thus, the Prohibition Amendment was repealed at a time when many were still opposed to widespread drinking, because the prohibition experiment had clearly failed. It had led to worse abuses than the problem it set out to correct. More recently, several states have relaxed their strict policies governing the use of marijuana, even though societal values remain opposed, because of the serious problems stemming from the unworkability of traditional policies.

A more positive, but closely related, approach to workability is concerned with the assessment of the credibility, on the part of professionals and policy makers in particular, that the results of the policy will be those actually sought. Will the probable results contribute significantly to the attainment of the policy goals? Is there a real likelihood of some kind of measurable payoff? Will the policy get the goods, services, or money to the desired groups or individuals? Is this alternative similar to any others that have been successful? These questions can be answered whether or not there has been, or will be, any scientific or rational study or evaluation. For example, we might consider the problem of starvation in some areas of the nation at various times. Few people would look with equanimity on such an occurrence, for humanitarian reasons. But how do we go about getting food to poor people in a workable manner in time to avert starvation and in appropriate quantities? Is the food stamp program workable? Cash payments? Use of surplus commodities?

Essentially, what we are talking about here is simply common sense, knowing that we are referring to a most uncommon virtue! When all other considerations have been taken into account, does the policy really work? If subjective evaluation (which this admittedly is) doesn't square with other more objective appraisals, the policy will not be enthusiastically received.

Is the policy efficient?

This criterion at first glance may seem to be encompassed in workability as well as economy. But it is a different dimension altogether. It is possible to have two workable and economical alternatives with one being much more efficient. Efficiency, according to Webster's Dictionary refers to: "1. ability to produce the desired effect with a minimum of effort, expense, or waste; 2. the ration of effective work to the energy expended in producing it." Both these definitions stress the accomplishment of the end with the least effort or energy. It is quite important that a good analysis of policy alternatives include attention to so vital an ingredient. If we are to go in to the marketplace or the legislative halls to sell a policy, it behooves us to try to make certain that it is the most efficient road to the goal. Perhaps the verb "try" needs underlining, because it is obvious that efficiency will not always be compatible with such criteria as societal values, professional values, or political feasibility.

Efficiency is measurable through evaluative research techniques. Social workers sometimes bristle at the thought of having their efficiency measured. We think that we must somehow master those feelings. Perhaps fears can be rationalized by considering that efficiency is due our clientele. Rendering a service or benefit in the same degree of quality for less money or time will be of benefit to the client.

Will the policy be likely to generate other social problems?

The literature shows clearly that some policies generate or exacerbate other social problems. Edwin Schur's book *Crimes Without Victims* gives clear evidence of this in the cases of abortion, homosexuality, and drug addiction.[34]

Our present laws against prostitution serve as a good example. Since prostitution is offensive to many people, all states except Nevada have laws against the practice. What happens? By policy, we have created a group of criminals whose crime has no victim. The customers of a prostitute are seldom, if ever, prosecuted but the prostitute herself is liable for arrest. Further, the corrupt policeman may demand money payments for protection of the prostitute. Customers may default on payment knowing that they have not incurred a legally collectible debt. The prostitute is vulnerable to blackmail should she "go straight" at some later point in her life. She can be robbed without great fear of the consequences on the part of the robber. While we are not endorsing prostitution, we are saying that the policy of legislating against prostitution has generated a whole series of other crimes that are clearly possible only because prostitution is itself illegal.

It would seem only reasonable that each policy alternative be examined, in the light of all available knowledge, to see whether there is a likelihood of new problems emerging or the aggravation of other existing problems.

This, too, is risky and subjective at best. There is no foolproof way to do it, since it is a judgment based on wisdom and experience. But the effort to estimate the negative impact still needs to be made and the possibilities weighted as a risk. It is, of course, conceivable that a policy could cause a new problem or exacerbate an existing one and still be desirable because of its excellent showing on other criteria.

This framework that we have just summarized is not the last word. Some of the criteria are tentative and subjective. Experience may cause us to reject some, revise others, or add to the list. We do believe that these considerations have utility, and we hope to establish their usefulness. In the next chapters we will apply this framework to several important areas of social welfare policy. It is relatively easy for us (as is true of all Monday morning quarterbacks) to discuss past policies. It will be more difficult to build a convincing case for present and future policies.

REFERENCES

1. David Braybrooke and Charles E. Lindblom, A Strategy of Decision (New York: The Free Press of Glencoe, 1963), pp. 6–8.

2. Yehezkel Dror, Design for Policy Sciences (New York: Elsevier, 1971), p. 141.

3. These requirements are adapted from Ian L. McHarg, Design with Nature (Garden City, N.Y.: The Natural History Press, 1969), p. 105.

4. Ibid., p. 34.

5. *Ibid.*, p. 52.

6. *Ibid.*, p. 80.

7. *Ibid.*, pp. 188, 197.

8. Winifred Bell, "Obstacles to Shifting from the Descriptive to the Analytical Approach in Teaching Social Services," *Journal of Education for Social Work*, Vol. 5, No. 1 (Spring 1969), p. 7.

9. *Ibid.*, p. 8.

10. Neil Gilbert and Harry Specht, *Dimensions of Social Welfare Policy* (Englewood Cliffs, N.J.: Prentice-Hall, 1974), p. 29.

11. David Gil, *Unravelling Social Policy* (Cambridge, Mass.: Schenkman, 1973).

12. *Ibid.*, pp. 18–23.

13. Alfred J. Kahn, *Social Policy and Social Services* (New York: Random House, 1973), p. 56.

14. Robert Perlman and Arnold Gurin, *Community Organization and Social Planning* (New York: John Wiley, 1972), p. 153.

15. See Charles Frankel, "Social Values and Professional Values," *Journal of Education for Social Work*, Vol. 5, No. 1 (Spring 1969), p. 35.

16. See Nathan E. Cohen, *Social Work and Social Problems* (New York: National Association of Social Workers, 1964), pp. ix–xiv, 369–372, for an analytical scheme in which there is a built-in recognition of the disparities between professional values and societal values.

17. *Ibid.*, p. 35.

18. See, for example, Elizabeth G. Meier, "Child Neglect," in Nathan E. Cohen, ed., *Social Work and Social Problems* (New York: National Association of Social Workers, 1964), pp. 156–160.

19. Alexis de Tocqueville, *Democracy in America*, trans. by Henry Reeve, Esq. 5th ed. (Boston: John Allyn, Publisher, 1873). See especially Volume II.

20. See, for example, Franklin M. Zweig, "The Social Worker as Legislative Ombudsman," *Social Work*, Vol. 14, No. 1 (January 1969), pp. 30–31.

21. James Q. Wilson, ed., *City Politics and Public Policy* (New York: John Wiley, 1969), p. 7.

22. David Greenstone and Paul E. Peterson, "Reformers, Machines, and the War on Poverty," in James Q. Wilson, ed., *ibid.*, pp. 167–292.

23. *Ibid.*, p. 267.

24. Wilson, *op. cit.*, p. 13.

25. *Ibid.*, pp. 11–12.

26. See Charles S. Prigmore, "Use of the Coalition in Legislative Action," *Social Work*, Vol. 19, No. 1 (January 1974), pp. 96–102.

27. Lela B. Costin, *Child Welfare: Politics and Practice* (New York: McGraw-Hill, 1972), p. 278.

28. *Ibid.*, pp. 111–119.

29. Gunnar Myrdal, "The Social Sciences and Their Impact on Society," in Herman D. Stein, ed., *Social Theory and Social Intervention* (Cleveland: The Press of Case Western Reserve University, 1963), pp. 151–152.

30. *Ibid.,* p. 154.
31. *Ibid.,* p. 159.
32. Samuel Mencher, *Poor Law to Poverty Program* (Pittsburgh: University of Pittsburgh Press, 1967), p. xv.
33. Eveline M. Burns, "Commentary," in Herman D. Stein, ed., *op. cit.,* pp. 170–173.
34. Edwin M. Schur, *Crimes Without Victims* (Englewood Cliffs, N.J.: Prentice-Hall, 1965), pp. 25–62, 82–102, 130–164.

QUESTIONS FOR DISCUSSION

1. Give one or two examples of the "naive criteria" and "naive priority" methods of policy formulation. What limitations, if any, do you see in these examples for the development of the most useful and viable policies?

2. What do you think McHarg means by the "solution of maximum social utility"? Can you think of an example of a policy that meets this criterion?

3. Do you recall any public policies that clearly coincide with the self-interest of most or all individuals in the society? Can you think of examples of clashes between public policy and individual self-interest?

4. Give some examples of instances in which social work goals may be at variance with politicians' or legislators' goals.

5. Is assessment and comparison of the economic cost of social welfare programs a criterion that can be reconciled with social work values? Defend your position.

6. Can you think of any social welfare policy firmly based on scientific research? Or one established for other reasons but not inconsistent with the results of scientific research?

7. How would you characterize the contemporary "style" in social policy in your state or community?

8. Distinguish between workability and efficiency as criteria. Which seems basically more important?

9. Can every power or interest group be benefited by any single social policy. If not, how can this problem be overcome?

10. Describe a social problem that is caused or aggravated by a social policy (something other than the examples given in the text). Discuss.

SUGGESTED PROJECTS

1. Choose a social problem of contemporary interest, such as poverty, mental illness, or juvenile delinquency, and examine it through the screen of criteria proposed in Chapter 3. Do current policies meet the criteria? Can you suggest other alternatives that meet the criteria more closely?

2. Interview a mayor, state or federal legislator, political analyst, or writer. Ask this person to evaluate the criteria suggested in the chapter. Does he or she consider that many of these criteria are actually utilized? If so, which are utilized and which are not? Does this person think that those that are not currently utilized should be put to use?

FOR FURTHER READING

Winifred Bell. "Obstacles to Shifting from the Descriptive to the Analytical Approach in Teaching Social Services," *Journal of Education for Social Work*, Vol. 5, No. 1 (Spring 1969). A thoughtful and well-organized discussion of the need to move toward a more systematic and analytical method of teaching social welfare policy and services in the social work curriculum. The article captures the spirit and substance of the shift in stress that started in the sixties.

David Braybrooke and Charles E. Lindblom. *A Strategy of Decision*. New York: The Free Press of Glencoe, 1963. The authors discuss various traditional methods of decision-making, which they find to be inadequate or impossible. They offer a strategy of disjointed incrementalism, which is simply the process of making policy choices by means of a series of small steps. Their strategy has the value of a built-in consensus of relevant interest groups. Their work is stimulating and useful.

Yehezkel Dror. *Design for Policy Sciences*. New York: Elsevier, 1971. A review of the weaknesses of the behavioral and management sciences as a foundation for policy studies. It lays out a rationale, parameters, and dimensions of a new field of policy sciences. It is carefully written, although quite condensed in almost outline form. Very useful for the serious student of policy analysis.

David G. Gil. *Unravelling Social Policy*. Cambridge, Mass.: Schenkman, 1973. A brief review of the social welfare literature bearing directly on social policy and conceptual model of social policies stressing the quality of life with a particular focus on human relationships. Gil finds the processes of resource development, status allocation, and rights distribution as the key mechanisms of social policies, elaborates a framework for analysis of social policy, and applies his model and framework to a specific problem, that of mothers' wages. A valuable book but difficult for students to read and grasp fully.

Alfred J. Kahn. *Social Policy and Social Services*. New York: Random House, 1973. A monograph delineating the latent and manifest functions of the social services, reviewing the costs of a variety of services, providing a framework of social service policy, and exploring the relationship between policy and program. Valuable for students interested in the relations between social services, policies, goals, and specific programs.

Harold D. Lasswell. *A Pre-View of Policy Sciences*. New York: Elsevier, 1971. A pioneer in the policy sciences movement, Lasswell provides a social process model as well as a decision process model for the analysis of social policy. Although perhaps more difficult for the beginning student than Dror's book, it provides a logical and systematic framework for understanding and participating in the analysis of social policy.

Richard M. Titmuss. *Commitment to Welfare*. New York: Pantheon, 1968. Titmuss has been influential in American approaches to social policy analysis, both in his stress on the redistribution function of social policy and in his incisive and original discussion of the components of social policy. Serious students of social policy should familiarize themselves with his writings, although recognizing his elevation of redistribution to being synonymous with social policy in general rather than simply a specific social policy.

Part II
Challenges to
Policy Analysis and
Formulation: Five
Examples

*In the next five chapters we look at specific areas of interest to
social welfare policy: income maintenance, poverty, health and
mental health care, housing, and service delivery. We discuss our
analysis of the current policies that guide programs in the area
and suggest innovative alternative policies. These new policies are
not necessarily recommendations, but are intended to provide
take-off points for the reader's own attempts at analysis and formulation. We have tried to be provocative in some areas and to
avoid being constrained by current policies.*

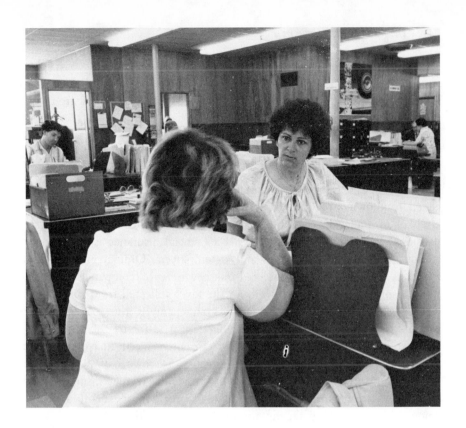

4 *Income Maintenance in a Money Economy*

The loss of earnings that occurs due to retirement, chronic illness, disability, unemployment, or death of a breadwinner is a severe problem for people whose income is solely from wages. These contingencies may be catastrophic for the person, but their impact is also great upon the whole society, illustrating the interdependence of individuals in a society. Modern societies have developed social welfare programs whose manifest goal is the maintenance of income. Some economists include programs designed to deal with poverty in income maintenance. We however have chosen to separate them. Under income maintenance we will address policies and programs designed to maintain income for those who ordinarily have earnings but have had an interruption in their working careers. In Chapter 5 we will address the problem of poverty and the programs and policies designed to deal with those who either have no ordinary income from jobs or who are underemployed. We recognize that the problems of income maintenance and poverty are interrelated, but we believe that separate treatment is justified since the policies that address the continuance of income for the ordinarily employed are quite different from the policies aimed at the question of poverty.

Definition of Social Insurance

The programs designed to maintain income by replacing earnings are generally known as "social insurance." Social insurance differs from the kinds of insurance that people know most about (life, annuities, private pensions) in several important ways. First, social insurance is financed by compulsory taxes on employees and/or employers. Ordinary insurance is voluntary and may be purchased from a variety of companies. Second, social insurance benefits are paid from the taxes collected from the current work force and/or their employers. As an example, the social security benefits that older people are getting now are paid for by the social security taxes deducted from the salaries of currently employed workers. The system has been on this kind of a pay-as-you-go basis since 1939. Although the original notion was to set up a trust fund like regular insurance, the decision was made to change to a policy of providing a socially adequate amount of money to make up for the lacks in existing old age pension programs.[1] Private retirement insurance (an annuity, for instance) involves the investment of the premiums so that the insured is paying for his or her own benefits. Third, because social insurances are governmental programs, legislatures can change the rules. In privately purchased insurance, the contract is binding on the company. Finally, social insurances tend to redistribute income from those who have it to those who no longer have it. Private insurance does not.[2]

The redistribution of income occurs as either a cash or an "in-kind" (goods or services) transfer. For example, older workers who retired at comparatively lower salaries gain the benefits of the contributions of present workers. In the process, cash is transferred from today's work force to yesterday's workers. Since the benefits for the retired worker exceed his own contributions, some income is redistributed from those who have income to those whose income is reduced.

The idea behind income maintenance is that the worker (and/or the worker's family) will be able to survive and so will most of the people with whom he or she does business. At least some cash will flow in the economy despite the contingencies of death, disability, retirement, industrial injury, or unemployment.

In this chapter we will identify the major policies that govern income maintenance programs in the United States. We will analyze them using the scheme that we developed in Chapter 3, and we will use this analysis as the basis for generating some different policy formulations. We want to remind the reader that we do not consider our formulations as the only ones that could be made. Some of them may look attractive (and some may not), but they are primarily for the purpose of illustrating the policy analysis and formulation process and to open rather than to close the discussion.

Income maintenance programs have developed in a piecemeal fashion in the United States. We can best understand the present income maintenance policies by briefly reviewing the major programs. This review is not a detailed description of the programs nor of their history. For details the reader should consult other sources.[3] Our purpose is to focus on what we think are salient policy issues. Our approach includes some issues that other writers discuss, but excludes some that others stress. This is due to the nature of our argument.

Workmen's Compensation

Workmen's compensation is based on state laws that require employers to compensate workers who are the victims of industrial accidents or occupational diseases. There are two kinds of benefits: (1) cash benefits to replace earnings and (2) payment of medical care. Employers usually discharge their responsibility toward their employees by purchasing insurance from private companies that specialize in workmen's compensation insurance. In many states the law requires the employer to carry insurance. In others, insurance is not required by law, but since employers must be able to meet employee claims, some form of insurance or risk pooling is necessary. In some states the state provides an insurance fund, but most do not.

There is also a workmen's compensation program for federal employees. This was, in fact, the first workmen's compensation law (the Federal Employee's Compensation Act of 1908). Most European countries had workmen's compensation laws before the United States. The earliest was Germany's under Bismarck in 1883. Bismarck did not promote workmen's compensation because of his humanitarian notions but to "cool out" the socialist opposition. The first state law in this country was passed in New York in 1910. By 1920, only eight states did not have such laws. In a few more years, all states had them.

Levy, Lewis, and Martin distinguish three major historical periods in the development of public policy.[4]

1. A period before social insurance developed, in which an employee's sole recourse was to sue his employer for personal injury damages under common law. To win such a damage suit, it was necessary for the employee to prove that the employer was negligent. This was difficult to do. Other employees did not want to testify against their employer. Moreover, the law allowed various possible defenses, including negligence of a fellow employee and negligence of the worker himself.

2. A period of ferment in which the common law remedy was rejected and efforts were made to enact compensation laws.

3. The period of legislative action in which workmen's compensation programs became institutionalized.

Under the present system there is no exhaustive search for negligence. The assumption is that occupational injury or illness is a social risk to be handled as a social cost through social insurance.

Universal coverage is a goal of any social insurance, but it is not realized in workmen's compensation. Most state laws still exclude domestic workers, farm laborers, casual workers, and employees of charitable and religious institutions. The present programs cover only about 80 percent of the labor force.

The operation of the workmen's compensation programs is deficient in several ways. There is great variability among states, and claims are handled in a variety of ways. Workers are often urged to settle out of court for an attractive lump sum which is not as much as regular income would provide. Benefits are uneven and do not replace lost wages, but are limited to about two-thirds of the worker's salary.

Perhaps an even more basic shortcoming is the narrow scope of judicial decisions over the years in interpreting the limits of compensation. Our examples come from the cases cited by Levy, Lewis, and Martin. The courts have held that compensation is not awarded for the injury but for the impairment of earning caused by the injury.

> The upshot of the prevailing doctrine is that pain and suffering and dignitary losses are not compensated, as such, whether or not employer negligence can be proved, and thus an employee may be disfigured by burns, *Morgan v. Ray L. Smith & Son*, 79 F. Supp. 971 (D. Kans. 1948), or suffer the loss of sexual organs, *Smith v. Baker*, 157 Okl. 155, 11 P. 2d 132 (1932) and have no remedy.[5]

Laws and courts in different states have viewed the loss of body parts in widely differing ways. In Hawaii the loss of the first finger is valued at $5,175. This is more than is allowed in Wyoming for loss of an eye, and just a few hundred dollars less than is awarded in Wyoming for loss of a leg at the hip ($5,800).

Even more restricting are the courts' positions on the necessary connection between work and injury. The courts have consistently held that the injury must arise "out of and in the course of employment." Thus, most injuries incurred while employees are traveling to and from work are not normally covered. The injuries may be covered, however, if it can be shown that a special risk was involved in going to and from the particular place of business (such as turning off a heavily traveled highway onto a small road). An emergency, special mission, a situation involving employer-furnished transportation, or a job that requires travel also might substantiate a claim that the injury arose in the course of employment. The courts interpret these situations in ways that may seem illogical to laymen. For example, in *Wiedenbach* v. *Miller*, a 1952 Minnesota case, the court ruled that a driver salesman with a varying route was not acting in the course of employment when he was drowned trying to save a man in a lake 250 feet off the route. This court, however, cited another case in which a man drowned and compensation was awarded. In this case the man worked for a contractor whose business site contained a recreation center for employees along which ran a dangerous channel forbidden for use. The man attempted to rescue two drowning people and was himself drowned. In this case the proximity of the recreation center to the dangerous channel created a "zone of special danger" affecting obligations and conditions of employment.

Consider the following decision. In *Lathrop* v. *Tobin-Hamilton Shoe Mfg. Co.*, a 1966 Missouri case, payment was denied after a woman was killed by a runaway driverless automobile which broke through the wall of the factory and hit her at her machine. The court ruled that the "injuries did not arise out of employment because they were not the rational consequence of a hazard connected with her employment." Or consider this situation. Normally employees hit by a stray bullet while on the street in an employer's interests are compensated. Yet in *Auman* v. *Breckinridge Telephone Co.*, a 1933 Minnesota case, a man was denied compensation because he was "hit by a stray bullet while crossing a vacant lot between his office and a garage." The moral of these two cases is clear. Stay on the streets rather than in vacant lots, and make sure that drivers around your business place are "rational."

State legislators and the courts have consistently felt impelled to broaden protection under workmen's compensation because of a lack of alternatives. It is this problem that has led to the hairsplitting decisions of courts. Levy, Lewis, and Martin conclude: "In retrospect, it seems clear that if adequate social or private insurance protection against nonoccupational disability had existed, workmen's compensation would not have been under the pressures constantly to expand its scope." [6]

It is clear that workmen's compensation did not develop as a wholly humanitarian policy, but primarily as a protection for employers. The frequent court tests suggest that boundaries are unclear. Consequently, workmen's compensation is not a certain way of protecting the work force against loss of income due to health problems.

Unemployment Insurance

Unemployment insurance is a federal-state program designed to insure the worker against periods of unemployment. In 1932 Wisconsin passed the first law of this type in the United States. Many European countries including England, Germany, and Italy had already passed such laws.

So that there would be coverage in all states, a provision of the Social Security Act imposed a tax on payrolls. If a state enacted its own program, the federal government forgave 90 percent of the tax. Very quickly, all states enacted unemployment insurance laws. Apparently, however, the designers of the Social Security Act really envisioned a federal approach. One of the chief architects of the Social Security Act, Edwin E. Witte, observed that a federal-state partnership could be more easily converted later to a federal system than could one operated only by the states.[7]

For the most part, states have limited their coverage to industrial and commercial workers. Generally excluded are agricultural workers, domestic employees, the self-employed, local and state governmental employees, and those who work for religious and charitable institutions. Only a few states cover any of these groups.

All states define unemployment insurance as a matter of right. For example, a recent publication of the Alabama agency states that "eligible unemployed workers should receive benefits based upon rights rather than as 'charity.' A test of 'need' is not involved." [8] Needs tests, in simplest terms, measure eligibility for benefits by some standard of income or assets.

To be eligible for benefits, a worker must be ready and able to work, unemployed, registered for work at a state employment office, and have been working in covered work over a base eligibility period. The base period is usually the first four quarters of the last five calendar quarters preceding the claim.

One cannot receive unemployment benefits if he or she quits a job without a legally acceptable reason, is fired for misconduct on the job, fails to register with the state employment service, refuses a job equal to or better than the one previously held, or goes on strike. Critics have argued that an unemployed worker should be required to take any job offered, but the law does not require a worker to switch occupations or to take a lesser job than that for which one is qualified. If this provision were changed, it would probably have a depressing effect on wages. This would not, in the long run, be a good policy.

Benefits are not equal to previously earned income. An unemployed worker generally gets about half as much in benefits as he or she previously earned. The low-paid worker who is unemployed for a relatively short time actually gets only slightly less cash than before. The worker gets more real compensation because he is not taxed during unemployment. This situation is relatively benign only if income is low and unemployment continues for a short time. The longer unemployment goes, and the higher the income, the more difficulty one has in making ends meet.

The program is not really designed to deal with chronic unemployment. The basic benefit period is twenty-six weeks. The state may extend this benefit period for another thirteen weeks if unemployment in the state goes over 5 percent. The federal supplementary benefit system, which was in force during the recession in the early 1970s, provided an additional twenty-six weeks of benefits in two thirteen-week stages, depending upon the percentage of unemployment. Under special circumstances, then, benefits have been paid for as long as sixty-five weeks—but this kind of coverage is only provided during a nationwide recession. This extended coverage does not pertain to individuals under ordinary unemployment circumstances. Normally, the unemployed individual will get benefits for twenty-six weeks—half a year.

Some believe that the system is generous enough to increase unemployment and that unemployed persons may delay seeking work. This opinion rests on the premise that there is no shortage of jobs:

> The large pool of long-term unemployed workers has been replaced by a much smaller relative number whose durations of unemployment are also much shorter. *Almost every unemployed person can now find a job in a very short time.*[9] (emphasis added)

We think that urban black youth, whose unemployment rate runs as high as 50 percent, may have a hard time comprehending this statement.

How have the courts responded to the unemployment insurance laws? Their interpretations have been very narrow in many instances. Such a narrow interpretation greatly reduces the impact of an unemployment insurance program, both on income maintenance and unemployment. For example, a carpenter with residences in Indianapolis and in Florida could not find work in Indianapolis and went to his other home in Florida, where he had always spent winters due to his wife's poor health. He could not find work in Florida either, although he tried diligently, finally returning to Indianapolis. He was denied unemployment insurance for his ten weeks in Florida on the basis that he should have known that work was more available in Indianapolis than in Florida.

Even more restrictive is the decision in *State v. Hix,* a 1949 West Virginia case, in which the court denied several claims in which the people left work because of illness. The court held that if they quit because of illness, they were not eligible to work and therefore were ineligible for benefits.

This case points up the inconsistencies and unreliability of unemployment insurance as an income maintenance measure. If a person must leave work because of illness but cannot draw compensation because his illness renders him unavailable for employment, how does society expect him to survive until the illness is sufficiently alleviated?

In another case a claimant was denied benefits because he refused a job which his union had forbade him to accept because the wages were not equal to the union scale. A higher court affirmed the decision, even though the worker would have lost group health insurance, retirement, and other benefits from the union if he had accepted the job. In another case a union had a mandatory retirement age, and persons filing for unemployment insurance benefits who were involuntarily retired were not considered eligible for benefits.

In a case concerning a dismissal for misconduct, an employee was denied unemployment benefits because he was fired for drinking during off-duty hours. The higher court upheld the decision on the basis that the employee knew that his employer was able to secure automobile liability insurance for the drivers in his vending business only on the basis of a written contract that drivers were not to drink alcohol either on or off the job. But three judges dissented on the grounds that there was no proof that the insurance would have in fact been cancelled for off-duty drinking.

In a case involving a labor dispute, a St. Paul plant of Ford Motor Company finally had to stop work due to lack of parts from the River Rouge and Detroit plants, where a strike was in progress. Although the St. Paul plant was not involved in any way in the strike, the court held that Ford had a master union contract and therefore unemployment insurance benefits were not available to workers laid off at St. Paul.

These examples [10] illustrate the fine line that often exists between eligibility and noneligibility in the operation of the unemployment insurance program. It is a rough and uneven tool at best for the handling of unemployment. It is also unwieldy as a mechanism of income maintenance since the eligibility question turns on issues other than loss of income.

Retirement, Survivors, Disability, and Health Insurance

What is generally termed "social security" is the federal social insurance program that covers retirement, survivors, disability, and health insurance (RSDHI). It provides cash payments to retired and disabled members of the work force and their families, as well as benefits to the families of deceased workers. RSDHI benefits are paid from taxes on incomes. In the case of wage earners, the employer and the wage earner each pay one-half of the tax. Self-employed people pay a tax on their incomes that does not quite equal the amount paid by employer and employee on a given income. Part of the tax goes to provide health insurance (Medicare), which we will discuss in Chapter 6 in connection with health and mental health policy.

Social security is a vast program with over 90 percent of the American work force covered by RSDHI at a cost of over $80 billion. As a whole, this is not a highly controversial program, but there are a number of policy issues that are generally brought out when RSDHI is discussed. One of these issues is the historic question of selectivity versus universality. That is, should social insurance be designed to provide benefits only for those in need or should the benefits be for all citizens? The American approach tends toward universality. A second issue has to do with adequacy of benefits. Should benefits be keyed to contributions or should they be socially adequate? As we mentioned, the United States has opted for social adequacy. However, it might be more accurate to describe this as a policy of *partial* social adequacy. Although benefits have increased, they are not enough to live on. Workers are advised (most recently in a radio spot delivered by country singer Donna Fargo) to save and to invest because social security will not be enough.

Alicia Munnel, an economist, has written one of the most recent evaluations of the retirement benefits under social security.[11] Two of her criticisms are pertinent. First, she suggests that social security may have a negative effect on saving, since workers may count too heavily on their retirement benefits. The second criticism is that the benefit structure overcompensates for inflation. In 1972 an automatic cost of living adjustment was made in the benefit payment structure. Munnel grants that this is sensible for presently retired workers, but since social security benefits are related to wages, today's workers' income will qualify them for extremely high benefits that will be hard to finance. Increases in the social security taxes passed in 1977 will lessen the problem. Further, these same legislative changes included eliminating the overindexing by a formula that will keep benefits to slightly less than half a person's former earnings. Even with the higher taxes, financing the system will be a problem due to demographic shifts. Today's declining birth rate suggests that when the baby boom children reach retirement, it will be difficult for the work force to maintain benefits.

In addition to the above issues, others have raised the question of social security's effect on the reduction of poverty. This is not a simple issue. Some believe that, although the current transfer systems are "considerably less than adequate," the social insurance programs have had an impact on poverty greater than those programs aimed especially at the poor.[12] This impact has been greatest on the aged. In analyzing the problems of the public assistance programs, the President's Commission on Income Maintenance Programs stated that social insurance programs (RSDHI, unemployment insurance, and workmen's compensation) "do not provide adequate benefit levels for the very poor." [13] This is simply because the poor have irregular work records and low incomes that do not yield the same tax contributions of higher paid and more regularly paid workers.

The history of the passage of the Social Security Act of 1935, which set up the present system, was a stormy one. There were many varied ideas and plans competing for attention. For example, the Townsend plan to give a flat grant of $200 a month to every person over age 65 acted as a spur to passage of the act. Southern senators forced the old-age assistance provisions of the program to be under state jurisdiction in order to keep federal authorities from influencing the size of grants to blacks.[14] The point of this discussion is that while social security is a well-accepted program, it is not without unsettled or unfinished issues.

It is not our intent to cover the development of the social security program. For a brief but detailed summary, the reader is referred to Munnel's Appendix, which traces the changes in the program over time.[15] Our focus is on the policies that guide social security as we now know it. We believe that the program currently follows these guiding principles:

1. The program should be financed by both employer and employee contributions (taxes).
2. Benefits ought to be work connected and based on earnings.
3. Coverage ought to be universal, and participation should be compulsory.
4. Benefits ought to be independent of need.
5. Benefits should move in the direction of social adequacy.

This last point is somewhat clouded by the notion that social security aims at providing a basic floor. Although the intent may be to move toward adequacy, it is certainly a minimal concept of what is adequate. The fact remains that many of today's retired receive extremely low benefits because their earnings were low during their working years. An older person of our acquaintance received monthly benefits of $237.30 in 1976. Benefits went up 6 percent for 1977. This means that the individual now receives $251.80. The percent increases may appear generous, but this only amounts to $14 a month. Social adequacy is still a long way off.

A Comparison of Current Policies and Selected Alternatives

We believe the major programs coping with income maintenance in the United States represent five major policies. They are characterized by the following: (1) A mix of state, federal-state partnership, and federal programs. (2) A mix of aims and purposes, in addition to income maintenance; for example, workmen's compensation and unemployment insurance both very clearly carry the aims of prevention of social problems through pressuring employers to adopt sound and workable safety measures and to stabilize employment.[16] (3) The clear intent to finance the social insurance primarily by employers (although RSDHI is financed equally through payroll taxes imposed on employer and employees. (4) A stress on work-connected benefits throughout all three programs. (5) A predilection toward minimum benefits, particularly in the employer-financed workmen's compensation and unemployment insurance programs. Even in RSDHI, the 1972 amendments which adjust social security benefits for increases in the cost of living start with such a low base that the adjustment will only gradually result in improved benefits. Other policies could be easily pinpointed, but these five give a fairly adequate summary of the major present policies.

Alternative policies that could be considered are (1) administering the programs solely at the federal level, or at the very least establishing uniform federal standards; (2) targeting more directly on income maintenance as the aim (rather than employment stabilization or industrial safety); (3) sharing of financing of all three programs equally among employer, employee, and general taxes; (4) gradually minimizing the stress on work-connected benefits; and, (5) providing genuinely adequate benefits.

Let us now look at the current policy and the alternatives in terms of the framework for analysis proposed in Chapter 3.

Is the policy compatible with contemporary "style"?

When the social insurance programs were first enacted into law, there was widespread fear of federal control. The southern states feared the racial consequences, as we pointed out earlier. The various states were considered to have widely different problems requiring different approaches. There was little experience in 1935 with federally operated programs, except for the post office, the military services, and a relatively small civil service. Today the situation is vastly different. Federal programs are commonplace. The states have become less dissimilar from one another as transportation and communication have improved. Many people consider federal administration more efficient and less corrupt than state administration. Contemporary style, in short, would favor federalized administration of the three programs, rather than the continuation of all three patterns.

In the 1930s it was considered necessary to induce and even pressure employers to adopt safety measures and a more stable approach to employment. There were few laws on the books to accomplish these objectives. Today the nation has a staggering array of laws and programs. For example, the U.S. Department of Labor has major divisions on employment standards and occupational safety and health, implementing laws requiring employers to conform to a variety of safety, health, and employment practices. Employers can no longer legally hire and fire because of sex, race, seniority, union membership, age, or religion. Employers can no longer ignore prescribed standards of health and safety. In the 1930s no such laws or programs existed, and it made good sense to build employer incentives into the new social insurance programs. Today the pressures on employers are redundant, unnecessarily cumbersome, and, worst of all, prone to create gaps and inadequacies in the programs. It is more in keeping with contemporary style to concentrate solely on income maintenance.

Similarly, the payroll tax on the employer was in keeping with the contemporary style in the 1930s. Employers were widely regarded as the chief architects of unemployment, work injuries, disability, and poverty in old age. Therefore, employers were expected to bear the burden of the social insurance costs. Today, in a more sophisticated world, these social problems are seen to relate more to actions and attitudes of government and the public as well as employees. It is more consistent with contemporary style to have a sharing of costs between the various forces involved.

Work-connected benefits were vital in the thinking of the thirties; but with ever-increasing automation, some are beginning to have second thoughts about work incentives. We are no longer sure that jobs can expand as rapidly as the working-age population. People are living longer, and in 1977 the Congress raised the compulsory retirement age for federal workers to 70. This will increase the competition for scarce jobs. The basic problem is that we are likely never again to have as many full-time jobs as we have able-bodied people ready and willing to work. Some reassessment of the work ethic is apt to occur by the 1980s. It is no longer compatible with our contemporary style to anchor the social insurance so immovably with work. It might make more sense to focus on other values—the need to maintain buying power, for example.

The provision of minimum benefits was clearly compatible with contemporary style in the early decades of the social insurances. But increasingly demands are being made to raise benefits to a level consistent with a decent life-style. As the work ethic begins to serve as a less vigorous prod, people will continue to demand higher benefits, and the Congress is more likely to accede to these demands. This will be particularly true in another decade when an even larger proportion of the voting public will be over 65.

Does the policy contribute to equity and justice?

The policy of having one of the social insurances administered at the state level, one a partnership and the rest at the federal level, produces a variety of gaps, inequities, and inconsistencies. A more equitable and just administrative procedure, which would ensure uniform and consistent coverage of all citizens, would be to turn to federal administration alone. As an example of inequities and inconsistencies in the present arrangement, some states have had conservative policies on workmen's compensation and unemployment insurance that have restricted the number and size of benefits. Others have been more liberal. Some states have had serious budgetary problems. Others have had less serious problems.

Similarly, it appears to be less equitable and just to expect the social insurances to serve a number of aims and purposes than to tailor programs specifically to meet income maintenance needs. If the aim of pressuring employers to adopt safety measures becomes paramount in a given state at a given time, the income maintenance objective may well be neglected. If the aim is largely or even partly to encourage industry to stabilize employment, more thought may be given to the needs of industry than to the needs of workers. Desirable as these other aims are, they may not serve the interest of justice and equity if they at times clash.

The targeting of financial support of the social insurances on payroll taxes on employers, particularly for workmen's compensation and unemployment insurance, may tend to make the systems more responsive to employers than to employees. "Who pays the piper, calls the tune." The present system tends to weight the operation of the laws, policies, and programs to employer needs and wishes, particularly when the administration of programs is at the state level. By and large, state governments tend to be more responsive to employer pressures than to the federal government.[17] Sharing the cost of income maintenance among employers, employees, and taxpayers may well make the system more equitable and just by ensuring that a more diverse set of pipers calls the tune. This sharing device may be a step toward progressive tax reforms, ultimately leading toward the financing of social security out of general revenue. Such a development, enlightened though it is in its removal of the connection between work and income maintenance, is not apt to occur soon.

Too heavy an emphasis on work incentives tends to skew the programs too far toward helping able-bodied workers in the so-called earning ages to the neglect of the disabled, the mothers with small children, minority-group youth, and the aged. Current benefits are low because they are based on wages earned before the inflation of the seventies.

The present minimum benefits policy is neither equitable nor just. True, the lower paid workers get more in benefits in proportion to their income than do higher paid workers, but the higher paid worker's lower proportionate return is unimportant if he or she has investments, stock options, and savings built on top of social security benefits. The minimum benefits are not enough to live on, and the lower paid worker is seldom in a position to have other resources on which to depend. Minimum benefits create the need for additional supports, adding the expense of additional programs. A more adequate social insurance benefit could be cheaper for the taxpayer, since only one social insurance program would have to be administered.

Is the policy compatible with social work values?

As indicated above, present policies tend to favor employers' input into decision-making, state control of programs in two of the insurances, a heavy stress on work incentives, and inadequate benefits. We think that all of these features seem to be opposed to social work values of worth and dignity of the individual. As social security is now administered, it is hard to maintain worth and dignity on such limited payments.

Is the policy compatible with other important values in the society?

There can be little doubt that the social insurances when they were enacted into law were consistent with the American values of achievement and success, activity and work, moral orientation, external conformity, nationalism, and racism. The social insurances clearly extolled work and achievement, have encouraged conformity and nationalism as they have been administered (such as denying benefits to the wife of a deported Communist), have supported conventional morality (as evidenced by a preference for providing benefits to widows who were absent from the home but still legally married over common-law wives who resided with the breadwinner). That these policies supported racism can be inferred from the concessions made to the South to make the insurances state-run rather than federal programs. The alternative policies we propose would show up somewhat less favorably in regard to this set of values.

There is little evidence that the social insurances are consistent with the American values of humanitarianism, efficiency, equality, science and rationality, and democracy. Although the programs were humanitarian in intent, at least in part, they were established with built-in biases toward employer interests and the rights of the middle and upper classes. The social insurances, taken collectively, are far from efficient, with their diverse administrative patterns, conflicting aims, and diverse methods of financing. One integrated federal system would be far more efficient from practically any standpoint. The social insurance policies are not egalitarian. The lower class is treated differentially and discriminatorily.

There is little evidence of the use of scientific data or rational thinking in the genesis of the programs, although the study of the programs since their inception has often been scientific and rational. Their beginnings owed far more to political and economic concerns than to any scientific or rational inputs.

They are democratic only in the sense that their birth and perpetuation have occurred through democratic processes. Their operation tends to be more bureaucratic than democratic, although the RSDHI programs in particular have undergone some thirty-one changes in coverage and thirty-two changes in benefits since 1951. These changes came about through congressional action, indicating a sensitivity toward voter interest in higher benefits and expanded coverage. One might reasonably conclude that the RSDHI programs tend to be more democratic in their operation, even though highly computerized and bureaucratized, than the other two social insurances. The alternative policies that we have proposed would show up far more favorably in regard to these values, being more humanitarian, efficient, equal, rational, and democratic.

The values of the individual personality and of freedom represent a somewhat unclear picture in their relation to the social insurances. There is a place for the individual in appeals within the systems, as well as to courts. There are certainly provisions for individual situations in the various social insurances, as they occur in frequently encountered patterns. Really unique situations, however, do not seem to be well handled, as demonstrated by a variety of court cases and administrative decisions. It is best, for example, not to fit into any unusual category if you are to apply for benefits under the social insurances. Rights are apt to be rights for the conformists rather than for the individuals, as we noted in discussing the problems of the common-law wife.

There is freedom in the sense that the individual can choose not to apply for benefits from workmen's compensation or unemployment. There is no freedom for one to decide whether to contribute or belong to the RSDHI program. There is no freedom for the employer to choose whether to take part in unemployment insurance programs or workmen's compensation programs, although a degree of freedom exists at the state level in choosing patterns of administration. Employers have freedom, as indicated above, to influence the operation of state programs. In sum, employers and states probably have more freedom than individual citizens in these social insurance programs. The alternative policies would probably redistribute these values somewhat, taking less account of employers and states and more of individual citizens.

Is the policy politically acceptable?

The social insurances were all politically acceptable, obviously, when they were enacted into law. They have retained a considerable degree of political acceptability, although with recurrent questions and crises. For example, concerns were voiced about the length of time unemployment insurance could be received during the high unemployment of the 1970s, and the length was increased by federal law. The RSDHI programs have come in for political criticisms from all directions, in regard to coverage, size of benefits, financial stability, and abuses of the Medicare program. It is perhaps fair to say that none of the income maintenance programs is politically secure from attack but none is in great danger of dismemberment or radical change. The current political climate appears to favor incremental changes rather than a radical upheaval of these programs.

The alternative policies we offered were conceived as incremental changes to existing programs. Some would favor a complete change in policy—those on the left propose a guaranteed annual income and those on the right want a negative income tax. We believe that the incremental changes proposed here, or equivalent incremental changes, probably would be politically acceptable if endorsed and pushed by influential groups. The shift to federal control is far more politically acceptable now than forty years ago. Targeting on income maintenance is more politically acceptable now that other laws are available to induce employers to have sound safety and employment practices. The sharing of contributions among all parties involved would be politically more acceptable now than the employer payroll tax alone. Minimizing work connection for benefits would admittedly be more politically risky than the other alternative policies, and only slight incremental changes would be suggested in preference to an all-out effort. Provision of more adequate benefits, particularly to the aged and disabled, is actually politically more acceptable today than the provision of minimum benefits, as a result of the increasing number of voters in the older age brackets and their emergence as a political force.

Is the policy legal?

Both the present policies and the proposed alternative policies are legal. However, we should recognize that some of the grounds underlying the choice of state as opposed to federal administration are no longer legal. Specifically, the South's preference to make workmen's compensation and unemployment insurance state programs rather than federal programs had clear racial motivations that would not be legally acceptable today. State administration of the social insurances is more apt to be discriminatory in race, religion, and sex than federal administration, because the federal laws are more strict. It is also less likely that federal administration would pursue diverse and illegal aims than would state administration.

Does the policy satisfy relevant interest groups?

The present policies no longer satisfy relevant interest groups as well as they did forty years ago. Blacks clearly have less to gain from state administration, from multiple aims, from employer control of programs, from a stress on work-connected benefits, and from low benefits. The same can be said of poor whites, women, citizens of Latin American origin, students, intellectuals, and perhaps labor. Labor, with the exception of the United Automobile Workers, has not fully realized the inequities in the social insurances. However, recent reflections on the social insurances suggest future labor support for changes. The primary support for present policies can be expected to come from business, with the exception of those identified with such groups as the Committee for Economic Development, as well as from farmers, the military establishment, and much of the civil bureaucracy. Such groups will support a mix of state and federal administration, work incentives, and minimum benefits. Payroll taxes on employers will be supported by business only if the programs are influenced by business. The mix of aims and purposes is probably "up for grabs."

Blacks and the other minority groups mentioned above should particularly push for federal administration, a single aim of income redistribution, sharing of financing of all three insurances, increasing benefits, and deemphasizing the stress on labor incentives. Organized labor can be expected to be less vigorous in support of these alternatives, although federal administration, raising of benefits, and targeting on income maintenance, should especially appeal to labor. Labor might well oppose, or be divided over a minimizing of work incentives, although that depends on how it is interpreted and by whom.

Is the policy scientifically sound?

The present policies were not based on clear-cut research, being largely motivated by political, economic, and moral considerations. Such research as is available casts doubt on all these policies. For example, in considering unemployment insurance, two social scientists stated over ten years ago:

> More specifically, there has been strong disagreement over proposals for federal legislation requiring minimum benefit standards. The resistance of state officials has been reinforced by employer opposition. We believe that such opposition is not justified when the states fail to provide adequate benefit programs. [18]

In short, on the basis of a generation of observation and research they found that states oppose federal standards due to employer pressure but sometimes fail to provide adequate benefits themselves. The clear implication of these studies is that federal legislation and administration is more likely to ensure adequate benefits.

Another researcher, Raymond Munts, cites considerable evidence to suggest that unemployment insurance "does not fully meet its economic security goals of supporting standards of living of the involuntarily unemployed." [19] He cites another study to show that "an increase in the size of unemployment benefits would not lead to longer duration of such benefits." [20] Workmen's compensation benefits vary widely between states. Turnbull, Williams, and Chiet conclude that the variations in benefits in all the programs administered by the states make "little sense by any standards." They find the administration of RSDHI to be "highly mechanized and efficiently conducted" but that the unemployment insurance systems approach dangerously low levels of funding at times, are overrestrictive in coverage, and equate benefits with loyalty to the company. They find that workmen's compensation programs fall short in rehabilitation, offer disincentives to workers to obtain rehabilitation, result in reluctance on the part of employers to hire the handicapped, and generally to be poorly administered.[21]

Is the policy rational?

In reviewing present social insurance programs, Schottland observes "the illogical division of responsibility among the various levels of government for administration and financing." [22] He also comments upon the state operation of some programs that are definitely in the area of federal interest without effective federal standards. It is clear from the later discussion that he is referring to workmen's compensation and unemployment insurance. Although he is not as sanguine as the present authors about the political feasibility of a gradual shift to federal administration, he strongly advocates federal standards for these state programs. Wilbur Cohen agrees that the present systems lack rationality. Cohen predicts changes in our ideas about work, for example, and suggests a retirement age of fifty-five and a thirty-hour workweek. He proposes a rational "double-decker" system of social security that would give all the aged a basic uniform grant with a work-related supplement, implying clearly that present policies of rewarding work only with minimum benefits are irrational. He also wonders if payroll taxes should not be supplemented by general revenues. Although he is primarily discussing RSDHI he thinks that "any government program should be administered by the federal government so that all persons in similar circumstances throughout the nation would be treated similarly." [23]

In discussing the irrationality of these separate programs, Turnbull, Williams, and Cheit concluded that the present system was makeshift and lacked comprehensiveness.[24]

On the other hand, the alternative policies are more rational. It makes better sense to integrate three related social insurance programs under federal administration. It is rational to limit goals to manageable and more concrete ones. It is perhaps less rational in one sense to have divided sources of income, since it is more involved and complex, but it is more rational to give the major interest groups (employers, employees, public) both a voice and a share of the cost. It is rational in an age of automation to look at the need to keep cash flowing even as jobs become harder to get. It is rational in an era of rising expectations and rising standards of living to give retirees and the handicapped more than a bare minimum income.

Is the policy economically feasible?

The present policy is quite expensive since the taxpayer is supporting over one hundred agencies to carry it out. Since each state and territory has an unemployment insurance system and a workmen's compensation system in addition to the federal social security structure, administration is a very costly venture. Obviously, there would be considerable savings in administrative costs if these programs were centralized in the more efficient RSDHI system. These savings would make more money available for benefits. The Social Security Administration now administers programs dealing with over 32 million accounts for an administrative cost of no more than 3 percent. Putting workmen's compensation and unemployment insurance under the Social Security Administration would result in more adequate grants at the same cost to the taxpayers.

Is the policy workable?

Present policies obviously work, although not without serious problems. Eveline Burns has noted two relatively new risks not dealt with by current income maintenance policies: risks resulting from family breakups due to causes other than death and long-term unemployment.[25] Such new risks could better be handled in an integrated federal system than in one hundred disparate state programs plus one federal program.

It seems to the present authors that programs of income maintenance might be more workable with fewer goals, with sharing of financing and inputs, with less stress on work incentives, and with a higher benefit level. They could easily be more workable in the sense of ensuring that citizens have more of their losses in earnings replaced. The federal government could best maintain uniformity of coverage, adequacy of benefits, and flexibility of programming to meet new needs. It takes many years to persuade or pressure fifty states to recognize a need, much longer to establish machinery to meet a need, and perhaps an infinite time to attain uniformity of coverage and adequacy of benefits. At the federal level, it can be accomplished far more easily and quickly.

Is the policy efficient?

This criterion relates to the question of how well an objective is attained. Efficiency is determined by cost, ease of accomplishment, and speed of accomplishment. The operation of the social security system in the United States is generally praised for its efficiency in terms of cost, ease, and speed. If benefits for injury, disability, and unemployment were integrated into the system, it is likely that the operating costs would be lower than the present systems in the states. Results would be achieved more easily and quickly with a computerized, centralized system. Because some degree of flexibility and variation is possible in a federal system, it is not necessary to assume that local needs would be automatically ignored. Social security offices have always existed at the local level, with possibilities for personal contact and flexibility of procedures.

Concentration on a single aim of income maintenance is clearly more efficient than concern with a heterogeneous set of goals. The program can be much more easily directed to the attainment of one goal, with corresponding savings in time and costs.

The sharing of financing between employer, employee, and taxpayer is not necessarily an efficient way to proceed, as compared with financing from only one source; yet RSDHI has managed to operate efficiently with such joint financing.

The concern with work incentives reduces efficiency in the present programs inasmuch as the program has to divide its interests and thrusts in multiple directions. It is cheaper, easier, and quicker to concentrate on income maintenance, without an overriding concern with work incentives. The attempt to decide whether or not a disability is work connected or not costs more than simply paying out the benefits.

Provision of minimum benefits is very inefficient in the long run, since supplemental programs have to be set up. The present hodgepodge of income maintenance programs in the United States is directly related to the inadequacy of benefits under any one program. People with temporarily reduced incomes who find themselves unable to make ends meet under one program quite understandably reach out for other resources. Food stamps and many other programs came into being in this way. The authors believe it is more efficient in the long run to face reality and provide more than minimum benefits. This can be done fairly readily if the preoccupation with work connectedness can be modified. We shall have to keep our eye on the goal—providing cash flow to protect both the worker and the worker's creditors.

Will the policy be likely to generate other social problems?

Turnbull, Williams, and Cheit give examples of how the present separate systems often seem to create more problems than they solve.[26] They discuss the difficulty in workmen's compensation in distinguishing between compensable occupational disability and noncompensable, nonoccupational disability, and state that often the medical profession has been split into opposing camps in trying to cope with almost impossible decisions in regard to heart and radiation cases.

The separate social insurance systems in the fifty states plus RSDHI contribute to problems of cost, bureaucracy, delays, and inefficiency, as well as to the development and spread of other social problems. Perhaps it is the failure to target directly on income maintenance that results in other social problems.

The assessment of taxes solely on employers in the unemployment insurance and workmen's compensation programs has led to overcontrol by employers and to failure to attain program objectives. In addition, employer control has led to change of emphasis in some state programs, underfinancing, very low benefits, and other problems. Diversity of the funding base would dilute employer domination, as has occurred in RSDHI.

The policy of work incentives has contributed to various administrative and social problems. For example, it has led to too short a period of benefits in unemployment compensation, deprivation of these benefits to a great many individuals not able to work, and omission of various groups from coverage under workmen's compensation. Frequently litigation results from the poor administrative machinery in the states.

Low benefits have resulted in personal and family hardships, health problems, deterioration in family relationships, and a variety of social problems. More adequate benefits should avoid these problems.

Conclusion

Several of the present policies associated with the three chief income maintenance programs have been identified: multiple levels of administration, diverse aims and objectives, financing through taxes on employers, stress on work-connected benefits, and minimum benefits. These policies have appeared to be less compatible with our criteria than was true forty years ago, and in many respects they are obsolete today. In some ways they are detrimental to the interests of people and to the attainment of income maintenance goals. On the other hand, federal administration (or at least federal standards), a single income maintenance goal, a more diverse financing pattern, a lessening of the stress on employment as a qualification, and more generous benefits all appear now to be more compatible with our criteria.

We do not say that any alternatives will be adopted next year or in the next decade. The changing alignment of political and economic interest groups is hard to predict. We do suggest that these alternatives represent viable incremental changes that may well be considered and adopted in some form.

Some of these changes appear to be too small and incremental. But there are radical shifts here, for example, in gradually minimizing work-connected benefits. We believe, however, that changes are politically and economically more feasible if they are incrementally accomplished within the present organizational framework. It is clear that more radical answers than those we propose are not acceptable at this time. We would rather improve benefits now than argue for some far-reaching change that has little chance of success. If, some day, guaranteed annual income or negative income tax programs are enacted, well and good; but must unmet needs continue until the resolution of the ideological differences of right and left?

REFERENCES

1. For a discussion by an orthodox economist, see Alicia H. Munnell, *The Future of Social Security* (Washington, D.C.: The Brookings Institution, 1977), pp. 5–24.
2. For a full listing of differences, see Claire Wilcox, *Toward Social Welfare* (Homewood, Ill.: Richard D. Irwin, 1969), p. 87.
3. June Axinn and Herman Levin, *Social Welfare* (New York: Dodd, Mead, 1975); Ronald C. Federico, *The Social Welfare Institution*, 2nd ed. (Lexington, Mass.: D.C. Heath, 1976); and Blanche Coll, *Perspectives in Public Welfare* (Washington, D.C.: U.S. Government Printing Office, 1973).
4. Robert J. Levy, Thomas P. Lewis, and Peter W. Martin, *Social Welfare and the Individual: Cases and Materials* (Mineola, N.Y.: The Foundation Press, 1971) p. 458.
5. *Ibid.*, p. 510.

6. *Ibid.,* p. 499.

7. Edwin E. Witte, *The Development of the Social Security Act* (Madison: The University of Wisconsin Press, 1963), p. 116.

8. *Employer Information Handbook on Unemployment Insurance in Alabama* (Montgomery, Ala.: State Department of Industrial Relations, November 1973), p. iii.

9. Martin Feldstein, "The Economics of the New Unemployment," in David M. Gordon, ed., *Problems in Political Economy: An Urban Perspective,* 2nd ed. (Lexington, Mass: D.C. Heath, 1977), p. 88.

10. These cases are cited in Levy, Lewis, and Martin, *op. cit.*

11. Munnell, *op. cit.*

12. Michael C. Barth, George J. Carcagno, and John L. Palmer, "The Coverage of the Transfer System," in Gordon, *op. cit.,* p. 324.

13. The President's Commission on Income Maintenance Programs, "Federal Public Assistance Programs," in Gordon, *op. cit.,* p. 318.

14. Witte, *op. cit.,* pp. 143–44.

15. Munnell, *op. cit.*

16. John G. Turnbull, C. Arthur Williams, Jr., and Earl F. Cheit, *Economic and Social Security* (New York: The Ronald Press, 1968), pp. 633.

17. See, for example, Donald C. Herzberg and Alan Rosenthal, *Strengthening the States: Essays on Legislative Reform* (New York: Anchor Books, 1972), p. 30, "Since they [employers] cannot get at the federal government, they vent their wrath at the state because they can get at it by withholding resources and denying authority."

18. William Haber and Merrill C. Murray, *Unemployment Insurance in the American Economy* (Homewood, Ill.: Richard D. Irwin, 1966), p. 500.

19. Raymond Munts, "Programming Income Maintenance: The Place of Unemployment Insurance," in Irene Lurie, ed., *Integrating Income Maintenance Programs* (New York: Academic Press, 1975), p. 246.

20. *Ibid.,* p. 247.

21. Turnbull, Williams, and Cheit, *op. cit.* See pp. 159, 258–268, and 339–344.

22. Charles D. Schottland, *The Social Security Program in the United States,* 2nd ed. (New York: Appleton-Century-Crofts, 1970), p. 181.

23. Wilbur J. Cohen and Milton Friedman, *Social Security: Universal or Selective?* (Washington, D.C.: American Enterprise Institute, 1972), p. 11.

24. Turnbull, Williams, and Cheit, *op. cit.,* p. 637.

25. Eveline M. Burns, "Welfare Programs in Evolution," *Monthly Labor Review,* CXXXVIII, No. 2 (March 1965), 294–295.

26. Turnbull, Williams, and Cheit, *op. cit.,* pp. 632–637.

QUESTIONS FOR DISCUSSION

1. Turnbull, Williams, and Cheit have suggested that increased litigation in workmen's compensation has thwarted the objectives of the program to the extent that injured workers sometimes do not want to be rehabilitated and employers sometimes do not want them back on the job. Can you suggest other changes in the present workmen's compensation program that could avert these outcomes?

2. Only about half the unemployed receive unemployment benefits. What are the pros and cons of changing the unemployment insurance program so that all the unemployed receive benefits?

3. Some writers suggest federal standards for state unemployment insurance and workmen's compensation programs as an alternative to federal administration of these programs. Which course of action appeals to you, and why?

4. Do you agree with the thesis of supporters of RSDHI that this program is politically strong enough to survive indefinitely, or do you agree with its detractors that it is apt to be bankrupt or otherwise unstable enough in the future to be politically vulnerable?

5. Are there additional programs you would like to see incorporated in RSDHI or additional groups of people, such as migrant laborers, that you would like to see added to RSDHI?

6. Do you agree with Wilbur Cohen that an RSDHI reserve of "about one year's benefit is sufficient as a contingency fund"? He takes that position on the basis that "social security is backed by the political, economic, and constitutional system of our economy and our government." Do you believe that a social insurance system should be backed to that degree by the government, or do you think RSDHI should have reserves like a private insurance company?

7. Can you suggest policy alternatives other than those suggested by the authors in this chapter? How would they measure up with the criteria?

8. The authors have confined their discussion in this chapter to income maintenance. Is it enough to maintain income alone? Would you agree, as many do, that real economic security calls for significant income redistribution?

SUGGESTED PROJECTS

1. Find two or three recipients in your community of one of the social insurance benefits (RSDHI, unemployment insurance, workmen's

compensation). What is their evaluation of the success and failures of the program? What changes in policy or administration do they suggest?

2. Compare the above survey of recipient attitudes with the perceptions of administrators or employees of social insurance programs. Ask how they feel the programs are working. What changes do they propose? What differences emerge? Can you account for these differences?

3. Talk with, or write to, your congressman to assess his or her view of the social insurances, including any recommendations for improvement. How does he or she differ from the perceptions of recipients and administrators?

4. Consult with your local Social Security Office to find the current benefit levels for a retired worker and the dependents of a deceased worker. Find out the current levels of unemployment benefits in your state. Check with state authorities on the usual payments made through workmen's compensation.

FOR FURTHER READING

Wilbur J. Cohen and Milton Friedman. *Social Security: Universal or Selective?* Washington: American Enterprise Institute for Public Policy Research, 1972. Stimulating presentations and rebuttals by two leading proponents of widely differing approaches to social security. Cohen, a former secretary of Health, Education, and Welfare, strongly supports the present system with minor improvements. Friedman, an anticollectivist economist and recent winner of a Nobel prize, just as vigorously proposes abandonment of the present system in favor of a negative income tax.

William Haber and Merrill G. Murray. *Unemployment Insurance in the American Economy.* Homewood, Ill: Richard D. Irwin, 1966. A comprehensive and scholarly analysis of the objectives, history, coverage, benefits, financing, problems, and progress of unemployment insurance. A valuable resource for the student interested in unemployment insurance.

Roy Lubove. *The Struggle for Social Security, 1900–1935.* Cambridge, Mass.: Harvard University Press, 1968. A history of social security, including workmen's compensation and unemployment insurance, that sets the system in a context of such value considerations as voluntarism, the work ethic, and individualism.

Charles I. Schottland. *The Social Security Program in the United States,* 2nd ed. New York: Appleton-Century-Crofts, 1970. A thorough, well-written review of the history, development, and operations of the various social security programs in the United States, including OASDHI, unemployment insurance, and workmen's compensation. Generally supportive of present policies but various incremental changes are recommended. Easy to read.

John G. Turnbull, C. Arthur Williams, Jr., and Earl F. Cheit. *Economic and*

Social Security, 3rd ed. New York: The Ronald Press, 1968. An almost encyclopedic review and analysis of the various approaches to economic and social insecurity and security in the United States, including not only the governmental approaches but private programs as well.

Edwin E. Witte. *The Development of the Social Security Act.* Madison: The University of Wisconsin Press, 1963. A detailed account of the events leading up to the passage of the Social Security Act by the executive director of the committee proposing and sponsoring the legislation. The first half of the book is a detailed review of the committee's work; especially interesting are 35 pages devoted to the congressional debate. The last half discusses the provisions of the final act and why the product came out as it did; the last 135 pages are especially informative.

5 Policies for Coping with Poverty

In Chapter 4 we discussed policies and programs that focus on maintaining income, the assumption being that the citizen has some income to maintain. This assumption is invalid for a good number of people. What of those who have no regular income? The rules of the game are different. In this chapter we will look at the major policies that address the question of poverty and then move on to a brief review of the major programs that flow from these policies. We will formulate some alternative policies and compare them with present policies using our policy analysis model.

What Is Poverty?

Poverty is a fascinating phenomenon. Everyone acknowledges that it exists, but there are disagreements about what the word "poverty" means and the numbers of people who are affected by it. The reason that poverty is such a mysterious concept is that there are different ways in which poverty is defined—and each definition yields answers that conflict with other definitions.

The most commonly used definition involves the notion of *absolute* poverty.[1] That is, a poverty line is drawn at a given income. The "official" poverty line in the United States is set by the Social Security Administration and is based on the U.S. Department of Agriculture's estimate of the cost for an "adequate" diet. This cost is multiplied by three (on the assumption that a poor family spends one-third of its income for food) to get a dollar amount. This figure is adjusted semi-annually. Currently, about 12 percent of American families have an income below the poverty line and so are counted as "officially" poor.

The second approach to defining poverty is the *relative* poverty notion. In this approach, poverty is relative to the standard of living enjoyed by most people in society. The amount of relative poverty in a given society depends on that society's attitude toward redistribution. The United States has never accepted the notion of relative poverty, and therefore has no official guideline on the matter. It has been suggested that a reasonable relative standard would be one-half the national median income. If this definition were followed, about 20 percent of Americans could be considered poor.

A third way of identifying the poor is the *social cost* approach. In this way of thinking, the poor are all those for whom society pays support—recipients of public assistance, criminals, patients in public hospitals and others in similar situations.

The answer to the question, "Who is poor?" then rests on one's definition. Our position is simply that, whatever the definition, the problem is large enough to warrant societal action beyond trusting to the market.

It used to be commonly accepted that, by absolute definitions, 20 percent of Americans were poor. The current absolute definition is, as we have said, about 12 percent. This looks like progress. After all, there are a number of programs that have transferred income from the earning members of society to the non-earning or less-earning citizens. But whether or not we are making progress or not turns out to be a highly political question. Supporters of the absolute poverty approach, most of whom tend toward political and economic conservatism, generally take the position that the United States is making significant progress. More radical students of the problem, Lee Rainwater and David Gordon, for example,[2] take the position that poverty should be viewed in relative terms and, therefore, there has been no decline in poverty. They argue that government transfers have had little real impact.

Because of the highly political nature of the poverty definition problem, we doubt if it can be settled readily. Coming to an agreement on a definition is not really relevant to our discussion. By any definition there are millions of people who will still be poor. Our past (and current) social welfare policy has not effectively eliminated the wretched conditions under which many Americans live. Any solution to the problem hinges, we think, on a change in policy approach.

Current Policies

We can isolate several major policies that guide social welfare programs for the poor in the United States:

1. Work is the best antipoverty policy. Recognizing that this is not a simple problem, society should provide some supports that will enable as many of the poor to work as is possible. These include:

   a. employment services directed toward the poor. These services include job training, job creation and placement, and relocation services.

   b. minimum wage law.

   c. counseling services.

   d. family planning services, since large families add to the burden of the poor.

   e. legal services and community action programs to procure justice in the courts and access to the political process.

2. For those unable to work, an unattractive minimum level of living should be provided. This should be offered in two ways:

   a. cash benefits (less than one would earn by working) and in-kind benefits (e.g., food stamps) should be provided according to need.

   b. low-cost housing should be available for those unable to obtain private housing.

Social services, family planning, legal services, and community programs also apply to those unable to work, but their thrust is clearly directed toward enabling the poor to function as workers if at all possible. We have not included medical services in our discussion because we have reserved that discussion for Chapter 6 which will deal with health policy.

There is an obvious moral tone in American policies toward the poor. Much of this centers around the accent on work. Many social workers have been critical of what they call the "work ethic," and yet the value of work is central to American society. It is unfair to say that only the poor are expected to work, since most middle-class people require it of themselves. Social workers themselves work hard and believe that their work is important and meaningful.

The work ethic as a concept is usually associated with the work of Max Weber, primarily *The Protestant Ethic and the Spirit of Capitalism.* This, however, is not fair to Weber. The two essays that make up *The Protestant Ethic* are Weber's attempt to deal with the role of moral thought in the development of modern capitalism. He concluded that, *although economic and political factors were predominant*:

> One of the fundamental elements of the spirit of modern capitalism, and not only of that but of all modern culture: rational conduct on the basis of the idea of the calling, was born—that is what this discussion has sought to demonstrate—from the spirit of Christian asceticism.[3]

Weber's writing on the influence of puritan asceticism on modern capitalism does not seek to explain the importance of work, as such, profit, or religion. Weber never said that work was a value exclusive to Western economic life. Nor did he think that acquisitiveness was unique to capitalism:

> The impulse to acquisition, pursuit of gain, of money, or of the greatest possible amount of money, has in itself nothing to do with capitalism. This impulse exists and has existed among waiters, physicians, coachmen, artists, prostitutes, dishonest officials, soldiers, nobles, crusaders, gamblers and beggars. One may say that it has been common to all sorts and conditions of men at all times and in all countries of the earth, wherever the objective possibilities of it is or has been given.[4]

Weber also tried to forestall criticism that he was saying that Luther and Calvin and their followers were personally responsible for the Protestant ethic:

> But it is not to be understood that we expect to find any of the founders or representatives of these religious movements considering the promotion of what we have called the spirit of capitalism as in any sense the end of his life work. We cannot well maintain that the pursuit of worldly goods, conceived as an end in itself, was to any of them of positive ethical value.[5]

Weber's point was that Christian asceticism of the puritan sort elevated work to the level of a calling or a vocation. This kind of devotion, coupled with political stability, good markets, and a sound money system, produced modern capitalism. Work and achievement, however, have been important in all human societies, even though few have pursued economic ends with the single-minded joylessness of those in the seventeenth and eighteenth centuries. All societies reward accomplishment and effort. While beggars are tolerated and even revered in some cultures, they are never accorded positions of authority. The importance of work is such a deeply ingrained value in the world that it is unlikely that it will be readily discarded. It should not be surprising that work is seen as the major remedy for poverty all over the world. It is not necessarily punitive to believe that work is important. It is punitive, however, to take the position that work is the only possible source of income (1) when work is not available, (2) when one is unable to perform it, (3) when one is prohibited from securing it because of his or her race, sex, ethnicity, or religion, or (4) when work is seen primarily as a morally redemptive activity.

We have made a major digression in our discussion on poverty. Only by bearing in mind the importance of work and achievement in human society can we understand the policies for dealing with poverty that have been developed in the United States. We will turn to an examination of the policies that we summarized at the beginning of the chapter. Since most readers will be familiar with the major events in the history of social welfare and will know something about current social welfare programs, we will only need to sketch our program examples.

Employment Services

The most conservative approach to employing the poor is to trust to the workings of the market. This has been the traditional approach and was American policy up through the Hoover administration. Trusting the market did not eliminate poverty in the past, and it is rarely offered as a solution today. Nevertheless, it is true that during periods of high labor demand, some of the poor benefit temporarily.

A more modern approach involves stimulating the economy by increasing the money supply. In theory, if more money is available at low interest rates, business will expand and hire more people, who will in turn spend money, thus creating more jobs. In the short run this works, but as we have seen in the past few years, the easing of the money supply has an inflationary effect that does little for the poor in the long run.

Another approach on the conservative side is the provision of tax incentives to businesses that will hire the poor. This is a later provision of the Work Incentive (WIN) program that was originally passed in 1967. Few employers have participated, and many are apparently unaware of the program.[6]

A fourth approach is for the federal government to provide jobs. The United States successfully employed people during the Great Depression in the Works Progress Administration and the Civilian Conservation Corps. President Carter has proposed similar programs to deal with today's unemployment. Such programs would not be addressed to the same population today. Many of the unemployed in the 1930s were skilled people who would ordinarily be part of the work force.

The provision of employment services in all states is another attempt to employ the unemployed. Although not limited to the poor, the services are directed principally toward the poor. The object is to match the worker with the right job through a program of testing, counseling, and referral.

Another set of programs involves training. The Economic Opportunity Act of 1964 contained a number of programs designed to prepare people, especially a number of youth, for employment. More recently, the Comprehensive Employment and Training Act of 1973 has provided employment and training opportunities.

Certainly any of these approaches will have some effect. However, they all run aground on several points. A great many of the poor are already working, but at very low wages. Most of the poor in this country are dubious candidates for regular employment since they are under eighteen, over sixty-five, or parents of preschool children. All of the employment programs together will only provide answers for some of the poor some of the time.

Employment of the poor is also addressed by a number of indirect policies. The policy of economic development of certain areas of the country has been used with some success. One example is the Tennessee Valley Authority, which provided relatively cheap power for large parts of the Southeast. Employment opportunities have increased in the region with a significant reduction in poverty over pre-TVA days.

The Minimum Wage and the Poor

The payment of a minimum wage is seen by many as an attractive weapon against poverty. Since many of the poor are employed, it would appear that the minimum wage would have been their salvation. England and some of the Commonwealth nations enacted minimum wage laws around the turn of the century. Some states in this country enacted minimum wage laws for women early in the twentieth century. After a stormy legal history, states now have minimum wage laws that apply to both men and women. However, the coverage of these laws is limited to local businesses.

The Fair Labor Standards Act of 1938 and its subsequent amendments govern the wages for the bulk of the jobs in the country under the constitutional power of Congress to regulate interstate commerce. Technically, only a few types of employment are not covered. There is a minimum wage for farm labor and a slightly higher rate for nonfarm labor.

The minimum wage law has raised the income of those who are paid according to its provisions, but it will not be enough to lift the employed poor out of poverty. Further, evasions are not uncommon. Policing is difficult, particularly in small, nonunion businesses.

Some economists consider the minimum wage a mixed blessing. Because an employer must pay the minimum wage, he or she may lack the capital to start a new business or expand a present one. Without the minimum wage requirement, it would be possible to employ more inexperienced, young, and marginally employable people.[7]

Counseling Services

Some social casework service has always been available to the poor—in the early days often of a moralistic tone—but counseling has not always been actively sought or offered. In 1962 the Social Security Act was amended to provide a federal contribution of $75 for each $25 of state funds committed to the provision of rehabilitative social services to those receiving public assistance. There is no evidence to suggest that these additional services have had a positive effect on reducing poverty. Even when counseling services are divorced from the administration of grants and rendered by skilled social workers from a voluntary agency, there is little evidence of great benefit.[8] This should not be surprising. Even if social workers were able to relieve all of the emotional conflicts, family problems, and service needs of poor people, it is unlikely that poverty would be ended. People are not usually poor because they have a disorganized personal life. It is more likely that poverty creates conflict and poor social functioning. While some individuals are undoubtedly helped, casework without the provision of adequate funds can only be a Band-aid approach.

The most recent program innovations regarding social services are embodied in Title XX of the Social Security Act. While Title XX continues the emphasis on rehabilitation and self-support (which is not new policy), states will now be expected to develop comprehensive services and must provide for citizen participation in the planning process. Delegating planning responsibility to the states is a "new" policy move, although states at one time did have responsibility for social welfare planning. Title XX is not a return to the old nineteenth-century policy of neglect, however, since too many things have happened to allow that to occur. Some services are mandated, but the people of a state theoretically have a good deal of freedom to select and design services that are considered important. Federal guidelines and federal funding as well as a provision for showing accountability should provide for some quality control. It is too soon to judge the effects on the poor. We are concerned because the services that appear to be most popular seem to have little to do with services that will improve the economic position of the poor. On the other hand, Title XX is a beginning. Perhaps it will spawn needed innovations in service delivery.

Family Planning Services

Family planning is a highly controversial approach to the problem of poverty. Some people are wary of family planning and equate it with artificial means of birth control. Some blacks have argued that family planning is a thinly disguised form of black genocide. There seems to be little objection to voluntary family planning by individuals for private reasons, but there is considerable objection to family planning as public social welfare policy.

Even in cultures where there is governmental support for family planning, it is hard to see that it has had a profound effect on poverty. Many of the poor are indifferent or opposed. Men, particularly, seem reluctant to change their values about contraception even when there is no religious objection to it.

There is also another stubborn fact that complicates the situation. Most poor families are small. Of course, there are dramatic examples of large poor families, but the *Statistical Abstract of the United States* for any given year shows that families receiving AFDC average between three and four members.[9] This is only about one more member than American families in general. Of course, to have one less child would be of help to both poor family and taxpayer. And, in those cases where poor people can be assisted in avoiding large families that they do not want and cannot afford, family planning can be of value. The point is, however, that we are not talking about millions of families with twenty children each. Most of the poor families that receive AFDC consist of a mother and one or two children. They are poor despite the size of the family. They will continue to be poor even if there are no more children. Family planning may prevent those women and children from becoming worse off, but it will not prevent them from being as poor as they already are.

It appears that the most effective family planning has been done voluntarily as a by-product of upward social mobility. As people earn more money (the one thing that most poor people are ill equipped to do), they control their family size and raise their standard of living. This phenomenon tends to support the argument that economic development is the most effective tool for the reduction of family size. With upward social mobility, value changes occur. Family planning is not successful without such a change. It is probably incorrect to blame large families (when they do occur) to ignorance or the lack of availability of contraceptives. People know about contraceptive methods, and condoms, at least, have been readily available for many years. People simply do not hold the avoidance of pregnancy as important until they can see where it will leave them better off. When there is some point to it, people find the information and use it. Without a change in values, family planning policy will fall short of the expectations of its supporters.

Access to Legal Services and to Decision-Making

It was widely recognized in the 1960s that the poor had little legal protection. It was also recognized that the poor were a politically impotent group. Therefore, the War on Poverty legislation of the Johnson administration provided for legal aid and community organization on behalf of the poor. At times there seemed to be more rhetoric than progress, but these programs did provide some access to both the law and the political process. The provision of legal aid to the poor has had some very grave funding difficulties at the hands of the Nixon-Ford administration. Legal aid services now operate in a much more restrictive arena. Reduced funding has also taken some of the steam out of community action programs.

Cash and In-Kind Benefits

The poor laws of England have provided the prototypes for most American policies. The Elizabethan Poor Law of 1601 (43 Elizabeth) provided for the local relief of the poor according to a categorical definition of eligibility. The "impotent" or helpless poor received relief while the able-bodied were punished if they refused to work. Work was available in workhouses for those unable to find it elsewhere. Relief was meager because it depended upon local citizens' willingness to tax themselves. Relief by category remains a central policy today, although there has been some modification.

A second policy was borrowed from the English Law of Settlement of 1662. This law said that one could only receive relief in his or her own parish. The parish could refuse relief to those who did not have legal rights of "settlement" and could order the poor to depart the parish. Although the concept of "settlement" gave way to "residence" in this country, such laws were still in use until struck down by the Supreme Court in 1968.

The English "reform" of 1834 was not so much a change in welfare policy to assist the poor as it was to help the business classes who felt burdened by the poor. The major policy to come out of the law of 1834 was the "doctrine of lesser eligibility." This is the notion that the poor should not receive as much as the lowest going rate for employed labor. The object, of course, was to make welfare unattractive—a job that hardly needed doing. From a policy point of view, it is interesting to consider that the doctrine of lesser eligibility ascribes great rationality to the poor. It assumes that the poor will pursue the course that will gain the most money.

Therefore, welfare must be low or the poor will make a rational decision to accept it. This neat bit of projection is at variance with another belief about the poor—that they are emotional children and are incapable of making rational decisions.

At the heart of English welfare policy (and American policy, too) there have been choices. First, if the poor are going to be given relief, should it be in the form of cash or should it be in kind (actual commodities)? Second, should relief be given "indoors" through some kind of workhouse or poorhouse system or should it be given "outdoors," allowing the poor to remain in their own homes? Having tried it both ways, American (and British) policy has gradually become one of cash relief (with some exceptions) on an "outdoor" basis.

American social welfare historically was based on the principle of local relief and private charity. Both "indoor" and "outdoor" approaches have been prominent at various times. Residence (or settlement) was required, and the benefits have been governed by the policy that the poor should be forced into work by the difficulty of living on what was provided. It is the placing of work in this context that gives rise to the criticism that Americans are too "hung up" on the work ethic. It is one thing to believe that work is good, fulfilling, and meaningful and that one ought to do it because tasks need to be done. It is quite another thing to structure a welfare program in such a way that work is regarded as punishment rather than as a useful way of reaching personal and social goals.

The Social Security Act of 1935 responded primarily to the needs of those who would normally be employed by providing the income maintenance programs that we discussed in Chapter 4. As a secondary concern, there were provisions for the public assistance of those who were not ordinarily expected to be part of the labor force. Originally, the public assistance provisions of the act provided for federal participation in state-operated programs for the old, the blind, and dependent children. Benefits for the permanently and totally disabled were added in 1950. We might note that these latter benefits were necessitated by the narrow focus of workmen's compensation and RSDHI on work-connected disability. The option of participating was, and still is, up to the state. A state could elect to participate in any or all of the public assistance programs under the Social Security Act. States did, in fact, selectively adopt programs, although all states finally came round to adopting programs for the old, the blind, and dependent children. The federal government sold the program to the states by providing a good deal of the money through the now-familiar device of the matching formula. Over time, the federal contributions have increased. In order to qualify for federal funds, a state program had to meet certain criteria. These criteria still apply to Aid to Families with Dependent Children (AFDC):

> [The federal government] requires that the program be in operation in every county in the state; that the state itself contribute to its costs; that it be supervised or administered by a single agency; that the employees of this agency be protected by a merit system; that benefits be available to all citizens; that they not be denied by imposing unduly restrictive residence requirements; that assistance be given only those who are in need; and that applicants be assured fair hearing, the right of appeal, and prompt determination of their claims.[10]

These categorical programs were supplemented in a number of states by a General Assistance program (GA), which functions to cover gaps in the public assistance program. The financing is from state and/or local funds. Some states pay cash benefits while others use a voucher system, and still others a combination of both.

Some changes were made in January 1974 when the Supplemental Security Income (SSI) program replaced the public assistance categorical aid programs of Aid to the Blind, Old-Age Assistance, and Aid to the Permanently and Totally Disabled. SSI is federally funded and administered, but states may make supplemental grants from state funds. Eligibility is more standardized, and SSI now looks more like the income maintenance programs. This is more than a cosmetic change. As a policy matter, the connection with the Social Security Administration makes some change in the status of the beneficiary by easing the stigma attached by public assistance. Second, the shift from public assistance to SSI represents a relaxation of the notion that these people really ought to be working. In the public mind "social security" is legitimate and is usually not confused with a demeaning kind of charity. The response of the public indicates greater acceptance of SSI than was true of AB, OAA or APTD. By April 1975 approximately four and a quarter million people were receiving SSI benefits, an increase of about a million and a half over the old categorical aid programs. Whereas it was assumed back in the thirties that, except for Aid to Dependent Children (changed in 1962 to Aid to Families with Dependent Children), the recipients of categorical aid would eventually qualify for work-connected benefits, there are still many who do not qualify for RSDHI or whose benefits are inadequate under current definitions.

AFDC continues in its old status as a federal/state categorical program. General assistance, where it exists, is also not affected. Both offer wide differences in benefits from state to state.

An interesting anachronism in welfare administration remains in the federal food stamp program. Although the program is financed by the federal government, application is made through the local offices of the state welfare department. Persons meeting a needs test may receive coupons that are redeemable for food. The value of the food coupons depends upon one's income and family size. A qualified recipient cannot normally exist solely on the coupons. This is only one step removed from providing "in-kind" relief. The food stamp program is an outgrowth of an older system of distributing food products that had been bought up by the federal government as a means of sustaining farm prices.

Low-Cost Housing

Since the 1930s the federal government has been involved in the provision of low-cost public housing for people with small incomes. (Public housing will be discussed more fully in Chapter 7.) It is enough here to note that low-cost public housing is available in many localities with rents based on income. To ensure that such housing will only be occupied by low-income tenants, an income limit is fixed. When one's income exceeds the limit, he or she must move into private housing.

Present Policy and Possible Alternatives

The present programs for the control of poverty are broad without being comprehensive. They are based on emotional values rather than on reason and knowledge. Society's misconceptions of the poor and their capabilities have so infected policy decisions that programs are irrational. Such programs do not work—nor can they work until people seriously consider what they are dealing with.

In our brief review we can see some change in the basic American policy of coerced work or stigmatized discomfort. Certainly the transfer of three categorical aid programs to the Social Security Administration is a progressive step, since the aged, the blind, and the disabled will appear to be beneficiaries rather than recipients. Supplemental security income is not the same as RSDHI, but will increasingly be identified with social insurance because it is administered by the same agency. We recognized in Chapter 4 that social insurance benefits are low; however, increases in RSDHI are less difficult to get than increases in public welfare grants. Regarding people as beneficiaries is an important symbolic change.

Those whose problem is plain uncomplicated poverty still face an uncertain future. What alternatives to coerced work and stigmatized discomfort are possible? After all, these policies are as old as the Elizabethan days and fit comfortably into a number of American values. Because the present policies feed self-righteousness, it has been possible to ignore the simple truth that *they do not work*. Coerced work and stigmatized discomfort have had a fair trial. If in 350 years these policies have failed to eliminate poverty, it would seem reasonable to try another approach.

First of all, effective policy should provide the poor with more money. Second, effective policy should reduce the stigma attached to being poor. Third, effective policy should be uncomplicated and easy to administer. Here is a policy package that we have generated:

1.

Redefine divorce, desertion, and unmarried parenthood as social risks just as death of the wage earner, unemployment and illness were defined in Chapter 4.

Americans assume that divorce, desertion, and unmarried parenthood are social risks that exist in a modern society. Certainly they are common enough in all social classes. Acting on the principle of mutual aid, society should insure citizens with custody of children against these risks through the tax structure just as one is now insured against the contingencies of death of a wage earner or disability. As in the so-called social insurance approach, this policy assumes need when the contingencies for which it is designed occur. One would not have to pass a "means" test, but the basis for eligibility would be the same as for RSDHI—when the contingency occurs, benefits can be claimed. These kinds of programs could be shifted to the Social Security Administration for ease and simplicity in administration. Financing, like SSI, could come from general taxation.

2.

Raise the level of benefits to adequacy.

No one would seriously suggest that the beneficiary of any social insurance should receive the same money as an employed worker. However, in the modern world with its money economy, we should insist that benefits ought to be enough for support that sustains life at a decent level. It is not in the mutual interest of Americans for people to be unable to pay their reasonable bills. If the poor had enough money, most of them would pay what was due. This provision would generate revenue on the money that would be paid to merchants.

3.

Make work as attractive to the poor—and as realistically available—as it is to the rest of the public.

There is nothing wrong with the general expectation that members of a society ought to find fulfillment in work and that work is important. The problem has been our inability or unwillingness to be realistic about work when we are talking about the poor. We have to bear in mind that the bulk of the poor are over sixty-five, under eighteen, mothers with small children, and marginally employed workers of both sexes. Therefore, we cannot expect to employ all the poor. However, work would be desirable to those who are able to work.

There are two subpolicies involved in making work attractive. First, we need to make realistic training available. We can do this by adding to the social insurance benefit an amount for tuition, books, fees, and materials for bonafide educational and training programs near where the poor are located. In the modern world, technical schools, colleges, universities, and other training programs are able to provide the necessary preparation for virtually everything. These institutions should be considered as a powerful weapon against poverty. The difference between what we are proposing and the WIN program is that we are suggesting that training be available to any person who is unemployed for any reason.

The second subpolicy that is needed in this area is that governments should provide jobs for those who cannot be absorbed into the private market or who choose not to enter the private market. In effect, we are suggesting a permanent set of public service jobs. The public work force could be expanded or contracted as economic conditions warrant. Private industry will always be more attractive for most people, but public service can be made more attractive. We could see the expansion of CETA, as an example, as a permanent umbrella agency that develops and staffs a whole series of public service occupations. These occupations would involve jobs that need doing. The point is that, if training and/or work that needs to be done are available, people will seek opportunity—particularly if it leads to career goals.

We see the need for both—easily available training and a permanent agency that provides public service employment. Obviously, when private industry needs workers, it will draw from the reservoir of people in public service. Private industry, we repeat, will always be more attractive because of the variety of opportunities available, the fringe benefits and perquisites, and the challenges. Because the work in private industry is apt to be more desirable to many and more complex, salaries will generally be higher and industry should not suffer from a lack of employees because of government employment. We also have to recognize that some people are not physically or mentally able to compete for work in private industry. Public employment could provide a source of income that would be considered less demeaning than being on the dole.

As a further extension of this point, we think that the minimum wage should be lowered for persons under eighteen. It is more important, in our view, that young workers be employed than on the streets. It is not likely that workers under eighteen would seriously displace experienced mature workers.

4.

Limited general assistance should be provided for emergencies and to pay for relocation of those who need to move to secure appropriate work.

We cannot totally do without an emergency grant system to fill in the gaps; however, we would also administer this kind of service through the Social Security Administration so that people deal with only one money provision agency. If everything else that we have suggested in this text were in place, we think that few people would be left in any permanent position of difficulty.

5.

We would retain certain existing policies, but would redefine them somewhat:
(a) counseling services should be available to all citizens who choose to have them;
(b) family planning services should be available upon request;
(c) legal services for both criminal and civil cases should be available to all citizens; and
(d) low-cost housing should be provided for those unable to afford private housing.

Basically, our proposal would make all counseling services voluntary and separate from any benefit program. We would leave family planning on a voluntary basis too. The improved economic future for the poor, we believe, would be the most important and effective motivating force for family limitation. We would also advocate the expansion of legal services beyond their present limitations. Our proposals about housing will be discussed in Chapter 7.

It should be noted that we have stressed the voluntary nature of these services. We do not think that citizens should be coerced into use of services unless their behavior is clearly harmful to themselves or others. Protective services for adults and children will still have to be maintained, and the criminal justice system will still be needed to deal with people who do harmful things to each other. We are addressing the problem of poverty, not protective services or crime. We do think that better economic opportunities created by the work and training program outlined would reduce some abuse, neglect, and antisocial behavior.

If these services were voluntary, who would pay for them? Services are better used when the consumer pays for them. Employed persons could use a prepayment system as is now done with health insurance. Persons receiving a social insurance benefit could pay for their services on a voucher system.

Although it is outside the scope of welfare policy, we think that welfare reform is somewhat contingent upon a sound national economic policy. We think that federal spending should be kept within reasonable limits. We believe that governments should be efficient in their operations and should give the taxpayers their money's worth. It is also important for the federal government to do what it can to promote intelligent economic growth in commerce and industry so that productivity and jobs can be created.

What Would This Approach Do?

We think that the above policies would produce upward social mobility for most of the poor and a decent level of living for those who do not qualify for training. These policies would also provide personnel for tasks that need doing at various levels of competence. They would provide employment for many—particularly women of child-bearing age and youth—who were formerly unemployable. And it would, we repeat, reduce the stigma of welfare to its irreducible minimum.

Such reforms would not produce the perfect society. There will continue to be antisocial people. There are always going to be persons with their eye on the main chance—but they occur at all levels of society, as we saw during the Nixon years. We do think that if human needs are met, those antisocial acts that are attributed to poverty will be reduced. We doubt that the poor are more dishonest than other people (though they probably are *just* as dishonest). We think that they are as interested in improvement as anybody else, but that we have been hampered in dealing with poverty because of the negative values with which we have approached the problem.

Analysis

We have, of course, generated these new policies for analytical purposes. We will now compare them with the existing policy of coerced work and stigmatized discomfort. For simplicity, we will refer to these two sets of policies as the "present policy" and the "proposed policy."

Compatibility with Contemporary Style

As indicated by the shift of the aged, the blind, and the disabled to SSI, the quasi-insurance approach is gaining in popularity. Divorce, desertion, and illegitimacy are common occurrences in all classes of people and are no longer seen as difficulties for "them." On the contrary, these are risks that all families run in contemporary society. Realistically, divorce, desertion, and illegitimacy are serious economic blows to all but the very well off. We cannot repeat often enough that poverty is not only disastrous for the poor, but it is also against the best interests of the nonpoor. Even the most hidebound conservative must recognize that his profits are maximized when customers pay their bills. It is far better to maintain people's buying power than to allow them to sink into poverty.

Further, the present system primarily punishes women. While divorce is generally more mutual than it used to be, men still desert women much more often than women leave men, and it is usually the woman who bears the financial burden resulting from a broken familial relationship. This kind of double standard is clearly unacceptable now and was always wrong, Women with children should not bear the social and financial responsibility that should, by the principle of mutual aid, be shared with men.

We think it is more in line with contemporary style to pay adequate benefits to victims of social risks. Everyone faces some or all of the risks of being unemployed, a single parent, disabled, blind, or old. The only way to guarantee avoidance is to be born wealthy, live alone, and die suddenly while young. If these are common risks, then adequate benefits ought to be the concern of all of us who are potential beneficiaries.

Since work is meaningful for most of us (at least as a means to an end if not for any other reason), contemporary style would dictate that it should be regarded as an opportunity rather than a punishment. Now that even skilled and educated people (teachers and engineers, for example) have felt the pinch of unemployment, we think it will be popular to provide practical training opportunities and alternative employment by government for all.

Voluntary services are also more in keeping with the American belief in individual worth than mandatory services. Americans no longer are willing to accept constraints on personal freedoms that are imposed when benefits are tied to counseling services. The increased use of private counselors by those who can afford to do so is a powerful indication of the public mood.

Emergency financial aid, as envisioned in the retention of general assistance, is likely to be unenthusiastically accepted, just as it is now. However, we would guess that if it were genuinely temporary, and administered as a kind of national traveler's aid, it would work and fit the contemporary style of the modern world.

Equity and Justice

Our remarks here are consistent with what we said in the previous section. Not only does the present policy violate contemporary life-style, it also is inequitable and unjust. Welfare programs now have widely varying benefit levels and eligibility rules. Our proposal would provide uniform benefit levels for those insured. The present policy blames the victims of poverty. Consider the father of a child born to a single woman. Although he is legally responsible, the law is virtually unenforceable. It is the woman who is left with the bills. She will be the one to apply for welfare and sign up for the WIN program. No stigma attaches to the man. In fact, having left a woman pregnant without support may be a source of sly pride in some circles. Since the woman should have "known better" (men are apparently not expected to "know better"), she alone becomes the financial victim. While women are less discriminated against morally than was true years ago, they are still left with the responsibility and the financial obligation. Insurance will help correct the financial injustice. Valid training and employment opportunities would help such women to build their own futures.

Compatibility with Social Work Values

The chief virtue of our approach in the proposed policy is that it is compatible with social work values. Clearly, the present policy of coerced work or stigmatized discomfort is unpopular among social workers. It is much more in line with social work values to provide benefits to citizens on an insurancelike basis. It is also much more in line with social work values to provide apportunities for self-fulfillment. It is also better, in social work terms, to provide attractive resources than to coerce the use of unattractive services. Social workers know, more intimately than anyone else, the debilitating effect of punitively low grants. Given the position of the welfare recipient in our relatively affluent society, it is a wonder to us that all recipients are not dishonest. Clearly, our proposal is more compatible with social work values.

Other Important Societal Values

Social values of human dignity and worth are not consonant with the demoralizing and depersonalizing means test now used to determine eligibility. While it is one thing to establish eligibility because of a contingency, it is quite different to strip people mentally naked as has been done in the name of determining financial need. Administration of all financial benefit programs as social insurances would avoid some of the invasion of privacy and promote a higher respect for human dignity. To its credit, the Social Security Administration's handling of RSDHI and SSI is not regarded as demeaning. However, we have been told by veteran social security people that the cost of determining need for SSI is more expensive than determining eligibility to RSDHI. So, we would formally abandon any form of "means" test.

The present policy of coerced work or stigmatized discomfort is compatible with societal values or morality, external conformity, and racism. The present policy is also compatible with values about work (but only to a degree) and achievement. The present policy is not compatible with humanitarianism, efficiency, equality, freedom, science, democracy, and individual personality. As we said earlier, the policy toward the poor currently in force is clearly based on a self-righteous morality. That this morality is also racist and sexist is apparent. Our proposed policy takes into account work and achievement as *most Americans see these things for themselves*. For most of us, work is opportunity, not punishment. Achievement is reaching some self-fulfilling goal, not a coerced end. Our proposed policy stresses the human aim of mutual aid. We think it would be efficient in administration. It is orderly but maximizes freedom and individuality. We are willing to take the position that people want to grow and be self-reliant rather than to be controlled. In short, we think that our policy reflects what most Americans would want for themselves if (or when) they face the contingencies that we suggest should be insured against.

There is little question in our minds that the moralistic approach toward the poor has been the most important reason for our failure to produce adequate programming. Otherwise, there would have been dramatic change, on the basis of other values.

Political Acceptability

The present policy seems to be politically acceptable—although this may be illusory. In the last presidential campaign, welfare reform was a popular goal for both candidates. Some form of change in the welfare system (always labeled "reform") is proposed before every Congress. The resulting changes are patchy or nonexistent. However, we think that the climate is clearly different today. Mayors of large cities have virtually begged for federal recognition that many of their problems, including poverty, are really national problems. Governors have recognized how limited the individual states are in their abilities to cope with the needs of their citizens. Therefore, we think that the dissatisfaction with the present system will break out even more prominently. The problems will not decrease if they are left alone. We think that our policy will look better and better to decision makers, and some variation of it may well be politically acceptable in time.

Legality

The present system still has many questionable legal points. A number of aspects of the traditional approach have been stripped away. "Man in the house" laws, "midnight raids," and residence requirements have been declared unconstitutional. How many other aspects of the present program will be challenged? Unequal benefits and variability of approaches would seem to invite suits. Our policy, on the other hand, would provide identical benefits and opportunities throughout the country, and we cannot see any ready basis for legal challenge.

Satisfaction of Relevant Interest Groups

The present policy satisfies only the self-righteous. Unfortunately, the self-righteous are a large interest group! Other than that, the present system does not satisfy any relevant interest group. Certainly, the poor must be the least satisfied. The present welfare system seems to be under attack from everybody with any stake in it at all, and there are few defenders. We do not agree with all of the critics, but in the process of policy analysis we have to take into account their criticisms. Despite our own beliefs that public welfare is not all bad, clearly a system that produces such emotional reactions in people could stand improvement. We are convinced, as we have said before, that the dissatisfaction that various interest groups have with present policies would have led to reform if the issue of poverty were not so value laden.

Scientific Soundness

We cannot present evidence of scientific soundness for either the present policy or our proposed policy. We think that pilot studies should be an important part of policy development and would test the soundness of the proposal.

One interesting study suggests by inference that our proposal moves in the right direction. Devendra Singh reported on a series of experiments in 1972.[11] The simplicity of the experiments does not detract from their importance. Using small children, Singh worked out a system by which one group got marbles by working for them while the other group's marbles came automatically. Singh found that "children, regardless of their culture, sex, I.Q., and need achievement, prefer to get their rewards by working." [12] Singh concluded:

> The important thing appears to be not that human beings get food, water and shelter, but that they get those things in ways that convey to the individual the sense that he is important, that he does control what happens to him. To achieve this goal, it will be essential to provide educational opportunities so that each member of the society can choose the work that will be satisfying instead of being forced to accept work that merely fulfills the biological needs, or take handouts. Otherwise, a person may feel compelled to seek satisfaction for this basic need, the need to control the environment, in ways that may be neither beneficial to, nor approved by society.[13]

Our proposal is consistent with Singh's beliefs about the importance of meaning in human life. We believe that people should exercise control over their own lives. Voluntary services, choice in work and training opportunities, and insurance against contingencies will, we think, promote the importance of the individual and give him or her a sense of mastery.

Rationality

Certainly, the present policy is irrational. It has grown in a piecemeal fashion, largely in response to beliefs about the poor rather than because of a rational attempt to deal with the problem of poverty. We believe that our proposed policy is clearly rational. We think that a recognition that poverty is a social risk, given the mechanisms of the industrialized society, is a rational position. We also think that adequacy of benefit levels is also quite rational. Clearly, the provision of work and training opportunities that lead somewhere are reasonable objectives. Again, we repeat that the irrational element in the control of poverty is the self-righteous morality that has infused what ought to be rational decisions. Poverty is the only non-criminal social problem so overladen with such a moralistic view. In contrast, we now have programs to assist people when they are old. We only require that the beneficiary be old; we do not require that they be Victorian in their behavior.

It is important to point out that we are not opposed to moral behavior. We do not advocate that people abandon their morals. What we do advocate is that social welfare policy aimed at dealing with poverty ought to assume that the poor are pretty much like other people in most respects and cannot be held to a moral standard that is "higher" than that for anybody else. We should plan for the reduction of poverty as we would plan for the reduction of any other social problem—with a rational approach based on knowledge and fact.

Economic Feasibility

Cost is a factor in any social welfare venture, of course. And no plan can be taken with a cavalier attitude toward the taxpayer. Using Skolnik and Dales' figures,[14] it appears that Americans received the following benefits (excluding medical care) in the various programs listed:

Public Assistance	$31,171,500,000
SSI	5,050,700,000
Food Stamps	5,691,800,000
OEO and ACTION	621,500,000
Work Relief, CETA, and EOA	5,534,200,000
Total	$48,069,700,000

As near as we are able to tell, then, about $50 billion was spent on the problem of poverty in 1976. Since about 25 million Americans are poor, this means that we spent an average of about $2,000 on each poor American (exclusive of medical care) in 1976. This does not mean that each poor American actually got $2,000. Administrative costs are included in this figure. Further, one must remember that not every poor person receives benefits from these tax-supported programs.

It is clear that our proposal would cost more than the existing policy. How much more would depend on how adequate the benefit levels were, how much training was desired by those who could take advantage of it, and how many jobs would have to be provided for those who could not or would not be upgraded by education. The probability of a cost that could easily run double our present expenditures is the major flaw in our proposal. This alone is enough to "shoot it down" unless the other gains made the cost worthwhile.

Workability

Our proposal is workable. We think that its simplicity makes it more workable than the present policy which is so complicated that it results in uneven benefits, high administrative costs, and frequent opportunities for error and sometimes fraud.

Efficiency

The efficiency of the present system is nil. The number of systems involved in public assistance, food stamps, and other programs cannot be cost-effective. Reduction to two systems (Social Security Administration and an expanded CETA) simply has to result in administrative savings, provided that the insurancelike approach is taken, as we have suggested, and the time spent in assessing needs is saved. In terms of cost/benefit, we think our proposal is sound. However, as we pointed out above, the country may not be interested in this proposal even if it were efficient simply because of the cost.

Effect on Other Problems

We cannot see how the proposal would make any other problem worse. It would reduce a good deal of the paperwork, provide more money to the poor, and provide an open opportunity structure.

Conclusion

In this chapter we have presented a rational but complicated proposal. It has several advantages over the present system, but the cost may be the hump that cannot be gotten over, even if the moral barriers could be surmounted. We do think that this approach, or something like it, could reduce poverty to a minimum—if Americans are willing to pay for it. Perhaps the cost will be worthwhile, if we continue to be plagued with the deleterious products of poverty.

In any case, we hope that we have energized the reader's critical apparatus with respect to the problem of poverty policy. We seriously believe that any proposal must be carefully thought out from the angles that we have used and must satisfy the criteria we have proposed.

REFERENCES

1. For a more technical discussion, see David M. Gordon, ed., *Problems in Political Economy: An Urban Perspective*, 2nd ed. (Lexington, Mass.: D. C. Heath, 1977), pp. 272–276, 293–300.

2. See *ibid.*, pp. 295–300, and Lee Rainwater, "Perceptions of Poverty and Economic Equality," *ibid.*, pp. 285–293.

3. Max Weber, *The Protestant Ethic and the Spirit of Capitalism*, trans. by Talcott Parsons (London: George Allen & Unwin, Ltd., 1930), p. 180.

4. *Ibid.*, p. 17.

5. *Ibid.*, p. 89.

6. See Marilyn Flynn, "Poverty and Income Security," Ch. 7 in Donald Brieland, Lela B. Costin, and Charles R. Atherton, eds., *Contemporary Social Work* (New York: McGraw-Hill, 1975), p. 104.

7. For an extended discussion of this point, see Clair Wilcox, *Toward Social Welfare* (Homewood, Ill.: Richard D. Irwin, 1969), pp. 211–227.

8. See, for instance, Edward J. Mullen, Robert M. Chazin, and David M. Feldstein, *Preventing Chronic Dependency—An Evaluation of Public-Private Collaborative Intervention with First-Time Public Assistance Families* (New York: Institute of Welfare Research, Community Service Society of New York, December 1970).

9. U.S. Bureau of the Census, *Statistical Abstract of the United States: 1977* (Washington, D.C.: USGPO, 1977), p. 346.

10. Wilcox, *op. cit.*, p. 230.

11. Devendra Singh, "The Pied Piper vs. The Protestant Ethic," *Psychology Today*, Vol. 6 No. 8 (January 1972), pp. 53–56.

12. *Ibid.*, p. 54.

13. *Ibid.*, p. 56.

14. Alfred M. Skolnik and Sophie R. Dales, "Social Welfare Expenditures, 1970–1975," *Social Security Bulletin*, Vol. 39, No. 1 (January 1976).

QUESTIONS FOR DISCUSSION

1. Pamela Roby has written: "The lives of the poor are shaped less by much-heralded poverty programs than by those factors in the U.S.

economy that cause some to be poor and others to be rich in the first place." Do you agree or disagree? What factors in our economy do you think she is referring to?

2. Discuss some of the pros and cons of a guaranteed annual income (or national income insurance) plan. How likely do you think it is that we will adopt such a plan in the next ten years?

3. Why might the lower middle and working classes be more critical of guaranteed annual income proposals than the upper middle class?

4. Why is redistribution of income different from redistribution of wealth? Would each take different policies? Which would you prefer, if either?

5. What are some of the pros and cons of the federal government serving as the employer of last resort? Do you support a full-employment policy?

6. How do you react to the authors' suggestion of exempting youth under 19 from a minimum wage law? What are some advantages and disadvantages?

7. Casework counseling with welfare poor has been a popular policy in this country over the past century. Can you account for its popularity? Do you agree that it lacks rationality, workability, and efficiency as a policy?

SUGGESTED PROJECTS

1. Discuss with a friend or relative their views on poverty and welfare. Does he or she perceive poverty as an individual failure or as an economic problem? Are his or her views toward welfare consistent with the perception of poverty; that is, does this person lean toward marginal grants, enforced work, regulation, and casework as responses to individual failure? Or toward full employment, guaranteed income, and other structural solutions as responses to economic problems?

2. Examine newsmagazines and newspapers for a week or so and read the articles and editorials on some aspect of poverty, welfare, unemployment, or a related issue. Do these seem like controversial topics in the media? Can you detect any consensus or trends? Are conservatives or liberals doing most of the writing?

FOR FURTHER READING

Peter Bachrach and Morton S. Baratz. *Power and Poverty: Theory and Practice.* New York: Oxford University Press, 1970. Two political scientists explicate an approach to power, stressing nondecisions, and apply it to the efforts of blacks to gain political access in Baltimore in the 1960s.

Eli Ginsberg and Robert M. Solow, eds. *The Great Society: Lessons for the Future.* New York: Basic Books, 1974. A series of articles by prominent economists, political scientists, attorneys, and educators assessing the War on Poverty and projecting future trends.

Dorothy Buckton James. *Analyzing Poverty Policy.* Lexington, Mass.: D. C. Heath, 1975. A collection of articles by political scientists, analyzing the current poverty and welfare policies, particularly the War on Poverty programs of the 1960s.

Sar A. Levitan. *The Great Society's Poor Law: A New Approach to Poverty.* Baltimore: The Johns Hopkins Press, 1969. A thoughtful and systematic review and assessment of the various programs of the War on Poverty.

Frances Fox Piven and Richard A. Cloward. *Regulating the Poor: The Functions of Public Welfare.* New York: Vintage Books, 1971. A well-documented account of the way in which relief-giving in the United States is utilized to maintain civil order and enforce work.

Lee Rainwater. *What Money Buys: Inequality and the Social Meanings of Income.* New York: Basic Books, 1974. An empirical study of the meaning of money and attitudes toward poverty and welfare in the United States. Among other findings, a guaranteed income is quite popular with the upper middle class as a solution to the burgeoning welfare bureaucracy and as an admission that the country cannot produce jobs for the unskilled undereducated.

Pamela Roby. *The Poverty Establishment.* Englewood Cliffs, N.J.: Prentice-Hall, 1974. Articles on the power structure that has controlled poverty policies and utilized them to regulate the poor and perpetuate economic and political inequality.

Albert U. Romasco. *The Poverty of Abundance: Hoover, The Nation, the Depression.* London: Oxford University Press, 1965. An account of the zenith of the voluntary approach to the handling of poverty, just prior to the Social Security Act and of other developments of the 1930s in the United States. This book will be of value to the student who wonders how poverty was handled before the thirties and what the prevailing attitudes of the time were.

Clair Wilcox. *Toward Social Welfare.* Homewood, Ill.: Richard D. Irwin, 1969. An economist examines the problems of poverty, insecurity, and inequality of opportunity, and evaluates the policies designed to cope with them. A comprehensive and critical analysis.

John B. Williamson. *Strategies Against Poverty in America.* New York: John Wiley, 1975. A very useful review and analysis of antipoverty policies. A standard scheme, utilizing twenty-six dimensions, is used to evaluate and compare the various policies. A national income insurance plan rates highest among the policies.

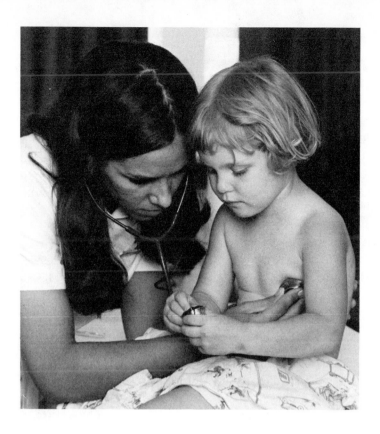

6 Policies for Health and Mental Health Systems

Health care was not excessively expensive until the 1960s. It has since become increasingly difficult for most Americans to receive adequate health care at a reasonable cost. Besides spiraling health care costs, the maldistribution of physicians and other medical care personnel has precipitated a call for government intervention in the health care system. Medical care has been compared to a national resource:

> Medical care is limited in quantity and is a service that everyone must have. It should be considered a national resource, or at least a public utility. It is unthinkable that electric power or the availability of power could be left to the vagaries of the market place, exploited by the producers. But what about

This chapter was written by Len Altamura, a mental health specialist, who is currently Director of Mental Retardation Services for the Calhoun-Cleburne Mental Health Board, headquartered in Anniston, Alabama.

medical care? A system would not be tolerated in which highways, postal services, and education were available only to those who could pay, or available more readily to those who could pay the most. But what about medical care? [1]

The history of health care policy in the United States is in actuality a history of no policy at all or at best a piecemeal set of guidelines. Today's emphasis on health care policy is a shift in goals in health care—a shift from health care for those able to pay to an emphasis on health care for all despite their means.

This health care goal is both simple and complex. It is simple in the sense that it may be easily stated: "An adequate level of physical well-being for all citizens at a reasonable cost." [2] On the other hand, it is complex in that there are at least two hundred federal health-related programs in existence. Each program has its own goals and policies, and in many cases these policies are in direct competition and conflict with each other.

"Social planning," in the words of Alfred J. Kahn, "involves a sequence of means-ends relationships. It is a process of policy determination for orderly development to achieve given objectives." [3] In effect, policies create those boundaries within which service programs exist in their quest to achieve given goals and objectives. In some areas of social welfare policy the student can review given programs and deduce the broad objectives of the program, as well as the policy decisions which have helped to shape those programs, for example, income maintenance (Chapter 4). Health care policies cannot be deductively reasoned quite so easily, for health care in the United States is in a transition period between major goals and, therefore, between policies and programs.

The goal of adequate physical well-being for all has within it two separate objectives. The first is that of preventing illness and disease. This is a task that the private sector (hospitals and physicians) finds to be less profitable, and therefore does not address. Also, prevention in our highly technological society is often at odds with the overriding goal of the free market system—profit. This is not to say that health care providers do not attempt prevention. Rather, it is more profitable to treat the ill—of which there are many—rather than to attempt prevention. When no private sector service provider is willing to perform the required services, the federal government usually feels compelled to intervene. This intervention takes many forms and can be seen in such programs as rat control, lead-based paint poisoning prevention, mine safety, immunization programs, nutrition for the elderly, and hypertension screening. These preventive tasks are often called "well care."

The second objective, after prevention, is that of remediation of illness and disease, often called "sick care." This objective of treating the ill and the handicapped is reflected in programs such as Medicare, Medicaid, community mental health centers, migrant health care, alcohol and drug abuse services, workmen's compensation, transportation services for the handicapped, Veterans' Administration hospitals, and military health care programs. In programs such as these, the federal government intervenes because the private sector, while providing such services, does so only for those who have the means to pay, or for those who live in areas that are attractive to health care providers, or for those who do not have special needs.

The thrust of this chapter will be to examine the goal of national health care; to examine past programs and policies which have led to the present goal; and to analyze and evaluate the policies that attend this goal.

The Goal: National Health Insurance

The goal of adequate health care can take one of two possible forms. One strategy is to provide a "national health service" in which the government would directly provide treatment and medical personnel. The national health service concept, sometimes referred to as "socialized medicine," [4] is already found to some minor extent in programs such as medical care for veterans, the armed forces, hospitals for persons with tuberculosis, and many medical services to native Indians. While this alternative may be viable for providing nonmarket services to needy groups, it will become obvious from the following section that the historical thrust is toward a health insurance scheme. This second strategy for universal health care—most often called "national health insurance" (NHI)—is the only alternative being seriously considered at this time.

National health insurance is presently only a group of proposals and concepts, and not a firm legislative package. Most of the national health insurance proposals that have received recent congressional attention involve several aspects of ordinary health insurance programs. For example, the insured would probably pay a premium, by having deductions taken at his place of employment, or if unemployed would receive coverage from the government. In the event of illness or the need for a physician or hospital visit, a certain percentage of the bill would be paid by the citizen (co-payment feature), with the remainder paid by the government. National health insurance would guarantee citizens that the majority of their medical care bills would be assumed by the federal government, upon the satisfaction of certain minimal expectations such as paying the premiums or assuming part of the total cost.

The very name, national health insurance, implies a cogent, coherent package; yet the truth is that the ultimate form of national health insurance will probably not become final until the mid-eighties. In reality, NHI exists only as an idea aimed at satisfying the goal of universal health care. The various proposals must be evaluated:

> The most frequently mentioned objectives of health insurance reform— though not necessarily all common to all of the current proposals—are: (1) enrollment should be universal but not necessarily compulsory; (2) coverage should be "comprehensive" (though definitions vary); (3) everyone should have an equal access to medical services, to the extent possible and to an extent consistent with other objectives; (4) medical cost inflation should be held to a minimum; and (5) the cost of administering the health insurance systems should be held to a minimum.[5]

Here we have a guide for examining the crucial issues in national health insurance. The first point mentioned is the universal coverage that many people consider basic to any national health insurance program. This is in keeping with the findings of a congressional task force which recommended that "no individual shall be deprived of needed health care because of inability to pay; . . . no one should be encouraged to delay care because of an insurance system that will not pay for ambulatory or preventive care." [6] The noncompulsory aspects of this issue, it would be suspected, relate primarily to the freedom of choice accorded all citizens in the Bill of Rights.

The second concept, that of comprehensive coverage, takes into account such possibilities as dental care, preventive services, eyeglasses, psychiatric care, and many other medical services that are often excluded from current federal programs and private insurance policies. The third point concerns equal access to medical services, and relates to such problems as inequalities in the distribution of doctors and other health care professionals and in the distribution of facilities and equipment. The goal here is toward an improved level of health care in all areas of the nation. Secretary of Health, Education, and Welfare Califano makes this same point:

> We have not done a very good job over the past 10 years of helping rural Americans get ambulatory care. The typical rural citizen is twice as likely never to have had a physical examination as the typical citizens of a large metropolitan area. . . . While some are starving for health care, obesity is common place for others. Nationwide we have an excess of some 100,000 hospital beds. . . . We have made progress in absolute numbers in ending the doctor shortage of 10 years ago, but doctors are unevenly distributed, geographically and by specialty. Manhattan has 800 doctors per 10,000 people; Mississippi has fewer than 80.[7]

The fourth issue, that of medical cost inflation, is one aspect of medical care that must be resolved prior to the acceptance of any of the fifteen or more national health insurance proposals. While the ultimate parameters of financing a national health insurance program will not be developed for a number of years, it is imperative that cost containment occur. Califano corroborates this point:

> If unchecked, total hospital costs could reach $220 billion by 1985. Health care is rising at a rate of 2.5 times the rise in the cost of living.
>
> This rapid inflation imperils the ability of uninsured people to get health care at all. It gobbles tax dollars at such a rate that they are not available for other public priorities. The federal government spends 12 cents of every taxpayer's dollar on health care—9 cents to the hospital industry alone. The average American worker works one month each year to pay health care costs.[8]

Finally, there is the consideration of the potentially enormous costs related to administering a federal health insurance program, whether administered by the government or by an organization such as Blue Cross. Many citizens have a great fear of any federal program, expecting a typically expensive bureaucracy that will be required to oversee it.

Precursors to a National Health Care System

The drive toward some form of national health care has been with us from the early part of the twentieth century. In the years 1915–1918, a group of academics, lawyers, and others attempted to have a model medical care insurance bill passed by several state legislatures.[9] Initially, this group had the cooperation of the American Medical Association but eventually lost this support. The AMA opposed the bill and it was never passed.

The next major surge for provision of government sponsored health care came in 1934 and 1935 with the provisions of the social security bill. It had appeared for a time that federal health insurance might be made a part of this landmark legislation, but the response from the medical community, especially the American Medical Association, was so negative that it appeared for a time that the entire social security program might be endangered if the health insurance provisions remained in the draft legislation.[10] The health insurance provisions were finally dropped, but this was the beginning of active interest in government participation in health care.

With the end of World War II and the beginning of President Truman's "Fair Deal," the issue of a national health care system was raised once again. The problem addressed continued to be one of unequal accessibility and distribution of health services. A number of legislative proposals were presented, with the strongest bill having five major specifications:

(1) insurance benefits were to cover all medical expenses;

(2) the plan would be contributory except for those who were destitute,

in which case federal grants to the states would provide for the poor;
(3) there would be a compulsory payroll tax to finance the program;
(4) administration of the program would be a national health insurance board; and,
(5) doctors and hospitals would be free not to join the plan, and patients would be free to choose their own doctors.[11]

This bill met the same fate as its predecessors. It was rejected by the 81st Congress in 1949.

Medicare and Medicaid

According to Marmor, those factions which had been proposing universal national health insurance finally decided that a more incremental approach might be successful. Accordingly, the thrust of government health insurance in the early 1960s focused upon medical coverage only for the aged. While much work and preparation went on throughout the entire Eisenhower administration, it wasn't until shortly after the inauguration of President Kennedy that a definitive proposal was sent to Congress calling for medical and hospital coverage for the estimated 14 million Americans over the age of sixty-five. Although the proposal was turned down in 1961, and again in 1962, 1963, and 1964, the concept of health care for the elderly began to gain momentum in Congress and in the nation. This build-up of support, coupled with the Kennedy assassination and the subsequent overwhelming support of Lyndon Johnson and his "Great Society" all contributed to making 1965 a turning point in government participation in health care.

After a seven-month struggle between January and July of 1965, with numerous efforts by various lobbies, congressional committees, and determined legislators, Public Law 89-97, the Medicare bill, was signed into law by President Johnson on July 30, 1965. While it is probable that Medicare would have become law at some future point, the enormous Democratic electoral victories in 1964 created a congressional and presidential coalition that assured passage of the bill, despite a number of attempts (some of them successful) at limiting the scope of Medicare.

The legislation that was finally signed into law by President Johnson added two new titles to the Social Security Act. Title XVIII has two parts to it. Part A provides hospital benefits to every person who has attained age sixty-five. This hospital insurance covers care in both hospitals and extended care facilities, as well as providing home health services. Benefits under Part A are subject to upper spending limits, such as coverage for only ninety days of hospital care per illness. Part A is automatically available to those who are eligible. It is funded primarily through the Social Security Act, which provided for deductions from employees' paychecks and contributions by employers. Additional funds come from general revenues and other sources. While there are no premium charges for Part A, benefits are subject to a deductible and a small co-payment which is paid by the patient.

Part B of Medicare is a voluntary program of additional services, either on an inpatient or outpatient basis, and is open to anyone covered by Part A who is willing to pay half of the premium for Part B. The remaining half of the Part B expenditures come from the general revenue of the federal government. If an individual is on welfare, that person's share of the cost for Part B services is paid out of federal funds. Physicians' services are covered, including services performed in the home, hospitals, or office. An annual deductible payment and a co-payment for certain expenses in excess of the deductible are also features of Part B.

The second title of Public Law 89-97, Title XIX, is best known as "Medicaid." The Medicaid legislation authorized comprehensive coverage —regardless of age—for those who qualify for public assistance (the "categorically needy") and for those who might become indigent as a result of medical expenses ("medically needy"). Financing for the Medicaid program is shared by the federal government, from its general revenues, and by the state, and in some cases, local funds are used.

One feature of Medicaid is that providers of medical services are not under any obligation to accept those eligible for Medicaid as patients. "As a consequence, many of both the categorically and the medically needy cannot gain access to medical services, even when Medicaid stands ready to pay the bill." [12] Another feature of Medicaid is that although the federal government established certain minimum eligibility requirements, procedures, and minimum standards, the individual states could impose their own eligibility and service boundaries. In effect, this led to not one Medicaid program, but to more than fifty different Medicaid programs. [13] Accordingly, there was, and continues to be, a wide variation in the eligibility criteria and the services offered between states.

With medical costs soaring and many state governments unable to keep pace with increasing Medicaid costs, a number of states have decreased their commitment to Medicaid by limiting the number of services available, lowering the eligibility ceiling for recipients, and reducing the amount that they will pay for certain medical costs.

The impact of Medicare and Medicaid on federal participation in health care is twofold. The first point is that they are important pieces of social legislation which point attention to the health needs of the citizens of the United States. While they deal with only two specific populations, the aged and the poor, the groundwork has nevertheless been laid for including health care as a "right" for all citizens. The second point, and perhaps the more important, is the now well-known consequence of increased health care cost as a direct result of the Medicare and Medicaid plans. Schorr, for example, states that

> enshrined in the law were the principles of paying "reasonable cost" rather than fixed prices, to hospitals and "reasonable" or "customary fees" to physicians. These concessions started a time bomb ticking. The price of health care, which had been rising at a rate of 3%, suddenly began rising at 6%. What had been intended as a price ceiling had become a price floor.[14]

The cost for medical care, aside from escalating enormously, has forced the premiums paid for Medicare to be increased. Unfortunately, as these premiums have risen, the benefits have been curtailed. The "deductible" has begun to rise, as have the premiums for voluntary medical services under Part B. Additionally, Medicaid coverage has been cut by eliminating certain services.

In summary, Medicare and Medicaid play an important part in the evolution of national health care by being pieces of legislation which acknowledge health care as a "right." Their impact on the cost of medical care is also important, for as we shall see, national health care is based on a moderate and sensible cost structure—a structure which Medicare and Medicaid have helped to weaken.

Community Mental Health

While Medicare and Medicaid were the first steps in the desired goal of overall health care, attempts were also being made to provide comprehensive care for another segment of the population—the mentally ill. It would be useful to review briefly the federal approach to mental illness, while keeping in mind the issues raised above concerning universal health care. There are decided differences between mental health policies and programs and the more universal health care of a nation; yet federal experience with mental health has provided a number of lessons that may be useful in implementing a national health care program.

Like other health problems, mental illness is seen as a social problem in the United States. Whatever standards are used to measure this phenomenon—time, money, unhappiness, or loss of human potential—the conclusion must be that this great loss constitutes a social problem. While estimates vary widely as to the incidence of mental illness in the United States, it is estimated that approximately 20 million Americans suffer from a psychiatric disorder at one time or another during their lifetime. Mental and emotional difficulties have no respect for the money of the rich or the misery of the poor. They are also color-blind. The threat which its random course poses is in itself a major factor calling for federal attention to the problem.

As Dentler so eloquently summarizes, "We can neither attack a mental illness effectively, nor have we learned culturally how to endure it." [15]

Historically, mental illness—like national health care—has had periods where it has appeared as a raging issue, or more commonly, smoldered beneath the surface. While some action has been evidenced over the past eighty years, it has only been in the last twenty years that a concerted effort has been made at a national level to deal with this major health hazard. Historically, mental illness has been viewed, ever true to the Protestant ethic, as the individual's problem. Until the decade of the 1960s, it was felt that the federal government should not be involved in the care of the mentally ill, but rather that their care should be left to the state and the private sector. A more liberal point of view espoused federal action on the grounds that the private sector was responsible for social causes of mental illness and that the government had allowed industrialization to proceed at a pace beneficial to the industrialists, but detrimental to the individuals in this society.

Very much like the debate over whether or not the federal government should be involved in overall health care of its citizens, so did the debate rage over government intervention in response to the needs of the mentally ill. The first concerted efforts toward a national mental health policy produced the Mental Health Act of 1963. This act was based on the report of the Joint Commission on Mental Health and Mental Illness, *Action for Mental Health*. This report was broad enough, and vague enough, to permit various interest groups to read what they wished into it. What resulted was a vigorous political battle at the federal level between psychiatrists with a public health view, advocating prevention and new precedents for mental patient care, and those psychiatrists maintaining the traditional medical model who advocated greater federal assistance in improving the quality of mental hospitals. This dichotomy still persists, but will probably not be a main concern in the future. As it turned out, the new—or community-based—services were adopted. Especially important was the governmental support of the proposed comprehensive community mental health centers. These centers were to be developed, for the most part independently of the mental hospital, and were to keep patients as close to home as possible.[16]

The approach advocated by the Commission included: (1) emergency and acute treatment services; (2) expanded resources for treatment; (3) community clinics as the major service provider; (4) psychiatric beds in the general hospital system; (5) emphasis on short-term hospitalization; and, (6) community resources for psychiatric illness. These items formed the basis for the comprehensive community mental health centers legislation of 1963.

The legislation took effect in 1963, and in 1965, 1967, 1970, and 1975, the federal government extended the programs and funds for these mental health centers. Coinciding with the original legislation was the invention of psychotropic drugs. With the advent of the phenothiozines in 1956, mental hospital populations began declining even though admissions were rising. This was mostly due to the decrease in the time being spent in the psychiatric institution. As patients left the institutions, they usually found no local psychiatric treatment facilities, outside of the private psychiatrist, who could treat them. By establishing comprehensive community mental health centers, it was felt that outpatient care would become more readily available—often with Medicare and Medicaid covering the costs. These centers would allow the patient to receive the support of family and community while still receiving the necessary psychiatric treatment. In effect, the emphasis was placed on facilitating the transfer of patients from distant custodial wards back to the community.

Politically, endorsement by both major political parties seemed to indicate that the nation's mental health needs, and especially the needs of the poor, would be listened to in Washington. Unlike the limited Medicare and Medicaid proposals, the community mental health centers were not created just for the old or the poor. In effect, this made them more palatable to the nonpoor, even though the poor needed and used the facilities more often.[17]

The original legislation of 1963 established a funding base for local mental health facilities. In order to qualify for federal funds, these organizations had to provide five basic services: (1) a consultation and education service intended to provide education to the community and thereby attempt to decrease the incidence of mental illness; (2) an emergency service that would provide around-the-clock psychiatric crisis care; (3) an outpatient service that would provide generic psychotherapeutic assistance; (4) a partial hospitalization service aimed at patients who needed more than outpatient care but who did not need to be hospitalized; and, (5) an inpatient service for patients who were acutely psychotic but who did not need long-term placement in a state-supported psychiatric institution. While the ravages of psychiatric disorders were to be the primary concern of these facilities, the mentally retarded were likewise to receive appropriate care, as were alcoholics and drug abusers. The services mandated through the mental health center legislation indicated that federal policy decisions were being based on, if not ideal solutions, at least on solutions that seemed more appropriate to the wealth of mental health knowledge: while new mental health buildings and facilities might not improve mental health in a community, shortened hospitalization and community support of the mentally ill were quite desirable.

Following Kahn's [18] format for evaluating relevant policy issues, we offer the following analysis. The services provided by the community mental health centers are available to all. In this sense, they are *universal* and apply equally to all. Payment is on a sliding scale, and is therefore *means-tested*. In a sense, *redistribution* occurs because the "haves" pay more for the services (taxes and fees) than the "have nots." Services are *in kind* through public, nonmarket facilities. The services to be available are determined in a general fashion at the federal level, and with some freedom, specific services are determined locally. As such, the legislation provides for both *discretionary, decentralized* services, as well as *statutory, centralized* control. Accordingly, the programs provided are custom tailored to the people they are to serve, so that there is a measure of *separatism* involved, and the emphasis for change can be aimed at either the individual or the community, depending upon the nature of the center.

While a number of changes have occurred in the community mental health center legislation, the basic concept of community-based care that would operate both to prevent mental illness and to treat it when it occurs, is still operative. The concept has withstood attempts at impounding funds (President Nixon, 1973), a veto of continuing legislation (President Ford, 1975), and significant congressional intervention and calls for reform, evaluation, and accountability. Nevertheless, the concept continues to be a viable one. With continuing success, these agencies should find continued financial support when some form of national health care is adopted.

It is apparent from the way the 1975 legislation (Public Law 94-63) was written that Congress finally became fully committed to the community mental health center concept and that federal mental health policy would be defined and executed through the proliferation and maintenance of these community-based facilities. A House and Senate subcommittee report stated: "the Committee does not consider the Community Mental Health Centers Act as a demonstration program. It is the Committee's intent that within the next five years the entire nation be served by an appropriate network of centers." [19] This Committee report is a clear statement that community mental health centers shall be the delivery system for mental health services.

This congressional commitment toward providing federally sponsored mental health services for the citizens of the nation is yet another step in the direction of universal health care. Of course, the funding of community mental health centers will differ significantly from that of national health care. To begin with, the mental health centers are funded as private agencies which receive federal financial support on a declining basis. At the end of the funding period, the mental health centers are expected to be financially independent of the federal government. Unfortunately, the system has not always worked well. In many cases, after mental health centers received their last year of federal support they were able to exist only through increased funding from the states and local governments or by curtailing services.

On the other hand, there are many similarities between a system of national health insurance and the community mental health centers legislation. To begin with, both programs aim at comprehensive care for the nation. Both would stress preventive ("well care"), as well as remediative ("sick care") efforts. Both programs are open to all citizens without regard to income levels, age, or other eligibility criteria. In this case, both are universal services. The sliding-scale fee now used in community mental health centers could possibly be adopted as a part of national health insurance, especially as a co-payment feature.

Of the numerous national health care proposals before the Congress, most feature inclusion of mental health services as part of the comprehensive care definition. While these proposals vary considerably from the reimbursement procedures of mental health centers, it is generally agreed that some incentive will be provided to users of community mental health centers. These incentives may take the form of lowered cost at a community mental health center. In any event, while the future of comprehensive community mental health centers is not overwhelmingly bright, there is every indication that continued federal funding will be available under a national health program, and that the concept of community-based mental health care will continue to flourish.

National Health Planning Act of 1974

"Since 1935, Congress has been passing laws having to do with health, health resources, environmental protection, and biomedical research at an accelerating rate." [20] To help coordinate and bring coherence to the more than 130 separate pieces of health legislation, Public Law 93-641 came into being. This law, the National Health Planning and Resources Development Act of 1974, establishes a national network of health planning bodies. These local health systems agencies (HSAs) are given the ultimate responsibility for local planning. HSAs, acting as a network, are to develop plans for health care systems in their localities, which in turn are to be coordinated at the state level through state health coordinating councils. These state councils, in turn, are to develop state health plans and medical facilities plans. Finally, the individual state plans are coordinated at the federal level, and form the basis for federal decision-making in the development of health care services. The HSAs, in conjunction with the state planning bodies, have virtually complete power over such areas as health facility construction, including mental health facilities, hospitals, and nursing homes; federal state and health planning programs, such as mental retardation services and health personnel training funds; and many other health-related services.

Public Law 93-641 mandated the HSAs to develop their plans and guidelines according to a number of congressional priorities, which can be summarized along the following six dimensions:

1. Health status, which covers such issues as infant mortality and life expectancy.

2. Health promotion and protection, concerned mainly with health maintenance and prevention.

3. Health care services, covering all medical, dental, and mental health problems.

4. Health data systems, including data collection, analysis, and utilization.

5. Health innovation, including areas of new procedures and products.

6. Health financing, including cost containment.[21]

These six dimensions viewed as a whole provide an insight into the direction of congressional intent: coordinated health care services; however, they also provide—if this coordination task is accomplished—the elimination of many problems associated with implementing a national health care system.

Indeed, there are many issues, some of which have been previously mentioned, that will impede the implementation of any national health insurance policy. Califano categorizes these pitfalls: (1) health resources are poorly distributed; (2) health resources are not organized as efficiently as they might be; (3) there is very little incentive to be cost-effective, with a consequent emphasis on treatment rather than prevention; and (4) health insurance in America is expensive and inequitable.[22]

To a great extent, the functions of HSAs and the entire health planning system is to assist in eliminating or reducing the impact of these four problem areas. With regard to poorly distributed health resources, HSAs are in a position to increase or decrease resources in a given geographical location. For example, in an area where excess nursing-home beds exist, the local HSA can refuse to authorize additional construction of nursing homes. Likewise, in an area where adequate hospital resources are lacking, the local HSA can make the acquisition of these resources a high priority for federal expenditures.

The second problem, that of inefficient organization of health resources, can be alleviated through the overall planning function given to HSAs. In this problem area, HSAs can, for example, provide incentives to physicians for staying in needy urban areas rather than moving to the more lucrative suburbs. The third issue, cost effectiveness, affords HSAs the opportunity to encourage the use of group practice settings, prepaid prevention programs, and health maintenance organizations (HMOs). Finally, again through the use of HMOs and other prepaid prevention programs, the cost of health insurance can be brought to a more reasonable level.

Health Maintenance Organizations

Thus far we have seen the evolution of a national health insurance program begin with Medicare and Medicaid, become more refined through the implementation of mental health centers, attempt to become coordinated through the use of HSAs, but still lacking the major ingredient for implementation, that is, reasonable cost. Providing health care at a reasonable cost can be best accomplished by the establishment of health maintenance organizations.

In its most simplified form, an HMO is a health care system in which professionals deliver comprehensive medical services to patients for a prepaid fee. The HMO delivers, or has delivered, all health services that a patient population may need. The population consists of individuals and groups who contract for the delivery of these services. They agree to pay a fee whether they are ill or well. The HMO and the consumer negotiate ahead of time the cost per person or per family.

Obviously, the HMO must provide for the prevention of illness if it is to succeed financially, for prevention is far less expensive than treatment. The provision of preventive services, through regular examinations, prompt treatment, and early detection of disease, makes the HMO a financially viable organization. This cost effectiveness of HMOs makes them attractive for inclusion into a national health insurance program. Indeed, one of the mandates for health systems agencies under Public Law 93-641 was to develop integrated medical group practices, health maintenance organizations, and other organized systems for the provision of health care.

Like the concept of community mental health centers, HMOs are intended to provide a complete range of health care services, including prevention. Cost is not based on income, or type of disability. Rather, by prepaying the consumer is actually encouraged to stay healthy. With the emphasis on prevention, the more expensive "sick care" system is consequently utilized at a lower rate, thus reducing the HMOs operating cost and the cost to the consumer.

HMOs provide a great potential for quality care at reduced cost—the necessary ingredient for a national health insurance program. The emphasis on establishing HMOs began in 1973 with the passage of the Health Maintenance Organization Act of 1973 and is being reemphasized through the mandate to HSAs. It may well be entirely possible that the passage of any eventual national health insurance proposal will be based on the future successes of HMOs as efficient, affordable, and quality health care providers.

A Comparison of Current Policies and Selected Alternatives

The present system of health care coverage results in numerous service gaps and shortcomings. The poor and elderly receive minimal—and in most cases inadequate—health care coverage under Medicare and Medicaid. Increasing costs and decreasing services under these programs have left the needy with only make-shift health care coverage. The financially well-to-do, on the other hand, pay increasingly higher costs for a full range of health care. The working poor and middle-income groups, while to some extent covered by private medical insurance, are medically underserved, paying an ever-increasing amount for shrinking coverage and receiving services only when ill. This health care system reflects the following practices: (1) health care is based on a free market system; (2) government services are provided on a selective basis; and (3) emphasis is on "sick care."

Alternatively, the movement toward a national health care program involves cost containment; universal care in the form of national health insurance; an emphasis on prevention as well as remediation; and a shift to a federal system. We will now move to a comparative analysis of these two policies.

Is the policy compatible with contemporary "style"?

Adequate health care in America is seen as a right by many people and no longer as a privilege. For the public to obtain these "rightful services," it is very much in keeping with contemporary style to allow the federal government to operate in the free market system. Precedents such as federal price supports for farm products, guarantees and loans to industries, and other federal interventions in the marketplace, all act to make a governmental health program acceptable. Virtually no one, including the American Medical Association, is willing to question federal involvement in national health insurance. The only question that really remains open to discussion is what form national health insurance will take so far as administration of the program is concerned. It is almost unanimously agreed that the present mixed system of federal, state and federal, and private insurance does not meet the needs of the public. When a problem such as the lack of adequate health care affects a majority of the population, it is seen as adequate reason for federal intervention.

If anything, the prospect of centralized federal planning and intervention in health care received a boost with the election of President Carter.

His platform included a program of national health care. We believe that the nation's mood is less one of sweeping social change such as under Kennedy or Johnson, and more one of contemplation, reasoning, and thinking before acting. Thus, replacing a fragmented system with a well-reasoned approach is in keeping with the nation's overall mood and style.

The comprehensive aspects of a national health insurance program, including prevention and remediation, are likewise compatible with contemporary style. Americans have become increasingly aware of the often piecemeal and incomplete results of many federal programs. It would be expected that a truly comprehensive health care program would be quite welcomed. Lobbying for specialized health programs would still need to continue for certain minority health care needs. That is, many Americans might consider mental health care a nonessential health service, while others would continue to lobby for its inclusion in a national health insurance program. The same case could be made for services to the developmentally disabled and cerebral palsied and for other groups that are not in the mainstream of American society.

The issue of preventive care through the use of HMOs is also in keeping with contemporary style—in concept. In reality, it is questionable whether Americans will be readily able to make the necessary intellectual and life-style changes to accommodate preventive medicine. It has been the practice for too many years to utilize health resources only when one is ill. Experiences with HMOs have shown this life-style change is possible, but that the process will be slow unless financial incentives in the form of reduced premiums are available.

Does the policy contribute to equity and justice?

The question of equity and justice refers to the distribution of services in a manner that is adequate for those persons least able to cope with our society. In the instance of medical and health care, equity and justice refer as much to the working poor and middle class as to the elderly and the unemployed poor—both groups who can least afford a health-related disability.

Medicare was one of the first steps in the equitable and just redistribution of health care services. Although partially financed by the employee, Medicare was nevertheless a redistribution process because of the additional funds contributed by employers and the government. Medicaid involved a larger redistribution process, but was inequitable in the sense that each state operated its program at a different level, and therefore denied equal access to services. Medicare and Medicaid were both movements in the right direction, but both have fallen far short of their potential.

The development of private health insurance contributed little to ease the burden on working persons, had no inherent redistribution system, and varied from company to company as to cost and coverage.

Even within the context of private health insurance, inequities exist.

> While insurance companies accounted for more than half of the total gross enrollment under private health insurance plans for almost all services in 1973, the population covered by insurance companies is overrepresented by a non-marginal, economically secure and healthy group including whites, the middle-aged or young, married and middle- and upper-income groups.[23]

This means that only the better insurance risks were accepted under private health plans, while the less desirable risks were encouraged to go to such plans as Blue Cross who tend to charge higher premiums or have lower benefits.

A federal system of universal health care at reasonable cost carries the previous programs one step farther in the cause of equity and justice. For example, the formation of HSAs assures an equitable distribution of government funds toward the provision of health services. By way of illustration, as pointed out by Califano: "In Southern California there are enough CAT scanners—a sophisticated X-ray and computer diagnostic tool costing $500,000 or more—for the entire western United States." [24] HSAs could prevent the reoccurrence of such waste and maldistribution.

Without such a constraining influence, the cost of medical care could only be expected to rise astronomically, thereby placing medical care out of the reach of even more people. The issue of cost containment is not so much one of providing increased equity and justice, but rather one of preventing a loss of equity and justice: if medical costs continue to multiply, services will become even less equitably and justly distributed.

The provision of comprehensive health care, including prevention, removes many barriers standing in the way of adequate health care. As movement occurs toward this comprehensive system, the increased range of services contributes to equity and justice in the system. To have a truly comprehensive health care program would mean redistribution of resources, both financial and human, and would provide for incentives to transfer resources from areas of excess to areas of need.

Is the policy compatible with social work values?

Perlmutter indicates that concern over health should be central to any discussion of welfare in the United States.[25] Her point is that health is but one of the areas with which social work must deal in order to bring about a society in which all can function adequately. Based upon this, there appears to be an overall absence of conflict between societal values and social work values on the issue of national health care. Clearly, comprehensive national health insurance is compatible with social work values in that it provides for universal service rather than service on a selective basis. A federalized health care system that includes "well care," and is based upon reasonable costs, is very much in keeping with the traditional social work concept for the proper functioning of individuals in a society.

Conversely, the present health care system is not compatible with social work values. To begin with, services are not equitably distributed and are fully available only to the wealthy. Likewise, those groups most disenfranchised by our complex and technological society are those who suffer most, yet can least afford health care services.

Is the policy compatible with other important values in society?

While concern for the poor, aged, and other minority groups is not always evidenced to a great extent, concern for one's personal physical well-being is often a high priority. Accordingly, the thrust toward adequate health care can be considered an important societal value. Although NHI would be a comprehensive program, the poor and elderly would still be the recipients of a redistribution process. It is felt that this is in keeping with societal values in that redistribution of resources is already occurring under the present system, and therefore would not be more costly. This desire for physical well-being is of such overriding concern that federal intervention and participation in the health care system would be seen as in keeping with present values.

One central value of the American experience—the free-market system —has proven itself inadequate to the task of providing a reasonable level of health care. As in past eras, such failures in the system bring about demands for federal intervention. In this sense, NHI would be perceived positively if it fulfills the needs of a majority of citizens. Related to this issue is that of reasonable costs. The decade of the seventies has increasingly shown citizen agitation over high federal expenditures that result in low-effectiveness programs. It is obvious that the current emphasis on cost reduction and cost control are aimed at satisfying this important value.

Quite often the sense of helplessness when dealing with the federal bureaucracy has tended to mitigate against any government program. In the case of health care, numerous attempts are being made to include consumers as a part of the entire health planning and delivery system. For example, the mandate that HSA boards be made up of at least 50 percent consumers is a step in this direction. Having adequate consumer representation at the local level is, again, very much in keeping with the social values of a federalized system responsive to local needs.

Is the policy politically acceptable?

Any system of national health care that includes a strong planning component, universal care provisions, preventive services, and reasonable costs cannot help but be politically acceptable. While this has not always been the case, it has become obvious that the lobbying of such organizations as the American Medical Association and the American Hospital Association, no longer carry as much weight and influence as the public outcry for a functional health care system.

One key factor in making NHI politically acceptable is the incremental, reasoned approach taken thus far. As stated previously, NHI will result only when the necessary foundations (planning, cost control, distribution, etc.) have been laid. Also, the call for health care reform has reached such proportions, that it would be politically unacceptable for a politician to argue too strongly against NHI.

This pressure for reform emanates not only from consumers, but from local and state officials as well. The cost of health care (including Medicaid) has driven many local governments to the brink of despair. In the case of New York City, the cost of health care is one of the primary reasons for its near bankruptcy. Of course, some resistance will be met as the final form of national health insurance is legislated. Schorr indicates the focal point of this resistance in his discussion of the Medicare legislation:

> Congress, back in the days of innocence, in 1965 had crossed its heart and sworn to organized medicine not to change how health services are delivered to Americans. There are weak grins now when one recalls the free-enterprise safeguard clause that was written into the Medicare law, forbidding the government to "exercise any supervision or control over the practice of medicine or the manner in which medical services are provided.[26]

In the case of national health care, political feasibility would work in favor of a national health insurance program rather than against it, for it is clear that there is a consensus emerging among the citizens to have such coverage. For the first time in the history of national health proposals, the citizens, lobbies, and politicians, all seem to agree that the time for action is at hand.

Is the policy legal?

There appear to be no legal constraints upon the implementation of a national health insurance program. None of the major policy issues would seem to be in legal jeopardy. Of course, some of the more conservative elements in the country might question the "socialistic" bent of any federalized health care system. These objections, however, would not be sufficient to threaten the legality of a national health insurance proposal. Similarly, the present system is also legally practical.

Does the policy satisfy relevant interest groups?

The expensive, fragmented system we now call health care certainly satisfies those who profit from the free-market system of medical care. It does not satisfy the poor, elderly, working class, or virtually any other health care consumer except the well-to-do.

The alternative policy of national health insurance, while not appreciably reducing the profits of some health care providers, appears to satisfy most of the consumer groups as well as most of the provider groups. Of course, as the final form of national health insurance begins to take shape, specific objections may be raised by any one of a number of interest groups. Indeed, loud objections are already being heard from many physicians and hospitals over the control of HSAs and congressional meddling in local health care provision.[27] These objections, and others, are likely to continue for some time, for the HSAs will be offering the first organized interference to the free-market provider community.

Is the policy scientifically sound?

While a fully operational program of national health insurance does not exist, many of the component parts of such a system are already in effect and are therefore being empirically evaluated. The issue of providing prevention along with remediation has been proven to be a viable one in the limited experiences of health maintenance organizations.[28] Although there have been some administrative and bureaucratic difficulties in the establishment and operation of HMOs, there have also been a number of such organizations that have been successful—financially and clinically—in providing health care.

Many foreign countries have experimented with national health insurance programs for many years. Germany, which has had a national health insurance system since 1883, was the pioneer in providing health care. Despite years of frightful mistakes and many struggles with the medical profession, Germany has a flexible national health insurance program of top quality. Great Britain, Sweden, West Germany, France, and Canada have each organized their national health care programs separately, but experience has shown that a nationalized system is scientifically sound.

Additionally, the experiences of successful HMOs and other prepaid group practices have contributed to the growing body of literature to indicate that such prevention-oriented programs can be viable. The prepaid group practices that are now in operation—Kaiser-Permanente, the

Health Insurance Program of New York, the Family Health Program of Southern California, and the Harvard Community Health Plan—have all been quite successful in providing quality care at a reasonable cost.[29] The Kaiser program is a chain of thirteen hospitals and numerous satellite clinics, serving well over 1 million members. The success of the Kaiser program can be seen in a number of indicators: lower costs based on increased preventive activities; avoidance of unnecessary operations because of preventive measures; the comprehensiveness of the service, with minor exceptions. The success of the Kaiser program and others indicate that prevention and cost effectiveness go hand in hand, and both will be required in any national health insurance program.

In summary, the experimentation necessary for a fully implemented national health insurance program is slowly taking place through the incremental development and implementation of the various parts of the NHI system, both in the United States and abroad.

Is the policy rational?

The question of rationality would appear to argue in favor of a cost-effective national health insurance program. Indeed, the question of rationality is one that would argue against the present costly system provided by the free market. Certainly, it cannot be considered rational for the federal government to finance more than 60 percent of all biomedical research, over 40 percent of medical school revenues, and about 30 percent of all hospital charges, while at the same time having virtually no overall plan to which to relate these expenses.[30] Furthermore, the irrationality is evident when one considers the enormity of those expenditures and the small amount of return for each of those health dollars. It would appear to be much more rational to spend federal dollars in a planned manner, providing for reasonable costs through prevention rather than remediation, in a manner that would serve all citizens regardless of ability to pay.

Is the policy economically feasible?

Health care is expensive and this cost is as much due to previous government intervention as it is due to the lack of government planning. Without adequate planning and a strategy for incremental implementation, national health insurance cannot exist. Already, federal health expenditures have risen from approximately $19 billion in fiscal year 1973 to $44.5 billion for 1978. The impact of these expenditures was commented upon by Senator Bellmon:

> It is clear that the Federal government has helped fuel the raging inflation in medical care costs. We have been too willing to turn large sums of the

taxpayer's money loose and we have paid far too little attention to the economic effects of what we are doing, or even to the extent to which our generosity was really helping people meet their legitimate health care needs.[31]

Quite obviously, the present medical care system is gradually becoming an economic impossibility. If HSAs, HMOs, and other federal strategies such as ceilings on spending for hospital facilities are successful, then a cost-effective national health insurance program is possible.[32]

While the current practices in medical care are not now economically feasible, the immediate implementation of a national health insurance program would be even more disastrous, for the proper groundwork has yet to be fully laid and implemented. The cost effectiveness upon which national health insurance must rely for eventual implementation will only come about through successful planning by HSAs and by increased federal incentives for health maintenance organizations to originate.

The following summarizes the hoped-for results of HSA planning and subsequent cost control:

> For health planning to be really effective, the government and we, the public, have to evidence at least a modicum of interest in health. Historically, and I'm afraid currently, we have been preoccupied by medical solutions to acute care problems. Throw in a good measure of concern for equitable access to the best quality care, insurance which takes away nearly any incentive for financially responsible decision-making by the consumer, a reimbursement system which encourages excess, and you have guaranteed cost escalation with little or no positive impact upon health.[33]

Is the policy workable?

The present system is workable, yet because of the social and economic costs, it cannot remain so for long. The alternative system of national health insurance can only be assumed to be workable until it is fully implemented and therefore verified as workable. That costs can be reasonable is a workable goal that has been demonstrated through the implementation of HMOs and other prepaid programs.

It is expected that with the implementation of a national health insurance program the change in policy goals from a piecemeal to a unified approach will indeed pay dividends in the level of health care in the United States. It would likewise be expected that, due to the universal coverage and cost-containment features, services would eventually be available to all groups and individuals.

Whether or not the total program will be workable will need to be left to the future; however, from limited experience, we can say that a program of national health insurance should be workable.

Is the policy efficient?

The present fragmented system of health care is neither efficient nor effective. By streamlining this system through the use of HSAs and incentives for efficiency, a much more efficient system than is current could be possible. Certainly, a centralized federal system would provide more clinically and financially efficient service than a mix such as is now available. The emphasis on prevention would also streamline the system by eventually removing the need for many complex and emergency services.

Will the policy be likely to generate other social problems?

This is one policy analysis area that is decidedly applicable to Medicare and Medicaid. These two programs were laudatory in their goal; however, within a few years of their implementation it became obvious that their cost would be excessive. Indeed, the federal approach to Medicare and Medicaid greatly contributed to soaring medical expenses, which in turn helped to fuel the inflationary spiral of the early 1970s economy.

Rising medical costs also meant rising premiums for private health insurance, and a closing-out of medical services to the working poor and to many middle-income persons.

The present proposed policy of national health insurance based on reasonable costs and a philosophy of prevention will probably have some unforseen social consequences, but would not at present seem to add any additional social burdens.

Conclusion

The changing health care scene in the United States is indicative of increased public awareness and lobbying for an integrated and unified health care approach. While national health insurance may not be the last answer to the problem of health care, it is the next evolutionary step toward solving the health care crisis. Certainly, the thrust toward a comprehensive and universal program fills a major need. Additionally, the emphasis on cost reduction and cost control through preventive services appears to be sound.

REFERENCES

1. Robert Gumbiner, *HMO, Putting It All Together* (St. Louis: C. V. Mosby Company, 1975), p. 1.
2. Joseph A. Califano, Jr. Taken from a speech to the American Medical Asso-

ciation, as reported in the *Congressional Record*, 95th Congress, 1st Sess., Vol. 123, No. 112 (June 28, 1977), p. S10862.

3. Alfred J. Kahn, *Theory and Practice of Social Planning* (New York: Russell Sage Foundation, 1969), p. 15.

4. John Krizay and Andrew Wilson, *The Patient as Consumer* (Lexington, Mass.: Lexington Books, D. C. Heath, 1974), pp. 11–12.

5. *Ibid.*, p. 157.

6. Quoted in Daniel Schorr, *Don't Get Sick in America* (Nashville: Aurora Publishers, 1970), p. 167.

7. Califano, *op. cit.*, p. S10863.

8. *Ibid.*

9. Theodore R. Marmor, *The Politics of Medicare* (Chicago: Aldine, 1973), p. 7.

10. *Ibid.*, p. 8.

11. *Ibid.*, pp. 11–12.

12. Krizay and Wilson, *op. cit.*, p. 82.

13. Originally, Arizona and Alaska did not establish Medicaid programs. Eventually Arizona, Alaska, Guam, Puerto Rico, the Virgin Islands, and other U.S. holdings all established Medicaid programs.

14. Schorr, *op. cit.*, p. 103.

15. Robert A. Dentler, *Major American Social Problems* (Chicago: Rand McNally, 1967), p. 420.

16. David Mechanic, *Mental Health and Social Policy* (Englewood Cliffs, N.J.: Prentice-Hall, 1969), pp. 59–60.

17. August B. Hollingshead and Frederick C. Redlich, *Social Class and Mental Illness: A Community Study* (New York: John Wiley, 1958), pp. 194–250.

18. Kahn, *op. cit.*, p. 204.

19. *Community Mental Health Centers News*, Vol. 6, No. 13 (September 1975).

20. U.S. Department of Health, Education, and Welfare, *Papers on the National Health Guidelines: Baselines for Setting Health Goals and Standards* (Washington, D.C.: USGPO, January 1977), p. 9.

21. *Ibid.*, p. 3.

22. Califano, *op cit.*, p. S10863.

23. Carol K. Morrow, *Health Care Guidance: Commercial Health Insurance and National Health Policy* (New York: Praeger, 1976), pp. 96–97.

24. Califano, *op. cit.*, p. S10863.

25. Felice Davidson Perlmutter, *A Design for Social Work Practice* (New York: Columbia University Press, 1974), p. 6.

26. Schorr, *op. cit.*, pp. 102–103.

27. John K. Iglehart, "Playing the Role of Doctor," *National Journal*, Vol. 8, No. 20 (May 14, 1977), p. 757.

28. Roul Tunley, *The American Health Scandal* (New York: Harper & Row, 1966), pp. 114–116.

29. Gumbiner, *op. cit.*, pp. 7–8.

30. U.S. Department of Health, Education, and Welfare, *op. cit.*, p. 9.

31. Senator Bellmon speaking in support of the proposed FY 1978 HEW budget allocation, 95th Congress, 1st Sess., *Congressional Record*, Vol. 123, No. 112 (June 28, 1977), p. S10861.

32. John K. Iglehart, "Stemming Hospital Growth—The Flip Side of Carter's Cost Control Plan," *National Journal*, Vol. 8, No. 22 (June 4, 1977), pp. 848–852.

33. Willie B. Goldbeck, "Health Planning: An Essential Ingredient in Cost Containment," *National Journal*, Vol. 8, No. 22 (June 4, 1977), pp. 876–877.

QUESTIONS FOR DISCUSSION

1. What services do you feel should be included in a comprehensive national health insurance program? How could these services be financed?

2. National health insurance will be a form of income redistribution. What groups do you think will finance the majority of the costs, and what groups will benefit most?

3. The AMA has indicated that any national health insurance program must be implemented gradually. Can you propose one or more methods of gradual implementation?

4. In an attempt to cut health care costs, it has been suggested that doctors use less expensive, but equally sound, treatment methods in areas such as kidney dialysis. Do you think that Congress should have a voice in how medical treatment is carried on, if the treatment is federally financed?

5. If health costs cannot be controlled through HSAs and HMOs, what alternatives would you suggest?

6. Some would argue that any consumer co-payment of health expenditures would once again discriminate against those least able to afford it. Others argue that co-payment is needed to avoid unnecessary hospital and doctor visits. How would you resolve this conflict?

7. What incentives can you develop that might motivate doctors to practice in rural or ghetto areas?

8. It has been proposed that under a national health insurance program, community mental health centers be given an advantage over private practitioners. How could these advantages be developed? What issues do you see as important? What values are operating in this example?

SUGGESTED PROJECTS

1. Visit a board meeting of your local health systems agency. Whose interests are being represented? What issues were discussed, and how were they resolved? Was the thrust of the meeting planning or playing politics?

2. Write to the Medicaid office in your state requesting a copy of services and eligibility requirements. Are these services adequate? Are the eligibility requirements stringent or relaxed?

3. Visit your local mental health center. Ask the administration and staff about funding patterns, services, and costs. How much does a client pay for services? How does the agency keep aware of the mental health needs of its geographic area? What roles do social workers perform in this agency?

4. Visit your local hospital and talk to the administrator or business manager. What do they see as the cause of high hospital costs? What remedies do they suggest? How do they feel about national health insurance? Medicare? Medicaid? Health systems agencies?

5. Visit the nearest federal repository library or other major library and find copies of the *Congressional Record* that deal with the annual HEW budget (your librarian can assist you in finding this). What are the major issues being discussed? Is the emphasis on expanding or reducing health care? On the basis of what you read, how would you advise your congressman or senator to vote on each issue? Why? (What are your major values?)

FOR FURTHER READING

American Enterprise Institute for Public Policy Research. *National Health Insurance Proposals.* Washington, D.C.: American Enterprise Institute, 1974. A detailed, excellent summary of the issues surrounding national health insurance. The text was prepared by a renowned editorial staff and reviews major NHI proposals. Six proposals are compared by considering issues such as distribution of services, manpower, and cost.

Bruce Denner and Richard H. Price, eds. *Community Mental Health Social Action and Reaction.* New York: Holt, Rinehart and Winston, 1973. A well-written contemporary approach to mental health services focusing on community involvement, accountability, and prevention. The authors present a strong case for community participation in the policy and planning stages. Includes a "how-to" approach for involving the community.

Robert Gumbiner. *HMO, Putting It All Together.* St. Louis, Mo.: C. V. Mosby, 1975. Written by the founder and chief executive of a prototype

HMO, the text examines every major aspect of HMO operation. Although intended as a guide for other practitioners desiring to establish an HMO, the book also provides many insights into the history, financing, and services of a HMO.

John Krizay and Andrew Wilson. *The Patient as Consumer.* Lexington, Mass.: D. C. Heath, Lexington Books, 1974. An examination of the financial aspects of U.S. health care written by two economists. A rather complete review of data related to Medicare, Medicaid, private health insurance, and health insurance reform. Although packed with statistics, the text reads well and provides the financial facts necessary to understand health care issues.

Theodore R. Marmor. *The Politics of Medicare.* Chicago: Aldine, 1973. The author has worked both in and out of the federal government, and is familiar with policy-making in the Department of Health, Education, and Welfare. He provides a detailed political look at the evolution of this Medicare legislation from impossibility, to possibility, to enactment. An excellent view of health care politics.

Daniel Schorr. *Don't Get Sick in America.* Nashville, Tenn.: Aurora Publishers, 1970. An entertaining, highly readable, fact-filled book written by a respected television journalist. Examines, from the consumer's point of view, the health delivery system in the United States, including Medicare, Medicaid, private health insurance, and national health insurance.

U.S. Department of Health, Education, and Welfare. *Papers on the National Health Guidelines: Baselines for Setting Health Goals and Standards.* Washington, D.C.: USGPO, January 1977. A compendium of primary health care data used in setting health policy guidelines.

7 Policies for Problems in Living Space

In this chapter we want to look at some problems in the living space of people. Principally, we will focus on housing, but living space includes the neighborhood, transportation facilities, and other amenities that are desirable to full human living. This topic may be seen as outside the mainstream of social welfare policy. Indeed, it is the province of other professions and interest groups who may have a larger stake in it than do social workers and social welfare planners. Nevertheless, this problem has an impact on areas for which social workers are responsible, though other groups may have more to say about the policies, programs, and delivery systems for products and services.

We cannot exhaustively discuss all the problems in living space in a single chapter. What we will do is to review some central issues of particular concern to social welfare and analyze these issues in terms of their impact on social welfare clientele. It is at these points of impact that social workers will find opportunities for intervention.

We discussed social welfare policy and poverty in Chapter 5 where our discussion centered on money. But lack of money is not the only thing that impoverishes the human being.

> The quality of the environment in which people live, work, and play influences to no small degree the quality of life itself. The environment can be satisfying and attractive and provide scope for individual development or it can be poisonous, irritating and stunting.[1]

Whether the conditions under which people live, work, and play are satisfying and attractive or poisonous, irritating, and stunting is not accidental. The quality of human life is a matter of policy—choices made on the basis of knowledge and values which result in a line of decisions over time. That some people live in substandard housing, walk unsafe streets, attend poor schools, and lack humanizing amenities are outcomes of policy choices that have alternatives.

It is not that we lack the technology to produce other outcomes. There is no technological reason why all Americans cannot live a decent life. One must look, as we shall see later on, at political, economic, and social values for insights into the reasons for policy being what it is.

We do not want to rest our case for concern about living space on the basis that "bad" living conditions cause "bad" people. The naiveté of this position is easily seen when one considers the number of "good" people who have come from difficult backgrounds and the "bad" people who were born into privilege. Chester Hartman provides a much less emotional basis for concern:

> While good housing can provide a supportive environment for change, it is unlikely that basic problems of employment, education, and crime will be swept away by moving into a good home in a nice neighborhood. . . . The country's serious need for improved housing cannot rest exclusively on arguments of health and safety or social pathology.
>
> A sufficient basis for concern and action with regard to housing is that most people feel that their living conditions are central to their lives, and millions of American families deem their current living conditions as onerous and unacceptable in view of what the society offers to the rest of its people.[2]

Hartman's position is compatible with our position that human survival is dependent upon mutual aid. We ought to be concerned that people live under onerous and unacceptable conditions simply because "they" are part of "us." We would reject an argument which says that we should be concerned because "they" live in a way that is a threat or an affront to "us."

The Federal Government and the Housing Industry

It can be said that most people in the United States live in better circumstances than members of any other society, although some people still live in squalid and substandard conditions. The present policy works for most people. In regard to housing, the current major policy is that the federal government guarantees the payment of a large number of mortgages, and provides for the liquidity of capital in the investment market. This policy makes it possible for many more people to have housing than would be the case otherwise—but among the primary beneficiaries are the lending institutions, the housing industry, and the realtors. There is little opposition to the policy of government-industry cooperation from the political right, given that the federal government plays a major role in the housing marketplace.

The role of government in the mortgage field is quite complex. Probably the feature best known to the general public is the function of the Federal Housing Administration (FHA). The FHA was established during the Great Depression. It insures lenders against default on mortgages. Ordinarily, lending institutions will loan a buyer 60 to 80 percent of the value of a house, requiring repayment to be made over fifteen or twenty years. Most home purchasers are unable to come up with down payments of 20 to 40 percent of the purchase price of a house. An FHA-guaranteed loan, however, permits the purchaser to make a down payment of 5 to 10 percent and pay off the balance over thirty or even forty years. Of course, the home purchaser with an FHA-guaranteed loan ends up paying a great deal more for the same house than does a purchaser with a "conventional" mortgage. Although the monthly payments may be lower for the FHA-guaranteed loan, lending institutions figure interest in such a way that for half the life of the loan, the purchaser is paying mostly interest. And, of course, one is making payments for a great deal longer due to the smaller down payment, which prolongs the life of the loan. On the positive side, FHA has made home ownership possible for millions who would otherwise not be able to afford it.

A second form of federal "intervention" is the provision of a system that guarantees availability of capital to the lending industry. There are a number of federal supports to the mortgage market.

> To back up the primary mortgage market, the federal government has a byzantine array of agencies and programs, many of which date from the collapse of the housing credit system in the 1930's. These include the Federal Home Loan Bank Board and its twelve regional banks, a central banking system for home-loan banks analogous to the Federal Reserve System for commercial banks, insurance agencies, the Federal Deposit Insurance Corporation and the Federal Savings and Loan Insurance Corporation, to protect

depositors in various types of savings institutions; and a secondary mortgage market, which permits mortgage investors to sell mortgages in their portfolios or convert them into securities acceptable to other segments of the investing public.[3]

The point is that the federal government is, heart and soul, committed to the success of the development of housing through its intervention in the money market. The trouble with all this is that the "feds" do very little else that has any positive effect on poor families.

The Federal Government and the Low-Income Individual

There is a rent supplement program in which the FHA pays a subsidy to owners of lower income property that is insured by FHA, theoretically permitting the owner to charge a lower rent. This program is small and not effective. In addition, there is public housing. In order to get a really good hold on these problems, it is necessary to know a bit of history.

Urban Renewal and Public Housing

Slum living has never been as charming as those who have been able to leave it have sometimes nostalgically described. Hartman summarizes the problems:

> Among the more notable hazards of slum living are a higher incidence of fires, related to poor heating equipment and wiring; higher rates of home accidents from broken stairs and other structural defects; rat bites . . . and hazards to personal safety resulting from poor lighting, inadequate locks, and the like.[4]

Hartman also lists the dangers of carbon monoxide poisoning from faulty heaters and lead poisoning from paint on old houses.

One of the most readable accounts of the development of federal attempts to deal with slum living conditions is by Ashley A. Foard and Hilbert Feffernan.[5] We have drawn heavily on their summary of federal legislation through 1960 in the paragraphs that follow.

Apparently the earliest that national attention was focused on housing and living conditions (aside from journalistic pieces and fiction) was the President's Conference on Home Building and Home Ownership in 1931. No legislation grew out of the work of the conference, and the United States had no national policy on housing until the Housing Act of 1937 (although some public housing was built under the National Recovery Act of 1933). The 1937 act's title was, "An Act to provide financial assistance to the States and political subdivisions thereof for the elimination of unsafe and unsanitary housing conditions, for the eradication of slums, for the provision of decent, safe and sanitary dwellings for families of low income, and for the reduction of unemployment and the stimulation of business activity, to create a United States Housing Authority and for other purposes." Foard and Feffernan say that the 1937 act was "intended to help clear slums through federal loans and annual contributions for the provision of low rent housing." [6] It is also clear that the supporters of the act thought that building low-cost housing would also benefit idle construction workers and the companies that employed them.[7] What seemed to be a sensible blend of altruism and practicality in 1937 gave way to a different purpose in the Housing Act of 1949.

The Act of 1949 had a stormy history. As one might suspect, the idea of clearing slums and replacing them with federally subsidized housing looked better in the Depression than it did after World War II. The chief provisions of the Act of 1949 included federal money for slum clearance and some public housing (which was the most controversial part of the bill) but focused on urban redevelopment which was broader in scope and not controversial. In essence, the bill provided for localities to generate a plan for urban redevelopment. A local community could acquire slum land, clear it, and sell or lease it but was not committed to replace whatever was cleared with housing. The act only required that new construction be "predominantly residential," which was taken to mean one-half. The federal government undertook to underwrite up to two-thirds of the loss that a locality would incur as the difference between what purchase and demolition cost and the sales price or lease value. The locality would have to underwrite one-sixth of the loss in cash but could count as its other one-sixth the cost of provision of parks, streets, and other improvements. In effect then, the relatively benevolent Act of 1937 which was designed to provide low-income housing and put the unemployed back to work, was changed into a policy to encourage urban redevelopment, which included the sale of land for purposes other than housing.

Another milestone was the Housing Act of 1954. This act reflected a further shift. First, the idea of urban redevelopment was changed to "urban renewal." Second, the local planning body had to present a "workable program" for eliminating blight and overall community development if it was to obtain federal assistance. FHA mortgage insurance was made available for private residential construction with the Federal National Mortgage Association standing by to purchase any mortgages not taken up by private investors. Another important provision of interest to us here was the removal of the requirement that an urban renewal area had to be rebuilt as "predominantly residential."

With the passage of the 1949 and 1954 acts, the way was cleared for cities to condemn slums, sell or lease the land more freely, and avoid public housing. Foard and Feffernan note that the additional low-rent public housing units authorized by the 1954 Act were made available only for meeting the needs of families displaced by government activities in a community where an urban redevelopment or urban renewal project was being carried out.[8]

While this provision was repealed in 1955, the policy intent was clearly opposed to public housing. Hartman is more pungent on the subject of urban renewal:

This program [urban renewal] was introduced in the 1949 Housing Act as "slum clearance" but was taken over at the local level by those who wished to reclaim urban land occupied by the poor for commercial, industrial, civic, and upper-income residential uses. Over half a million households, two-thirds of them non-white and virtually all in the lower income categories, have been forcibly uprooted. A substantial percentage of these persons were moved to substandard and overcrowded conditions and into areas scheduled for future clearance, at a cost of considerable personal and social disruption.[9]

It is clear that the 1949 act was a turning point. It has been downhill since, as far as public housing goes. Congress failed to appropriate enough money for the amount of housing authorized until the Kennedy years, and even then the best that could be done was 100,000 units in 1961. There was a modest upswing in public housing during the Johnson administration, and some innovations appeared in 1968.

The Housing Act of 1968 contained two provisions that are of some novelty. Section 235 provided for the purchase of a home by low-income people. The purchaser was supposed to pay only 20 percent of his or her income in payments including taxes and insurance. The federal government, through the FHA, guaranteed the loan and made up the difference between the purchaser's payments and the ordinary payment that would ordinarily be required by paying all but 1 percent of the interest. While moderate and near-poor people secured housing, the very poor were not affected. Even though the down payments were low under the program ($200), the poor could not manage them.

Section 236 of the act made it possible for rental units to be built using private capital with the federal government subsidizing the interest. Since interest makes up a good part of the payment on housing loans, the government subsidy made it possible, in theory, to rent to low-income people at a price they could afford. The catch was that it was still necessary for the Local Housing Authority or a nonprofit sponsoring body to collect rents sufficient to pay the mortgage and upkeep, so it was never financially realistic to admit tenants who were too poor.

Another popular innovation from about the same time was the "turnkey" approach. Using the turnkey technique, "a builder arranges to construct or rehabilitate a development to housing authority specifications and then turns the completed units over to the authority at a prenegotiated price." [10] This approach proved to be popular, since it provided the private builder a guaranteed sale of the product.

Since 1965 the practice of leasing units became part of federal programming. This approach did not build new housing; it leased standard housing units from existing stock and rented them to low-income tenants for a fixed proportion of their income (20 to 25 percent). The Local Housing Authority, using federal funds, covered the difference between the tenant's payments and the market value of the housing.

These last two approaches were the mainstays of the Nixon administration, particularly since the 235 and 236 programs ran into problems. Simply put, too many builders cut too many corners. The 235 housing was often shoddily built, but the builder got his money just the same. It was not uncommon for a family to purchase a house under the 235 plan and simply walk away when they needed to move. They had built up little or no equity, and could only lose their very modest down payment. A number of housing tracts built under the 235 provisions fell into disrepair simply because the tenants had walked away and left their houses. Since foreclosure takes time, the house deteriorated and was often vandalized. The 236 program did not always work out well either. In one such operation, which is unfortunately typical of most, a private not-for-profit corporation built a very attractive set of townhouses for rental to poor families. Although the federal rent subsidy kept the payments low, the payment on the principal and the upkeep still had to be paid out of rents. Poor tenants simply were not able to pay regularly, so the operation continually was on the edge of going broke and reverting to HUD by default. The pressure was to rent to dependable tenants with as high an income as was possible. By 1974, defaults from 235 and 236 programs were costing HUD $2 billion annually.[11]

Finally, the Nixon administration declared a moratorium on federal housing programs and new subsidized housing. The difficulties came to a head in the early seventies as attention turned to the so-called Brooke amendments (sponsored by Senator Edward Brooke of Massachusetts), which would have increased governmental subsidies and limited the amount that the poor would be expected to pay for housing to a maximum of 25 percent of their income. These amendments were designed to counter the finding that tenants were paying, in actual fact, more than 25 percent of their income for housing and related costs. The Office of Management and Budget stalled on implementing the Brooke amendments and the provision of housing for the poor ground to a halt. Since the moratorium, the Ford administration did little that profoundly affected housing policy, and no new programs have come from the Carter administration. The Act of 1973, which governs current programs, continues the community development idea but is "soft" on the provision of housing. Some federal funds are available for the reconditioning of dwellings, but this is not a significant policy innovation.

It is easy to see that housing the poor is a highly troubled issue. The real estate industry, the home building industry, and the lending institutions of the country have never been behind the idea of housing provided by the federal government. They have been much more cooperative with federal programs that offered them a chance to participate in the housing market—and guaranteed a return on their money.

Further, public housing has not been well received by the tenants. The now classic case is that of Pruitt-Igoe in St. Louis. Built in 1954, this housing complex was a model of its kind; however, when Lee Rainwater wrote about it in 1967, the complex had a vacancy rate of 20 percent.[12] It was unsafe and unsatisfactory. Whites had moved out, and the only blacks who would move in were those who were desperate for housing. The residents had become discouraged and alienated. Rainwater's suggested solution was to provide more income to the lower class and to discard the idea of ancillary services to the poor that he believed were predicated on the notion that they would remain poor. Though he does not say so, one would presume that if this were done, the poor would find their own housing and services on the private market and the need for public housing would decline. All Pruitt-Igoe units have been torn down, and Pruitt-Igoe is no longer the shining example of effective social planning. Though many public housing units are still in use, the idea of replacing slums with new units for the poor is an idea whose time is past.

What is wrong with public housing?

A number of critics have tried to answer this question. Martin Anderson in his book *The Federal Bulldozer*, published in 1964, gave the answer quoted most often.[13] Although the specific demon that Anderson felt compelled to fight was urban renewal as a whole, he made several points concerning the 1949 Housing Act. In essence, Anderson noted that urban renewal was tearing down about four times as many homes as it built. Further, the homes built on urban renewal lands rented for much more than the original tenants could pay. Therefore, most of the poor were forced to move into neighborhoods of about the same quality as they moved from—and at higher rents.

In another article, Anderson raised constitutional issues.[14] Slum clearance is done under the constitutional doctrine of "eminent domain." This rests on a phrase in the Fifth Amendment of the Constitution, which says "nor shall private property be taken for public use without just compensation." It is Anderson's position that the condemnation of private property, which is then resold to private developers after it has been cleared, is not *public* use but is clearly *private* use. Robert Groberg, one of Anderson's critics, maintains that public use is equivalent to public benefit and that it has been of public benefit to rid the communities of slums.[15] While this is not the place to argue the constitutional merits of the case (the Supreme Court having already ruled in favor of urban renewal), Anderson's point remains that urban renewal has not been a very effective tool in providing housing for the poor, but it has been a boon to the land developer.

Bellush and Hausknecht make a slightly different argument.[16] In their view, Americans have taken seriously Jefferson's idea of "the virtues of the yeoman farmer and the sterling pioneer" and have made of home ownership a symbol of success and achievement. Public housing runs counter to this symbolism. It also runs afoul of the interests of powerful groups in real estate and home building.

Other writers have mentioned that public housing is barren, lacks the character of neighborhoods that it replaces, and has a stigmatizing effect on its inhabitants. Still others point out that public housing has failed to serve the very people that it supposedly sought to serve. Since the payments on the principal and upkeep costs must be paid, Local Housing Authorities tend to rent to families and individuals at the upper end of the income range of eligibility. For instance, in all public housing there is an income limit. Let us say that in a given project one must make less than $4,000 to qualify. Most LHAs prefer to rent to those making as close to $4,000 as they can and tend to discourage the very poor from renting simply because they know that there is a better chance of getting the rent from those with more income.

All of what we have said points to the simple fact that governmental activity in the provision of housing for the poor has generally been unsuccessful.

First, federal policy is clearly in support of home ownership by private individuals shopping for housing using private capital whose investment is insured by the government. This policy bias is bolstered by the tax structure that allows the home purchaser to use interest on the mortgage and property taxes as deductions on the income tax. Even though the number of single family dwellings built is only about half of the new living units built per year and many people live in apartments by choice, the federal government continues to subsidize home ownership.

Second, it is clear that federal policy is opposed to public housing. It only supported public housing with any great positive effort in the thirties when the unemployment of skilled people was high, construction was down, and the poor were the temporary poor of the Depression. Since 1949 there has been a marked trend away from public housing in urban renewal programs which had other purposes than providing housing for the poor anyway.

Third, the poor do not accept public housing with the gratitude that its proponents would like to see. The poor have become aware that urban renewal is a threat and that the public housing that they have seen is no paradise. Consequently, it should be no surprise that the building of public housing units has resulted in what some writers have called the "transfer of the slum."

And fourth, the American public does not approve of public housing. The proponents of public housing could never really count on a solid backing from the public. Again, this seems most likely to be related to the moral attitudes about poverty that we noted in Chapter 5.

Present federal policy may change due to the pressure of events. High interest rates and the tremendous cost of land and materials (not labor, since labor costs have not increased as much as other costs) are slowly driving the price of single family dwellings out of the range of many Americans. The citizen who can pay for it can still, of course, buy comfortable housing. Many people of modest income may be all right—as long as they stay in their present housing, provided they bought it before the inflationary 1970s. The higher costs of today's new housing will be most detrimental to the generation that is just now forming family relationships. Surely the inflation in land and interest (which is not a hardship on those who sell land and those who lend money) is largely responsible for the increase in apartment living and mobile homes. Clearly, federal policy in housing has benefited the nonpoor, but has failed miserably to provide decent homes for the poor.

Other Concerns in Living Space

We have spent many words on the subject of housing. This is because housing is a primary concern in the whole subject of living space. Housing is not just a concern of the middle-class person but also of the poor. Hartman says that the poor consider housing their first or second most important problem. But while housing is a primary concern, it is not the only problem that one faces in his or her living space.

The surroundings have a great deal to do with whether or not the quality of life is genuinely human. For most Americans the environment is satisfactory. In addition to comfortable housing, most Americans own serviceable automobiles and have access to shopping. Most Americans can go outdoors at night without great fear—although this is not as certain as it once was. Most American children attend good, if not distinguished, public schools. And most Americans are able to find satisfying work that pays a salary that allows the personal luxury of fashionable clothing, color television, sports equipment, and other trappings of the good life.

It is true that air pollution, water pollution, potentially dangerous chemicals, energy shortages, and political corruption plague the citizenry of the United States, but by and large these problems, though they may get our attention from time to time, seem remote from daily life. Besides, the citizen can tell himself or herself that someone is working on them. The rest of life is rewarding enough to keep our minds busy and our bodies comfortable.

For the poor, too, some of the problems we have listed seem remote. But not because they are comfortable. We have already catalogued some of the problems that the poor have with housing. We should also mention that the poor, as a consequence of their powerlessness, put up with a good deal more frustration in their living space. The poor do not generally have access to dependable transportation. The myth of the welfare Cadillac is well entrenched. But if the Cadillac Motor Car Division of General Motors manufactures only 300,000 units per year and there are around 3.5 million families who are recipients of AFDC, then obviously they cannot all own new Cadillacs! We do not think that these facts will destroy the myth. Actually, the poor often have to depend upon friends who have cars and public transportation. Consequently, they are often unable to shop for bargains. Forced to depend upon neighborhood stores for merchandise, they are victimized by high prices, bait and switch merchandising, high interest charges, and contracts that the average citizen is too sophisticated to sign.[17]

Residents of poor neighborhoods fear to leave their homes in *daylight*, let alone after dark. The children of the poor still attend inferior schools which, in many cities, are patrolled by police. If the poor own any luxury goods, they will be making payments that will outlast the goods—or they buy "hot" merchandise from professional thieves who cater to the lower income market. There are even gangs who steal on contract. The thieves will find a desired item, steal it, and deliver it to the client at the agreed-upon price.

There is little to be gained by detailing the horrors that impinge on the living space of the poor. The reader will find Claude Brown's *Manchild in the Promised Land* listed in the bibliography at the end of the chapter. There is little charm in Brown's childhood living space, and his description of growing up is still reality for far too many Americans.

Where Are We in Policy Regarding Living Space?

Let us recapitulate present housing policy. The federal government pursues two related classes of activity. First, it insures mortgages for home buyers and provides a structure that guarantees the availability of capital. Second, the federal government, aided by local government initiative, has developed a mechanism for securing property, clearing it, and reselling the land to private developers. Both classes of activity are based on a single policy: government support of the real estate, construction, and lending market.

Isolating a national policy that covers other aspects of the living space is only a little more complicated. Probably Daniel Moynihan's famous phrase "benign neglect" covers it best. It may very well have been unnecessary to have advised President Nixon to follow this policy. We believe that it was, and continues to be, the policy already in force. In all fairness to Moynihan, who was a special adviser on urban affairs, it is clear that he had no malignant purpose in his advice. He apparently believed that forces were in motion that would bring about social change and that government's best policy was to stand aside and let things happen.

It is easy to see that this is not a serviceable policy. So far it has neither cured poverty nor provided low-cost housing, nor improved any neighborhood. The lack of an aggressive policy has allowed further decline in those neighborhoods that have become "poisonous, irritating and stunting." Again, as we argued in Chapter 5, social welfare policy (or, in this case, public policy with respect to housing and neighborhoods) continues to be inhibited by certain value positions. Recall the central values in American life that we discussed in Chapter 2. Achievement and success, activity and work, efficiency and practicality, progress, individual freedom, secular rationality, and group superiority are all very strong values in this culture.

Feudal and agricultural societies may often be poor. Generally, such societies lack the resources or the technology to provide widespread abundance in the Western sense. But, as we have said before, there is no such limitation in Western societies, particularly in the United States. We think therefore, that we are up against the same value dilemma that we posed in Chapter 5. With the accent on materialism and success, we should expect that governmental policy would lend support to those processes coherent with economic and social "progress," and to leave the poor out of it. Lawrence Friedman has pointed out that societies are not organized for the poor:

> Laws for the poor, we have suggested, are unlikely to be generated unless (a) the poor are a majority and have fair and adequate political representatives, or (b) on balance, proposed legislation serves the interests of some class larger and broader than the poor.[18]

Friedman goes on to remind us that most laws in this country favor the middle class:

There should be no cause for surprise in these facts. The United States is a middle-class nation and will remain so. However one defines poverty, the poor are a minority of the nation. The middle class is so numerous that the "general good" is apt to be identified with middle-class interests.[19]

Of course, there are opposing value currents in American society—humanitarianism, democracy, and altruism. But these, as we pointed out in Chapter 2, are less dominant than other values. Consequently, social welfare intrusions into the slum, the ghetto, and the barrio are fragmentary, insufficient, and limited in their success. There is never enough money or enough personnel—and there has been insufficient national will to invest heavily in the solution.

There are, of course, zoning laws; but they come after the fact of the city's existence and are nonexistent in most rural areas. Generally, they are only influential in new areas. There are building codes; but they largely affect new construction, requiring only that the oldest structures be brought up to code when major alterations are made. Owners of old buildings avoid making major alterations and may simply allow the building to fall apart when it no longer provides income.

In summary, things are as they are because most of us are busily achieving and succeeding. The public policies that we support and demand as a nation are those that result in supports for achievers and succeeders.

All of this is not intended as an angry indictment of capitalism. It may be an indictment of uncaring progress, or, if one wants to take a theological position, attribution of our living space dilemma to the presence of greed and avarice in the human soul. We think, and we have played this theme before, that the American drive toward success and progress and the moralistic outlook toward the poor have so influenced policy makers that they have not been able to address social welfare concerns in a direct and rational fashion. We suspect that if a socialistic system were highly achievement-oriented it could fail to take the poor into account in much the same way, so we are not going to suggest that radical social reform is the answer and "cop out" on the hard question of what can be done.

What Can Be Done About the Problems in Living Space?

We have taken the position that mutual aid is the most important basis upon which human societies can exist if they are to survive as historical entities. "Dog eat dog" is not an appropriate or successful way to build a genuinely human society. Insofar as societies have avoided the extremes of internal conflict, they have survived. Therefore, we want to look for an alternative to the present policy that is based on a cooperative ethic. We will not offer an ultimate solution, but will try to identify one that has a realistic chance of working in the real world. Again, we will remind the reader that we are trying to spark thinking, not to present a solution, so our suggested policy may or may not suit all ideologies.

We will focus on the housing problem as the key issue. We think that if we could "get cracking" toward a solution to housing then the problems of the neighborhood would come along. Of course, nothing that we propose (or anyone else proposes) would clear up the problem of the opportunists who prey upon the poor. If, however, people can secure decent housing and adequate neighborhood amenities, some of the frustration and hopelessness that sets up the climate in which people are deceived and fleeced may disappear.

Rather than generate our own policy proposal regarding housing, we will cite various housing strategies listed by Arthur P. Solomon:[20]

1. Eliminate all federal government support for housing, and rely solely on the private market.

2. Abolish direct federal housing subsidies, but retain favorable income tax and mortgage-insurance provisions.

3. Continue to rely on new construction programs for the poor.

4. Develop subsidies for using the existing housing stock such as direct consumer subsidies or management and maintenance incentives.

5. Develop a mixture of subsidies for new construction and use of the existing stock.

All these alternatives may sound complicated to the reader. Indeed, they are. If the goal is simply to provide housing for the poor, why could not the federal government simply buy a tract of land, put up relatively inexpensive houses on it, rent the houses to the poor, and absorb any losses? Technically, the United States could do this. It might sound cheaper and simpler than the proposals. However, such a program has no guarantee of working any better than the current programs.

First, there are few available tracts of land that are not geographically remote. One cannot, for example, find a vacant tract of land in Manhattan that could be turned into low-cost housing. One would have to go out from the city a considerable distance. If one cleared the commercial enterprises from Manhattan so that housing could be built, then the businesses and factories would have to be moved out from the city and the poor would still be isolated.

Second, if one could find an unused piece of land and build on it, could anyone guarantee that the poor would move to it? And, if they did, would we not be simply transferring the ghetto or barrio from one place to another?

Third, if the federal government underwrote all rental losses, why would anyone pay any rent at all? It would not be popular to underwrite a program of free rent for the poor which left the poor free from responsibility. Economically and politically, such a gesture, while sounding humane, would create greater monsters than it would replace. Further, it is patronizing and would do little to improve the condition of the poor.

We are afraid that there is no simple answer and that we are left with the task of choosing from among complicated and imperfect alternatives. Let us move to the task of examining the alternatives that Solomon suggests, using our criteria. Because there are five alternatives, we will try to keep the discussion of each as short as possible.

1. Eliminate all federal government support for housing, and rely solely on the private market.

This, as one might suppose, is not compatible with contemporary style. Unlike some other areas where governmental "interference" is resented, FHA-guaranteed loans and secondary supports for the money market are so in style that they are taken for granted. Few would seriously propose that the "invisible hand" of the market be the sole policy. We would guess that the lending institutions, the construction industry, and the real estate interests would oppose a free market in housing—so would most citizens who are in the market for a house.

This policy does not contribute toward equity and justice, except that it is theoretically true that anyone can participate in a free market for housing. Actually, it would discriminate toward all but the upper classes who can afford "conventional" home financing.

Since this policy is not equitable and provides no service for the bulk of the citizenry, it is not compatible with social work values. The policy is compatible with individualism and a certain number of conservative values —except, as we have noted, it would lack the support of a number of conservatives in the lending, real estate, and construction business. It would seem that this policy would not be compatible with most liberals either.

This policy would not be politically acceptable. Neither political party has espoused it, nor are there significant power groups working toward this end. The alternative is legal, or could easily be made so. It obviously will not satisfy many relevant interest groups. It would not have the support of labor or of upwardly mobile members of the working class and lower middle class.

Science can give us no guidance to answer this question. Given that only the upper income groups could afford contemporary housing, it is not a rational policy, since it would create dissension and conflict that could be avoided.

The policy is not economically feasible. This is a rare case where more expensive alternatives may be more economically sound. The elimination of all federal support would change the housing industry drastically. Less money would move in the real estate market. Most Americans would have to settle for smaller, less amenable homes, and there would be repercussions in the whole construction and home products industry. While the well-to-do could continue to build and purchase luxurious homes, those not so well off would have to settle for a lot less or have no housing at all, since federal intervention is all that enables the bulk of Americans to buy homes. Such a policy would be workable in the short run, but would have such an effect on the work force and the construction industry that it would be unworkable in the long run, and hence, not really efficient. This policy would no doubt aggravate other problems and produce chaos in housing.

The appeal of this policy is probably limited to a few doctrinaire and reactionary people.

2. Abolish direct federal housing subsidies, but retain favorable income tax and mortgage insurance provisions.

This policy fits contemporary style because it would continue to give tax benefits and insurance benefits to home purchasers and people who provide rentals. It would eliminate only subsidies that benefit lower income groups. Since this would make housing available only to the nonpoor, it would not be seen by most liberal people as contributing to equity and justice. Clearly, the policy would be antithetical to social work values. It would, however, be compatible with the values of most home purchasers, since it would continue their benefits and negatively affect only the poor.

This policy would probably be in trouble politically, except among conservative constituencies. The policy is probably legal and would be satisfactory to many interest groups except the poor and those whose political life is tied to the poor.

As in the case of most of the policies discussed in this book, science is of no clear help. The policy is, however, not rational since it would create social dissension which rational people would not want to happen.

Again, this policy is economically feasible and would save some money in the short run. The policy is workable, since it simply means not funding some currently funded programs. The policy could be efficient in the short run, but it would make the condition of the poor much worse in the long run.

3. Continue to rely on new construction programs for the poor.

This policy is clearly not in tune with contemporary style. It does work toward equity and justice. Most social workers would approve of providing housing for the poor, but it clearly runs afoul of most values in the United States since such housing would not be the product of work and achievement.

This alternative is clearly not politically acceptable, although it is quite legal. The policy would not satisfy many relevant interest groups, including the poor. The poor do not support public housing with any enthusiasm, but regard it as a last resort.

One could plead that the provision of public housing has no scientific support on the basis that the data available suggest that housing for the poor has not solved many problems connected with living space. Rationality suggests that this alternative is not viable, since it has not worked well in the past.

The construction of housing for the poor is expensive, and is clearly not superior to other alternatives. Because of the political way in which urban renewal has developed, reliance on new construction is probably not workable, nor is it efficient. The policy would not improve the social problems connected with poor housing, but would only transfer their location.

4. Develop subsidies for using the existing housing stock such as direct consumer subsidies or management and maintenance incentives.

This alternative would continue the benefits now enjoyed by the middle and upper classes and subsidize the housing of the poor by direct grants to consumers. It would have the blessing of the middle class and offers something for the poor. Thus it would be compatible with contemporary style. This policy contributes to equity and justice, even though it favors the nonpoor. The policy is fairly compatible with social work values and is compatible with other values, with some reservations on the part of doctrinaire conservatives regarding the subsidies for the poor.

Coupling subsidies for the poor to the benefits for the nonpoor keeps this policy within the realm of political acceptability. It is, of course, legal. The policy satisfies all powerful interest groups: home purchasers, lending institutions, realtors, contractors, and to some degree the poor and their advocates. This is a rational policy to the extent that it is possible in the present climate of values and can be made to work.

This is an expensive policy, but cheaper than the alternative that would depend on new construction. It is more expensive than alternatives (1) and (2) which left out any housing for the poor. It is workable in economic terms, since the country has been doing it for several years. The policy could be efficient if properly administered—since by paying grants for housing to the consumer instead of the housing industry it maximizes the participation of the poor in the housing market. The industry would have to compete for the poor's housing dollar. Unfortunately, this policy, unless funded at far greater levels than is true at present, stands a good chance of prolonging the present situation in which a number of critical housing problems remain unaffected.

5. Develop a mixture of subsidies for new construction and use of the existing stock.

This policy would do what (4) would do, but would add in the provision for some new construction of low-cost housing. The only difference would be the added expense of new construction. Our analysis of this alternative would be identical to what we have said about alternative (4) except that this might make economic feasibility less, and would not be politically popular.

Solomon, after a careful, but rather complicated analysis, opts for alternative (4). His argument is that the middle and upper classes will take care of themselves, given the federal supports already available. Lower income people will be best served by direct subsidy that allows them to shop for housing, thus encouraging more efficient use of existing housing stock. New construction, Solomon says, should be limited to special circumstances. Besides, as we have seen, new construction tends to benefit lenders and builders more than consumers.

Solomon admits that his choice defies conventional wisdom. The conventional approach has involved government payments to builders and lenders as well as funds for land clearance. Alternative (4) would involve a subsidy of the consumer, allowing the consumer some choice in housing and the status of tenant rather than beggar. Solomon cites six arguments for changing to a more consumer-oriented strategy: [21]

1. Twice as many families can be moved into decent standard housing for any given federal dollar commitment.
2. Short of bulldozing and rebuilding (which has already proved itself politically, morally, and financially unacceptable), it is the only strategy designed to stabilize and modestly upgrade declining inner-city neighborhoods.
3. Tying the subsidy to the family rather than the dwelling permits a flexible response to changing local market conditions and programmatic needs.
4. Direct subsidies to consumers offer the most practical means for dispensing low-income households outside impacted, blighted areas.
5. Using the existing supply of older housing minimizes vertical and horizontal inequities.
6. The choice of housing type, structure, and location is placed in the hands of the tenants themselves rather than the government.

While Solomon reached his choice primarily from an economic analysis, it can be seen that he took into account morality (values), political angles, and rational or practical factors. Therefore, it is no surprise to find that on our criteria, alternative (4) also appears to have the best chance of working.

Concluding Comments

After briefly surveying the history of the provision of housing and living space for Americans, we have looked at some alternative proposals and their merits. Our conclusion for the present (remember that few policy conclusions can be regarded as final for all times) is that Americans would be best served with a combination of the present provision of insured mortgages and federal supports to the money market coupled with the provision of a housing allowance for those who are beneficiaries of financial payments. The only innovation involved is the provision of a housing subsidy directly to the consumer as opposed to subsidizing the builder or lender. The reader will recall that this is consistent with our earlier recommendations for the minimization of poverty which provided direct grants to the poor, coupled with the provision of educational grants and job opportunities.

If we could characterize an overall policy direction in our policies, it would be toward the idea of consumerism. We believe that the best remedy for poverty, whether it be in income, educational opportunity, housing, or services (as we shall argue in Chapter 8) is to provide mechanisms that will allow the poor to be consumers rather than the recipients of charity from the nonpoor. Our society is clearly oriented to middle-class norms. It will continue that way for some time. The most effective war on poverty will involve coupling the needs and wants of the poor to the kind of policy that can be understood and supported by the middle class.

This approach will not be popular on the political right. Our proposals involve the provision of buying power to the poor without onerous moral overtones. It is our policy that if one is poor, unemployed, disabled, ill, or in need of any kind of counseling service, then he or she should be given the opportunity of purchasing services as he or she sees fit. We think that it is more effective to provide these things in such a way that the consumer has a choice and a decision to make about the kind of service provided and the conditions under which it is provided. The food stamp program has not been as effective as its supporters had hoped, but one interesting thing has come out of it. The consumer can use the stamps in a variety of stores. Merchants even try to attract food stamp business by advertising that they take food stamps. They know that if they act in an inappropriate way toward the recipient then he or she will take the business to a competitor. We simply propose to use the general principle of putting purchasing power in the hands of consumers and involving them in more decisions about how benefits are spent. We are willing to concede that politically it may be necessary to have funds earmarked for certain purposes (for example, educational allowances and housing allowances), but in principle we would prefer no earmarking at all.

The left will not like our proposed approach either, because it does not require a total restructuring of society and it continues benefits to the middle class. It is necessary to remind the reader that we are interested in *practical* results that will most likely improve the conditions under which some Americans live as soon as possible. We do not think that we should pin our hopes on the revolution, since it is apt not to come in time, if ever. What we espouse is simple—the expansion of a mechanism that works, but which has had only a limited use, on the grounds that it is the best mechanism for getting the job done right now. We would assume that if we subsidized the consumer directly then the consumer would be able to find good, serviceable standard housing that would not necessarily be restricted to slum property. We think that this is a revolutionary enough idea as it is, and we believe it has more promise than something based on "pure" ideology. If the fires of revolution were ever high in this country, it is clear that they are dying down or are at least banked.

The only innovative thing that we are proposing is that the consumer be given the right to determine his or her own future with respect to the spending of money. In the next chapter we will explore the implications of this principle for social services.

REFERENCES

1. Harvey S. Perloff, "Preface" in Harvey S. Perloff, ed., *The Quality of the Urban Environment* (Washington, D.C.: Resources for the Future, 1969), p. v.
2. Chester W. Hartman, *Housing and Social Policy* (Englewood Cliffs, N.J.: Prentice-Hall, 1975), pp. 2–3.
3. *Ibid.*, p. 29.
4. *Ibid.*, p. 2.
5. Ashley A. Foard and Hilbert Feffernan, "Federal Urban Renewal Legislation," in James Q. Wilson, ed., *Urban Renewal: The Record and the Controversy* (Cambridge, Mass.: The MIT Press, 1966), pp. 71–125.
6. *Ibid.*, pp. 78–79.
7. Lawrence Friedman argues that this was the only motive. See Lawrence Friedman, "Public Housing and the Poor," in John Pynoos, Robert Schafer, and Chester Hartman, eds., *Housing Urban America* (Chicago: Aldine, 1973), pp. 449–450.
8. Foard and Feffernan, *op. cit.*, p. 99.
9. Hartman, *op. cit.*, p. 107.
10. *Ibid.*, p. 120.
11. *Ibid.*, p. 145.

12. Lee Rainwater, "The Lessons of Pruitt-Igoe," in Pynoos, Schafer, and Hartman, *op. cit.*, pp. 548–555.

13. Martin Anderson, *The Federal Bulldozer* (Cambridge, Mass.: The MIT Press, 1964).

14. Martin Anderson, "The Sophistry that Made Urban Renewal Possible," in Jewel Bellush and Murray Hausknecht, eds., *Urban Renewal: People, Politics, and Planning* (Garden City, N.Y.: Doubleday, 1967), pp. 52–66.

15. Robert P. Groberg, "Urban Renewal Realistically Reappraised," in Bellush and Hausknecht, *op. cit.*, pp. 67–73.

16. Jewel Bellush and Murray Hausknecht, "Public Housing: The Contexts of Failure," in Bellush and Hausknecht, *op. cit.*, pp. 451–461.

17. See David Caplowitz, *The Poor Pay More* (New York: The Free Press, 1967).

18. Lawrence Friedman, "Social Class and Housing Reform," in Pynoos, Schafer, and Hartman, *op. cit.*, p. 27.

19. *Ibid.*

20. Arthur P. Solomon, *Housing the Urban Poor* (Cambridge, Mass.: The MIT Press, 1974), p. 32.

21. *Ibid.*, pp. 182–183.

QUESTIONS FOR DISCUSSION

1. Do you agree or disagree with the author's position that while slums are bad, they do not cause social pathology? Why do you take the position that you do?

2. Can you build a case for the idea that urban renewal is a good thing?

3. What is a slum? This is not as easy as it sounds. Is it poor housing? A high crime area? A subculture? Where are the boundaries?

4. Contrast the attitude of Congress at the time of the Housing Act of 1937 and the Housing Act of 1949.

5. Why has there been so much opposition to the idea of public housing?

6. Why would tenants of public housing be opposed to it? Shouldn't they be supportive since they benefit from the program?

7. Given the tremendous inflation in housing costs (see *Time*, September 12, 1977), what do you think the homes of the future will be like? Where will the poor and aged live?

8. Which of Solomon's policies do you favor? Why? Build a case for your choice.

9. Do socialistic societies have housing and neighborhood problems? Do all citizens enjoy comfortable housing at reasonable cost?

10. Is there a way to eliminate federal intervention in the housing market?

11. Is there a practical way to provide housing for the poor without also providing benefits for the nonpoor?

SUGGESTED PROJECTS

1. Assume you want to buy a house for $40,000. Talk to a real estate salesperson or a loan officer at a lending institution and find out how much you will actually pay for the house, the down payment, closing costs, and interest rate.

2. Interview a local public official involved in urban renewal. Find out about a local project. How much has it cost in public funds? How long did the project take? What was done with the property? Where did the residents go?

3. Arrange a visit to a local public housing unit. Your instructor may be able to arrange a visit to a vacant apartment for a small group.

4. What makes a slum? Try to devise a means of identifying just what "inadequate" housing is.

FOR FURTHER READING

Martin Anderson. *The Federal Bulldozer*. Cambridge, Mass.: The MIT Press, 1964. An important seminal study of urban renewal by one of the first critics of the federal program.

Jewel Bellush and Murray Hausknecht. *Urban Renewal: People, Politics and Planning*. Garden City, N.Y.: Doubleday, 1967. Although ten years old, this book is an indispensable collection of articles on urban renewal, housing, and politics.

Claude Brown. *Manchild in the Promised Land*. New York: Macmillan, 1965. A first-hand experience of life in difficult living space. Highly controversial when it was published, this book upset many people when it showed up on high school reading lists.

Chester W. Hartman. *Housing and Social Policy*. Englewood Cliffs, N.J.: Prentice-Hall, 1975. A useful introduction to the area of housing. An excellent first book to read on national policy toward living space.

Arthur P. Solomon, *Housing the Urban Poor*. Cambridge, Mass.: The MIT Press, 1974. Important critical study of federal housing policy. Solomon is highly technical, but there is enough interpretation to enable readers who are not economists to follow the argument.

James Q. Wilson. *Urban Renewal: The Record and the Controversy*. Cambridge, Mass.: The MIT Press, 1966. Another valuable collection of readings on urban renewal; a good companion to Bellush and Hausknecht.

8 *Social Welfare Policy and Social Service Delivery*

In our introduction we made the point that service delivery systems were related to social welfare policy both as outcomes and as sources for policy change. The relationship of service delivery to policy is probably most clearly seen in those agencies that are committed to the delivery of concrete services related to a more or less clearly defined social welfare program, for example, financial aid, employment, or adoption services. These kinds of services are directed toward relatively well understood ends, and it is easy to see that policy considerations shape the questions of eligibility, the nature of the service, and the goal. It may be a little harder to grasp the relationship of service delivery to policy in "pure" counseling services. In this chapter we want to think about social welfare policy as it relates to those aspects of service delivery most relevant to clients or patients—the service act itself. If the aim of social welfare policy is human survival through mutual aid, then service delivery should reflect that concern.

Social workers have been helping people for so long that they may not see that the direct treatment of individuals and groups takes the form that it does because of policy choices. Here we are not talking strictly about eligibility determination or the content of the service, although these elements are involved. We are interested in the *milieu* in which service takes place—the interaction between client and social worker in some kind of agency or institution. While this part of the social welfare enterprise is usually seen as strictly a clinical matter, it is possible to discern patterns in the various acts of service delivery that are the result of choices. These choices, whether explicit or implicit, follow guidelines that properly are matters of social welfare policy.

A Simple Illustration

In order to make this discussion concrete, let us consider what happens in a visit to a social agency. We will use a family counseling agency for our example, but one might have a similar experience in some other setting.

Mr. X thinks that something has gone out of his relationship with Ms. X, to whom he has been married for ten years. They seem to be growing apart, and their communications have become increasingly cold and hostile. Mr. X has talked to the pastor of the church that he sometimes attends. The pastor has suggested that a family social agency might be of help. Accordingly, Mr. X telephones a local United Way family counseling agency and is offered an appointment.

At the time of the appointment, Mr. X appears at the agency office. He is courteously received and after a brief wait, is ushered into an office where a social worker invites him to discuss his difficulty. Mr. X feels encouraged to talk about how things look to him, and the social worker helps him define his problem into a manageable form. During this interview, certain things will be tentatively decided. The counselor and Mr. X will try to arrive at some kind of working hypothesis about what the problem is. Some kind of beginning approach will be initiated. The advisability of the participation of Ms. X will be discussed. Further appointments, if there are to be any, will be scheduled. After about fifty minutes, the interview will be ended with the social worker's promise that the discussion will be resumed at a later scheduled time.

While we do not argue that the above scenario is either typical or universal, it does happen consistently. There will be other elements in the process, depending on the nature of the problem or the nature of the agency. That is, if the problem had been financial instead of interpersonal, and if the agency had been a public welfare office, there would have been forms to fill in and a process initiated by the social worker that would (or would not) result in some kind of cash payment. If the agency had been primarily a group-serving agency, there would be additional variation because a set of people would be involved as client. In principle, though, the "intake" process would not ordinarily be very different.

What occurs in encounters between the social worker and Mr. X (or Ms. X or group Z) is influenced by a number of social welfare policy decisions. The example is so commonplace that the policy choices that have been made have become obscure as *policy choices*.

Policy Choices in Service Delivery

Putting to one side our example, let us look at some choices that have to be made by a service delivery system. We will return to the example later on in the chapter.

James K. Whittaker, in the first chapter of his *Social Treatment*, identifies several "Dilemmas of the Helping Person in an Age of Ecological Crisis." [1] These dilemmas are essentially policy questions, and their resolution will involve policy skills.

1. How does one continue to justify any form of treatment or remediation when massive social problems like poverty, inferior education, and urban blight so clearly demand large-scale programs aimed at basic systematic change? [2]

Whittaker has raised the old, but still quite valid, question of the social engineering vs. the case-by-case approach to helping people. William Schwartz has addressed the same issue and has suggested that "the practitioner is required neither to 'change the people' nor to 'change the system' but to change the ways in which they deal with each other." [3]

The field of social work has not resolved this dilemma formally. It is clear, however, that as a matter of implicit policy the social welfare enterprise is firmly committed to the case-by-case approach. The general social welfare system has been slow to invest in social engineering; and Schwartz's "mediator" concept, despite its appeal and clear rationality, has not been used very often as the basis for service delivery organization.

2. At what point, then, should the "rights" of society supersede those of the individual? [4]

Although Whittaker poses this dilemma in the context of the ecology movement's campaign for limiting family size vs. the notion of self-determination, it obviously has a larger focus. This, too, is an unresolved dilemma. There are social workers on both sides of the issue. Some social workers see their function as carrying out the policy of the agency which is a sanctioned agent of society, while others see themselves as involved in a professional role wholly on the side of the client. And, as one would suspect, there are some who take a middle position identical to Schwartz's "mediator" approach. While an individual social worker may take an extreme position, it is clear that most social workers accept payment for their services from a social agency, government department, hospital, clinic, or an educational institution. They are clearly agents of society's concern. Very few make a living as an agent of the client, even when one includes private practice.

> 3. How does one continue to work within the system (in this instance, the social welfare system) when in many instances the most serious pathology lies not within individual clients, but within the very social service network of which the professional is a part? [5]

Whittaker has captured a long-standing dilemma. During the 1960s, one was most acutely faced with this question in very dramatic ways. On one campus in the Midwest, students tied colored cloths around their arms during demonstrations; those who were still willing to work "within the system" had one color and those who were for tearing it down had another. Actually, while this discussion once occupied a good many people, it may be false. Effectively, everyone who continues to remain in the United States works within the system unless they are employed as an agent of a foreign government or are members of a guerrilla movement. This is so, simply because since the days of Thomas Paine and Henry David Thoreau, American society has legitimized a certain level of radicalism. Civil disobedience is really "within the system," since for this to be an effective technique, the system must operate by recognizing one's disobedience and moving to censure or imprison the disobedient. Although there are sanctions against radicalism when it is perceived as extremely threatening, American society has allowed people to take more extreme positions than any other country and still retain a wide degree of freedom of speech and freedom of movement. While we cannot settle this issue here, it is clear that most social workers have opted for "working within the system" and have in fact maintained a fairly conservative posture in the classic delivery system. It appears that much of the anger exhibited by social workers in the sixties has been dissipated or at least suppressed. There are few social workers who have left the social welfare system for the purposes of making changes in social welfare from some new power base. Congressman Ron Dellums of California, a social worker, is exceptional in this regard.

It is difficult to work for change as an employee, but a few social workers do it. Many simply leave the social welfare field and follow some new occupation. Most, unfortunately, simply come to terms with things as they are.

> 4. But how valid is this concept of target philosophy today? Have not many of the social problems we face been shown to be interrelated? [6]

In this dilemma, Whittaker is raising the question of whether or not it ought to be social work's policy to continue to identify pieces of a problem for intervention or to try to work with the whole problem. Should we continue to offer services to individual poor people, or should we try to focus on the problem of poverty? Whittaker suggests that we may still need to think in terms of targets, but we may have to carefully redefine what we mean. Reality seems to be that in the years since Whittaker wrote this book clinically oriented people have by and large quietly recommitted themselves to working with a traditional target population rather than being concerned with an overall problem. This shift may seem more apparent when we consider Whittaker's final dilemma.

> 5. A final dilemma for the helping professional concerns his commitment to social action. Given the maze of problems besetting our social welfare system and the particular dilemmas faced by the practitioner operating within that system, is it any longer possible to separate social concerns from professional life? [7]

It seems to us that this question is increasingly answered "yes" by most social workers.[8] While on the one side (as we have mentioned before) there are growing numbers of people interested in social policy and planning, there is an even larger number who have retreated into purely clinical concerns, except for brief outbursts. We have seen, on the national level, the development of the Clinical Register. There are a number of state organizations of clinical social workers. The journal *Social Work* seems to have fewer papers on social change although there is still an encouraging emphasis on women's issues as an area of wide social concern.

There is no clear evidence that these policies have been consciously adopted. They are none the less real. And they are none the less policy choices. These choices are clearly the ones that have been made in agencies that follow the hypothetical service example that we presented earlier in this chapter.

A Sample Analysis

Let us return to Mr. X and his problem. We have stated our example in as general a way as possible. Almost any treatment method would fit into the service framework as we have outlined it. This is deliberate, since we want it to be clear that we are talking about service *policies*—something that is at a more abstract level than specific treatment *methods*. Given Whittaker's dilemmas as background, we will now extract some of the policy issues involved in the example. For emphasis, we will state them as guidelines.

1.

Service is to be rendered on a case-by-case basis.

If we had been talking about a group-serving agency, the above statement would have to be revised to reflect the nature of the service. Excepting that possibility, the current practice in social work usually involves initiative on the part of the client in locating the service. Even when a referral is made (as the pastor did in our example), the client still usually must initiate contact. The client comes to the practitioner by appointment, and most encounters take place in an office. This service pattern follows the policy of most professionals and semi-professionals. Only in rare cases does any service come to the consumer in the modern world. Unless one is dealing with an emergency or repair of a large appliance like a furnace, everything comes into the shop! The use of house calls, either by a physician or by the television repair service, is discouraged by staggering charges. In an older day, the physician went to the patient, the "law merchant" was available in the marketplace, and the social worker made home visits.

2.

A determination shall be made of the appropriateness of the service requested.

When a social worker talks to a client, a decision must be made about whether or not the client meets some criterion for eligibility for an agency's service. The agency has some kind of mission; it may be protective services, counseling, or homemaker services. The service delivery world is a specialized one, and clients must be eligible in some sense for the service. "Eligibility" can be understood from a number of angles. In one agency, a client is eligible if he or she is poor and falls below a certain income limit. In another agency, eligibility rests on whether or not the client displays certain problems or symptoms. In still another agency, one would be eligible because he or she had marital difficulty. In any case, the determination that a need exists is an essential condition of the service. One must be part of a target group.

While those of us in social work would like to think in terms of prevention, the plain fact is that the service delivery system is attuned to a remedial approach. The same, of course, is generally true of other professions, semi-professions, and technologies. For instance, while medicine has tried very hard to get people to think of maintaining health, most people will not relate to health professionals when they are well. In another area, only the sophisticated consult an attorney to *avoid* legal entanglements. Prevention may not be really possible except in a very limited sense.

3.

Evaluation and interventive action (or diagnosis and treatment, if the reader prefers) should be based on an accurate understanding of the client as revealed in the case material.

As the social worker and the client spend time together, a good deal of material will accumulate about the client's problem. This may include how the problem has developed, how it manifests itself, some inferences of the cause of the difficulty, and what the client has done about the problem. This material is intended as the basis for thinking about how the case should be handled. In most treatment approaches, some kind of record of all of this is kept. While there is great variety in the material (for example, a psychosocially oriented social worker's data may differ from that gathered by a behaviorally oriented worker), it will all find its way into a more or less stylized case record. Entries will also be made, as time progresses, on any changes that take place.

4.

Treatment consists of a series of fifty-minute sessions that will continue at appropriate intervals until client and worker agree that treatment goals have been met.

Regardless of the treatment orientation of the social worker, a more or less common policy can be discerned. Few social agencies deviate from the standard fifty-minute hour. The weekly appointment has become traditional for clients that are involved in any intensive treatment process. This policy is followed by both publicly supported and privately supported agencies for both individuals and groups (although groups may have longer sessions). Public agencies whose load is too heavy to actually see clients weekly would follow this policy if they could.

It would be possible to extract more policies from the service delivery act, but these will suffice to show the direction of the discussion. It is important to remember that we are not looking at the service delivery process with an intent to judge one treatment method over another. Our interest is limited to the policy issues that guide the provision of any or all treatment approaches. These common patterns constitute social welfare policy even though social workers do not always explicitly acknowledge them as such.

THE OFFICE-PRACTICE MODEL If we could put a name to the constellation of policies that we have extracted from the service delivery example that we used above, it might be best considered as the "office-practice" approach. The question then becomes, "How good or how desirable a service delivery policy is the office-practice model?" We could proceed to answer this question, up to a point, by applying our policy analysis model to this model alone. However, policy analysis and subsequent formulation makes the most sense when done on a comparative basis. As an exercise, we will compare the office-practice policy of service delivery with what we will call the "drop-in" counseling model. Bear in mind that we are not espousing any particular service delivery model. We are "pushing" a policy analysis process.

THE DROP-IN MODEL Suppose that you are on the staff of the agency consulted by Mr. X for his marital difficulty. At a staff meeting, the question is raised about the efficiency of your service policy. Is "office practice" the most desirable service delivery approach? A staff committee is formed to look into the problem. Let us further specify that there is only one other possibility (of course, in reality there are several, but we want to keep the example as simple as we can). This possibility is the drop-in approach. In this approach, the agency assumes that the community is the client. We will assume that need for the service is solely determined by the client and the staff in such an approach would have to agree to deal with any problem that the client defines regardless of the previous mission of the agency. Since need is assumed to be determined by the client, no formal need determination is made by the social worker. No history is taken, and therefore no "diagnosis" as such is made. Treatment consists of an informal, ongoing discussion process on a drop-in basis rather like an ongoing crap game. The clients can come in whenever they like and talk to a social worker. Instead of offices, the agency has converted its space into a series of lounge-type rooms. The clients alone decide when they have had enough and may come and go at any time the agency doors are open. Sometimes they might see the social worker alone; sometimes there may be other clients present. If clients request a specific resource (protective services or financial aid), the drop-in worker would have to refer the person to a specialized resource.[9]

Analysis of the Office-Practice and Drop-in Models

Now that we have a "standard" policy (the office-practice model) and an alternative, we can proceed to apply our policy analysis model as an aid in making a policy decision. A warning is in order. Because we are working at a general level of analysis for the purposes of illustration, our supporting data are not so precise as they would be if we were actually analyzing a policy decision in a real agency where actual data could be obtained. With that in mind, we can begin.

Is the policy compatible with contemporary "style"?

There will be little argument with the notion that the office-practice model of service delivery is compatible with contemporary style in the culture. In many areas of their lives, Americans receive services based on the office-practice model. We might use the example of the automobile repair shop. The customer brings in the car because he or she is dissatisfied with its performance. The service manager listens to the engine, asks some questions about the car's performance, and writes down the symptoms. The service manager then decides if the needed repairs can be made in the shop or if more specialized work needs to be done elsewhere. A record is kept of the work done as "treatment" is undertaken. Periodic maintenance at regular intervals may be suggested in order to ensure optimum functioning. This example is not intended to compare people with automobiles or service managers with social workers to the detriment of people, mechanics or social workers. The point is simply that people in technological societies are quite accustomed to obtaining services in this format. There is no clash with contemporary style when services are rendered in this way.

Now, how about the drop-in model? Few services now work this way, but there are some. Crisis clinics, drug abuse centers, and some services to the aging are structured to take advantage of our emerging more casual life-style. Certainly the bar, coffeehouse, or disco are frequently used institutions that operate on the drop-in principle. As other parts of the society become attuned to "dropping in," this kind of an approach to social service delivery may look better and better. In terms of style note the dramatic difference in the retail grocery business that has occurred since World War II. Very few people now shop in a grocery store where one waits to see a clerk behind a counter who fills individual orders while the customer waits. In a sense, the supermarket concept (which is now extended to hardware, notions, and even clothing) is the largest drop-in service model imaginable!

Therefore, our agency planning committee could agree that the drop-in model fits the contemporary life-style as well or better than the office-practice model. Insofar as we can judge the mood of the country, there seems to be a favorable response to the more relaxed style of the Carter administration. Perhaps, if our agency considers the drop-in approach, the staff committee would be very much in fashion with the times. The office-practice model may not be the most acceptable model for service delivery.

This is a good time to remind the reader that (and this will be true throughout the analysis) because one policy is inferior on given measuring points does not mean that it cannot be selected. It simply means that, when all factors are considered, the one with the most favorable evaluations will be more likely to succeed. An alternative policy may look very bad on one or more points, but strong enough on others to be worth the risk. The reader will recall that we said that policy-making involves choices. All choices involve a certain risk. The analytical process helps to avoid risks, but it also helps to *take* risks by identifying areas of high uncertainty.

Does the policy contribute to equity and justice?

The answer to this is not clear-cut. Some years ago the question was raised that social work was moving to an increasingly middle-class orientation.[10] Recently, the question of private practice has resurfaced as a very live issue.[11] On the other hand there have been indications of support for the drop-in practice approach as we mentioned earlier in the chapter. These signs lend support to an argument that a significant number of social workers are highly supportive of a more consumer-oriented concept of service delivery. This leads us to think that the office-practice model and the policies which make it up tend *not* to contribute to equity or justice. Service may be increasingly remote from the mass of people. While middle-class and upper-class Americans are highly mobile, there are segments of the American population that are not able to seek out services. Many are not able to reach downtown offices; others are not socialized, as are the upper classes, into the fifty-minute appointment every week.

While we are sure that most of those who engage primarily in office practice, whether private or agency based, would support norms of equity before the law, equality of opportunity, and equal justice, it is hard to escape the conviction that their practice tends to support middle- and upper-class behavior patterns.

On the other hand, the drop-in pattern seems more likely to be based on democratic norms. Particularly, this will be true if the agency is willing to decentralize geographically. Even without decentralization, the drop-in service model is still more democratic so long as it has flexible hours and the clients can come and go when they are able to get there.

A drop-in service is also democratic in that there are no inherent priorities in service, no limits on eligibility, and little formal structure in the service process. Therefore, the drop-in approach appears superior in terms of equity and justice.

Is the policy compatible with social work values?

There is nothing in the National Association of Social Workers' code of ethics that would invalidate either the office-practice or the drop-in approach. On the other hand, social workers have a historical tradition of carrying service to people "where they are" geographically and psychologically. The question is whether or not this value can be realized in a service delivery system that requires the clientele to seek service in a conventional class-based way. We cannot really offer any certainty on this issue as yet. The field has not reached significant closure on the question. We are left to conclude, tentatively, that neither model has a clear advantage in compatibility with social work values.

Is the policy compatible with other important values in society?

No obvious incompatibilities present themselves with either the office-practice or the drop-in approach, other than the possible elitist bias tendered in the previous section. It may be reaching a bit to suggest that the office-practice model may appear to be more work oriented since service takes place in a clearly defined workplace. Both are humanitarian. The drop-in model may allow the individual more freedom, since there is less structure imposed on the client. An office practice may appear to be more compatible with a technical and scientifically oriented society. We can probably conclude that neither would cause a great groundswell of opposition because of values involved.

Is the policy politically acceptable?

The more traditional or historical approach almost always has a political advantage over an innovation. While there is no hard evidence that either approach would seriously offend any influence group, it is probably true that the office-practice model would have more support among decision-making centers of influence simply because it is traditional. If the drop-in approach were to be seriously put forward as an alternative to the exclusion of "office practice," we are sure that extremely hard opposition would develop. If a single agency were to consider making such a change, it would be wise to count heads as politicians do in order to size up the number and strength of the opposition. This question would have to be decided by knowing the flexibility of staff, board, and administration.

Is the policy legal?

Both approaches are legal. We are aware of no lawsuits that have challenged either format. There could be a problem having to do with confidentiality or information in certain circumstances in the drop-in approach, since privacy would be at a minimum. However, in present-day practice, clients and social workers can usually find a relatively private place if the matter warrants it. Also, if an agency were to change its style, the clientele would have to know that the rules of the game were different. Clients would have to agree to a more open form of communication in much the same way as members of encounter-type therapies do now.

Does the policy satisfy relevant interest groups?

Obviously, those social workers who have a heavy investment in office practice would not be satisfied, but that does not really count here, because we are assuming that the drop-in policy is being looked at for its potential by a group who seriously considers it as an alternative to its own present office practice. In other words, we are not considering this decision as an adversary proceeding where one group of social workers is trying to defeat another group.

The real questions that would have to be answered by an agency that was considering changing its service delivery approach would have to do with how a number of groups would be affected in some very practical ways. Would the present clientele use the service if the structure of delivery were changed? Could the clerical staff adapt to changes in hours? What would maintenance people be able to do and when if the agency were open, say from 8 in the morning until midnight? What would be the concerns of neighbors of the agency? How would contributors and volunteers react? Would the significant people in the community believe that the appropriate service needs are being met? If satisfactory answers to these questions can be obtained, the drop-in model would be viable on this point.

Is the policy scientifically sound?

Unfortunately, we cannot answer this question for either alternative. While there is research on the merits of various treatment methods, we know of no dependable evidence that would support either delivery pattern over the other. We said earlier that the office-practice approach *looks* more compatible with scientific or technological norms, but we know of no proof of efficacy that would help settle the question. The use of our policy analysis model has, in this case, raised a question that ordinarily in the real world ought to be answered (if at all possible) when making a policy choice. However, in anticipation of just such situations as this, we can move on to the next question.

Is the policy rational?

In the absence of scientific input to the policy decision-making process, we can at least raise the issue of rationality. Leaving aside any considerations raised through application of other parts of the analysis, both policies are rational. One could build a logical case for offering service to people in either mode. Neither idea depends upon technology or materials that do not exist, and both have a reasonableness about them that would not shock anybody's logic. Neither policy would seem to have any clear advantage when the test of rationality is applied.

Is the policy economically feasible?

Here there is a problem. Our example is hypothetical, but the same problem arises if it were real. We have no data on our proposed alternative. The office-practice approach is more easily "costed out," since we know what it costs to run the agency now. A real agency would have to project the costs of doing business in the alternative way and arrive at a dollar figure. It would be possible to get some comparative data using a neighborhood center's experience with an analogous drop-in program, but the costs for any new policy will be uncertain. This is clearly an area of risk for any new policy.

Is the policy workable?

Given what we mean by workability (see Chapter 3), both policies are workable. No new technology is needed to implement the alternative drop-in approach, although, as we mentioned above, some schedule changes might need to be made.

Is the policy efficient?

In order to answer this question, a cost/benefit study would have to be made. Certainly, it is possible for both approaches to be economically feasible; however, this does not mean that they have equal cost/benefits. The office-practice approach might have a high cost but a high "cure" rate. The drop-in approach may treat more people per hour, thus reducing the cost, but few people get better very quickly. Obviously, this is another question for which answers are needed but which do not now exist.

Will the policy be likely to generate other social problems?

There is no evidence to suggest that the new approach would make things worse than the office-practice model. Logically, the drop-in approach would sound superior on the grounds that instant help would be available without delays caused by the waiting list. No costly diagnostic screening would slow down an immediate entry into the agency's program. However, if some factor, such as the lack of privacy, were to get in the way of treatment by preventing people from using the service, then some kinds of problems that might have been successfully treated by the office-practice method might become exacerbated by an agency's reliance on the drop-in method.

What Policy Decision Should Be Reached?

This hypothetical run-through is of limited usefulness because it is only an example. In the real world there would be some firmer answers—or the direction would be shown for the acquisition of data that would give some guidance. From this example it can be seen that the application of our policy analysis model has provided a rational basis for dealing with a policy choice even when some of the inputs are nonrational (for example, questions of style and values). Our analysis reveals some important considerations for service delivery policy. The office-practice approach does not have an unassailable position. When soberly considered, its chief advantage lies in its being traditional. Even without hard data which is often missing for both models, the reader can see that there are ways to approach innovation by comparing proposed service delivery changes with existing practices.

While in a number of programmatic areas of social welfare there are a number of new alternatives, there is a relatively smaller number of innovations in service delivery policy. The major arguments center around *clinical* methods that should only be evaluated for their scientific effectiveness, efficiency, legality, and morality. While a firm conclusion cannot be reached for our hypothetical case, we think that an innovative agency might do well to consider the following argument.

Following the office-practice model would be safe. However, its chief advantages are in areas that would be expected of the status quo. Since the drop-in model (1) supports equity and justice, (2) supports some social work values that office-practice does not, (3) has something different in it for some interest groups (primarily clients), and (4) is rational and workable, an agency might decide to try it out with some staff for a specified period of time. This would allow a cautious appraisal of the innovative policy and allow the agency to test out the scientific basis of both policies, the economic feasibility of the drop-in policy, and the efficiency of both. Of course, clients would have to understand that there could be some sacrifice in privacy, since the drop-in operation would cause them to encounter people coming and going during "treatment" that they might not have encountered in the office-practice mode. Obviously, clients would have to know the rules of the game and be able to choose not to play.

In other words, while the existing practice still works and will continue to receive wide acceptance, an innovation can be tried, and the areas of risk are known. Even if the agency were to decide not to attempt the innovation, the staff would have reached that conclusion through a rational process that has considered the issue from a number of viewpoints. Decision-making about programs ought to be enhanced because of the process of policy analysis.

A number of service delivery policy questions can (and should) be subjected to policy analysis. In the absence of adequate attention to policy, it is our impression that most service policies are set by trial and error, tradition, and/or a certain amount of faddishness. This is unsound. It is every bit as important for service delivery to be good policy as it is for it to be good practice.

Gilbert and Specht in their book *Dimensions of Social Welfare Policy* have summarized the policy effects of current social service delivery networks:

> In the heat of controversy, the criticism of service delivery intensifies. Such criticism tends to focus upon the characteristic failings of local service-delivery systems which include *fragmentation, discontinuity, unaccountability,* and *inaccessibility.*[12]

Given these criticisms, it follows that "the ideal service-delivery system is one in which services are *integrated, continuous, accessible,* and *accountable.*" [13] The difficulty is that this is not a simple choice. Gilbert and Specht point out that "taken separately each of these ideal elements strains against one or more of the others." [14]

Gilbert and Specht summarize the policy choices as they see them:

> 1. *Reduce* fragmentation and discontinuity by increasing coordination, opening new channels of commuication and referral, and eliminating duplication of services (possibly *increasing* unaccountability and inaccessibility).
> 2. *Reduce* inaccessibility by creating new means of access to services, and duplicating existing service efforts (possibly increasing fragmentation).
> 3. *Reduce* unaccountability by creating means for clients or consumers to have input into, and increased decision-making authority over, the system (possibly *increasing* fragmentation and discontinuity).[15]

Policy selection based on either the "naive criteria" or the "naive priorities" method would miss the complexity that Gilbert and Specht's more sophisticated approach correctly identifies.

In a closely reasoned discussion, Gilbert and Specht have summarized proposals for change into a neat typology:

> A. Strategies to restructure authority for, and control of, policy making
>   1. Coordination
>   2. Citizen participation

    B. Strategies to reorganize the allocation of tasks
       3. Role attachments
       4. Professional disengagement
    C. Strategies to alter the composition (i.e., number and types of units) of the delivery system
       5. Specialized access structures
       6. Purposive duplication [16]

In the discussion that follows the articulation of this typology, Gilbert and Specht engage in an analytical comparison of each position on the three strategies above. We will summarize the main points below.[17]

Coordination vs. Citizen Participation

There are two basic ways in which coordination can be brought about. One is through administrative centralization of services, exemplified by the Local Authority and Social Services Act of 1970 in Britain. This act created Local Authority Social Services Departments which integrated a number of governmental services on the local level. While this appears to provide better coordinated services, there are two dangers: intraorganizational conflict and the limiting of accessibility to one organization.

A second approach to coordination is the development of neighborhood service centers as has been done in the United States. This is a federated approach, since each agency retains its own organizational structure while it shares a geographical location in a neighborhood center. This will only work if agencies can surrender some of their autonomy—a development that does not always occur.

Coordination efforts are agreements among or between agencies. The citizen participation movement would redistribute decision-making among the agencies and the clientele. While this appears to honor the important value of democracy, in practice it has been difficult to ensure a genuine broadly based citizen representation.

SOME COMMENTS First, the above summary does not do justice to Gilbert and Specht's cogent discussion. The reader should consult the original. Gilbert and Specht have certainly captured a great many of the pitfalls awaiting those who wish to participate in policy analysis and formulation.

We will try, briefly, to contribute something to the solution of this dilemma from the viewpoint of our analytical model. It seems to us that citizen participation, despite its failings, is more compatible with contemporary style than the coordination approach. Consumerism is not a passing fancy, but an idea whose time has clearly come. Americans are weary of solutions "from the top." Citizen participation clearly is the most equitable and just policy. It is more compatible with social work values, and is clearly more compatible with other important values. Citizen participation is not, however, politically acceptable. Citizens will like it, but entrenched professional groups may really not like the idea of citizen control over public policies, any more than physicians or attorneys do. Both policies are technically legal; however, the proliferation of consumer lawsuits suggests that experts and decision makers are under attack when they exceed their authority or fail to fulfill their obligations. Citizen participation may reduce the occasion for lawsuits against service systems. Citizen participation also ought to satisfy the most relevant interest groups other than professionals. While scientific soundness is lacking for either position, it is clearly rational to provide for citizens to participate in decisions that affect their lives. Citizen participation may be more costly from an economic feasibility point of view; for decision-making may be slower, and costly mistakes can be made. Workability and efficiency may suffer in the short run, but in the long run policies in which citizens participate will be more advantageous on these criteria. It is possible that citizen participation in service delivery policy will create some problems; for example, fragmentation and discontinuity as Gilbert and Specht suggest. On the other hand, it seems to us that a policy of citizen participation has so much going for it to ensure accessibility of services and accountability that social welfare decision makers at all levels ought to support efforts to improve the quality and quantity of citizen participation rather than to support coordination efforts.

One can argue that, as a by-product of citizen participation, private practice will increase as a response to some groups of service consumers. While middle-class consumers are the group most likely to use private practitioners, third-party payments may bring social work services within the reach of many. This alternative would enhance the autonomy of the social worker and lead to the decrease in the present semi-professional status of social work. Some kind of payment system could be provided for those unable to pay as is currently done (admittedly imperfectly as yet) in medicine. Or perhaps social service clinics could be provided on the model of the legal aid clinic for those unable to pay. Of course, certain public services of a protective nature (child welfare, probation and parole services, and some kinds of mental health work) would have to be continued. This will not threaten professional autonomy any more than the presence of public health and employment of attorneys by government threatens medicine and law—if the bulk of trained social workers were in private practice as other professions are.

Role Attachments vs. Professional Disengagement

Gilbert and Specht here deal with the problem of reallocation of tasks to come to terms with the problem of accessibility. The central idea in the notion of role attachment is that "professionals" have too much social distance between themselves and their clientele. Therefore, the indigenous nonprofessional aide role has been created as a bridge or attachment service for the lower class client. There are three problems. The poor may end up getting amateurish services. Second, the indigenous aide may not be accepted by the profesesionals. Third, the indigenous aide will want to become professional and move out of the aide status for reasons of money and prestige.

The second policy, professional disengagement, involves simply a turning away from traditional agencies by practitioners into private practice supported by fees from those who can pay and a voucher system for those who cannot. The trouble is, as Gilbert and Specht point out, professional disengagement will not turn people who have specialized in some field into generalists. Therefore, accessibility to needed services will not necessarily be enhanced nor will fragmentation be lessened.

COMMENTS Here again, we have oversimplified Gilbert and Specht's careful explication of the issues. It appears that Gilbert and Specht have looked at these two policies from the standpoint of what we have called equity and justice, workability, economic feasibility, and to a lesser extent, efficiency. However, they have been unable to reach closure.

From our vantage point, professional disengagement with a few modifications seems the more satisfactory of the two policies. We think that there are better ways to deal with the problem of task allocation, for example, specialization or bureaucratic structure vs. team practice. However, we will try to keep our comments as close to Gilbert and Specht's phrasing of the issue as we can.

Of the two policies, a movement toward professional autonomy, *subject to consumer control* (see the previous issue) seems more compatible with contemporary style. With the provision for consumer control, equity and justice are better served by the professional who is forced to deal with the public directly. The use of an indigenous professional as a go-between cannot help but emphasize the gulf between client and social worker. The autonomous professional is compatible with social work values and most other important positive social values; the use of indigenous nonprofessionals is not, in that it is exploitative on the part of professionals and obviously unsatisfactory in the long run for the nonprofessional. The disengaged professional is becoming more politically acceptable to social workers. Both are legal. The indigenous nonprofessional system cannot really satisfy client groups simply because the nonprofessional does not have access to goods and services. He or she merely has access to those who have access, and this is not good enough. Clients want to see someone who is in charge. There is little in it for nonprofessionals themselves, as Gilbert and Specht point out, since nonprofessionals do not want to stay in the role. An alternative to the use of nonprofessionals ought to satisfy more involved interest groups. The autonomous professional, while not perfect, is certainly a better choice.

Again, there are no scientific studies that help in this decision, but rationality would favor the detached profession since it means a better chance for genuine advocacy and service to one client instead of agency loyalty to the exclusion of client interests. The use of indigenous nonprofessionals has not proven workable, nor has it proven economically feasible. Any time a role is not acceptable to an occupant, he or she will try to leave it. The impermanence of the occupants of the job means that one is always hiring replacements. This is not economically feasible, and it is not going to be efficient either. The frequency with which people leave agency services in the public welfare field is sufficient testimony to the unworkability and inefficiency of our present system. The addition of the indigenous nonprofessional aide on any wide-scale basis would not help an already unwieldy service delivery system. The continued use of indigenous aides complicates matters, thus perpetuating and expanding this kind of role attachment, and can be counted on to make the problems of clients worse. The autonomous social worker who is forced to come to terms with the clientele in order to earn his or her bread and cheese ought to reduce service problems.

Gilbert and Specht raise two more "workability" problems that we have not discussed. They suggest that private social services would not prevent the "private practitioner from imposing his particular brand of service upon the client" and it might tempt the practitioner to continue service in order to collect a fee. Actually, there is nothing to prevent a practitioner from pursuing an unproductive approach at all costs under any system. The practitioner who ignored the needs of clients in favor of an ideological commitment to a particular kind of service that was inappropriate would be out of business. His rather narrow focus would not be protected by an agency as now is the case. As for the fee question, only the extremely gullible would continue to pay a fee for a service that is of no value.

We think that the problem of role allocation would be best served by the organization of service professionals into a fee-for-service group practice, again excepting those professionals employed in protective services. Eligibility determination, for those concrete services where needs must be demonstrated by law, is an administrative function and should be handled by skilled management-oriented people. Human service is a professional job and should be handled by persons trained in human service. Rather than depending upon indigenous nonprofessional aides, it is more productive to train intelligent, flexible, service-oriented people who are able to relate to the poor either because of background or socialization to the task. Specialization of members of the service group would speak to the problems of access and continuity of service.

Specialized Access Structure vs. Purposive Duplication

With this issue, Gilbert and Specht deal with the problem of fragmentation, inaccessibility, and discontinuity of service. They see two current ways of speaking to the problem. One is the information and referral service, which performs a sorting and brokering function. The other approach is purposive duplication, in which a number of agencies perform the same function. Information and referral services, say Gilbert and Specht, only add to fragmentation. Duplicating services is "enormously expensive."

COMMENTS As one might suspect, we strongly support purposive duplication. It fits contemporary style in that most services in other areas of human life in the United States and the Western world are duplicative. One may shop in a number of grocery stores, and in most towns there is more than one garage. Only in very remote areas does anyone have a monopoly on any kind of service, and even in these cases, some options exist. Gilbert and Specht make a distinction between two forms of purposive duplication—competition and separatism. Competitive services increase choice and keep competitors on their toes. Separate services do not seek to enter into competition with existing services but seek to provide an alternative for disadvantaged groups that cannot or do not care to use existing services. Either format fits contemporary style. It is analogous to, say, the clothing industry. One can purchase off the rack or go to specialty shops that have unique (but not always expensive) fashions for particular groups of customers.

Equity and justice are more nearly served by purposive duplication if there are both competitive and separate services (using Gilbert and Specht's terms). Purposive duplication is compatible with social work values and is especially cohesive with social values in the United States. Duplication is politically acceptable to major influence groups in most areas of life. Duplication is legal and flexible enough to satisfy interest groups of all kinds. Such a policy is rational. Distribution is economically feasible and theoretically superior to other alternatives because of the competitive feature. Of course, competition may mean that inefficient and ineffective services would go out of business, but we frankly think that this is entirely appropriate. The alternative is to maintain services that are inefficient and inappropriate simply because they have always been there. This is a luxury that is not defensible. Mutuality in survival is the key. No agency, service, or social work practitioner should have a *unilateral* right to continue when benefits do not accrue to the consumer. Both social worker and client will survive when they are interdependently related. Duplication is workable and has a better chance of efficiency than monolithic services that are the only game in town. Access services may only add another screen between the client and service and may make problems worse. Duplication of services would put all social workers on the firing line with no screens.

Conclusion

This has turned out to be a rather radical chapter. It will help for us to summarize where we are in order to effect some closure. Obviously, we think that service delivery policy needs a good shaking up. In our opinion service deliverers have made the most conservative and least risky choices possible. There is some danger, we believe, that service delivery can slip backward thirty years unless some new elements are considered. We think that this task can be best accomplished by raising questions about our present practices through the application of a multidimensional model, however imperfect.

If we take seriously Gilbert and Specht's contention that fragmentation, discontinuity, unaccountability, and inaccessibility are the major problems in service delivery, we think that one is led into a radical stance toward practice. It is certainly true that more of the same will only intensify these problems. It appears to us that a different delivery system is worth a trial. We recognize that the whole delivery system will not change overnight, even if we could prove our case absolutely. We do think, however, that some innovative practices are in order.

It seems to us that the innovation with the best chance of success is the autonomous group of specialized social workers who earn their living by fees. This kind of service delivery system would maximize citizen participation, result in professional disengagement from its current semi-professional status, and create a situation of purposive duplication with the elements of competition and separation (some groups might want to use the drop-in approach, others office practice!).

This innovation is not without its dangers. We think that Gilbert and Specht's recognition of the dangers is pertinent and persuasive of their existence as factors to be watched. We take the position that these dangers are preferable to the present regressive tendencies in social welfare service delivery. Some change is involved, but there is some drift toward private practice now. Certain precautions must be observed. Protective services, as we have noted, will have to be continued. Eligibility for certain benefits will remain, but would be handled by a new breed of social accountants who could be trained to administer financial services, employment services, and other benefits. Most services of this type are now staffed by persons not specifically educated to provide counseling or treatment services. Unfortunately, they are not trained in the adminstration of benefits either. Specific training for the actual task as we have defined it would certainly result in improved benefit administration. Gradually, we would see persons trained in counseling, therapy, group methods, and policy and planning services moving to "private practice." Fees, vouchers, prepaid services and third-party payments would promote citizen participation and even control over the nature and quality of service. Peer review (instead of supervision) could be built in for additional quality control. It would be more compatible with our criteria than the present system where the consumer has very little to say about services that affect his or her life. Professional disengagement from traditional agencies and governmental services would render social workers truly autonomous and even bring status to those who remained in protective services. A physician is still respected as a practitioner of an art, even when he or she work for a governmental body. The independence of physicians in general supports this respect. Finally, the existence of more than one firm of social workers would mean competition, but would allow for separation of distinctive and particular services.

We realize that what we propose is a dramatic change. We do think that it would work to the benefit of clients and their families. We think that it represents a genuinely professionalized social welfare service delivery system.

REFERENCES

1. James K. Whittaker, *Social Treatment* (Chicago: Aldine, 1974), Ch. 1.
2. *Ibid.*, p. 7.
3. William Schwartz, "Private Troubles and Public Issues: One Social Work Job or Two?" in Robert W. Klenk and Robert M. Ryan, *The Practice of Social Work*, 2nd ed. (Belmont, Calif.: Wadsworth, 1974), p. 97.
4. Whittaker, *op. cit.*, p. 11.
5. *Ibid.*, p. 14.
6. *Ibid.*, p. 17.
7. *Ibid.*, p. 19.
8. David C. Phillips, "The Swing Toward Clinical Practice," *Social Work*, Vol. 20, No. 1 (January 1975), pp. 61–63.
9. Of course, the drop-in model would have some limitations as a mode of approach in public welfare. One possible adaptation would be for eligibility determination to be handled as an administrative task with service personnel free to interact with clients.
10. Richard A. Cloward and Irwin Epstein, "Private Social Welfare's Disengagement from the Poor: The Case of Family Adjustment Agencies," in Meyer N. Zald, *Social Welfare Institutions* (New York: John Wiley, 1965).
11. See Arnold M. Levin, "Private Practice Is Alive and Well," and Paul A. Kurzman, "Private Practice as a Social Work Function," in *Social Work*,

Vol. 21, No. 5 (September 1976) and the "Letters" section in *Social Work*, Vol. 22, No. 1 (January 1977).

12. Neil Gilbert and Harry Specht, *Dimensions of Social Welfare Policy* (Englewood Cliffs, N.J.: Prentice-Hall, 1974), p. 109.

13. *Ibid.*, p. 110.

14. *Ibid.*

15. *Ibid.*, pp. 110–111.

16. *Ibid.*, p. 111.

17. This material is summarized from *Ibid.*, pp. 111–123.

QUESTIONS FOR DISCUSSION

1. Is the office-practice model applicable to public welfare practice?
2. Discuss the question of whether or not social workers should concentrate on social reform or individual treatment.
3. Can one change service delivery policy from within an agency? How?
4. Could social welfare agencies be restructured in some way to deal with interrelated social problems?
5. How compatible are contemporary practice models to alternative forms of service delivery: office practice, drop-in, or home visits?
6. Would the creation of multiservice centers really be a change in service delivery policy? In what way?
7. Is social work practice becoming more "customer oriented" as the authors contend?
8. Is science really an important consideration when considering social work delivery policy?
9. Why would anyone worry about morality in social work practice? Aren't efficiency and effectiveness enough?
10. How do you react to the idea of a service delivery system whose main service component is private group practice? Would you consider this "real" social work?

SUGGESTED PROJECTS

1. List several policy issues, other than the ones in the text, that affect social work practice.
2. Select one of the above and analyze it using the policy analysis model outlined in this book.
3. Invite a practicing social worker to class to discuss the relation of social policy to practice.

4. Design your own innovative service system. Use the analysis model presented in this book as your guide.

FOR FURTHER READING

Neil Gilbert and Harry Specht. *Dimensions of Social Welfare Policy*. Englewood Cliffs, N.J.: Prentice-Hall, 1974. A provocative, scholarly treatment of social policy and the social service delivery system. See especially Chapter 5, "The Structure of the Delivery System."

————. *The Emergence of Social Welfare and Social Work*. Itasca, Ill.: F. E. Peacock, 1976. A book of readings that relates social work and social services to a policy background.

Alfred J. Kahn. *Social Policy and Social Services*. New York: Random House, 1973. Chapters 3, 4, and 5 are most pertinent although Kahn is really talking about social service program issues rather than a policy of service delivery.

————. *Shaping the New Social Work*. New York: Columbia University Press, 1973. A thoughtful collection of essays edited by Alfred Kahn on the impact of social policy on practice concerns. Gloomy about the future of social work in spots, it will be interesting to see if the shape of social work will be influenced by the currents identified.

Arnold M. Levin. "Private Practice Is Alive and Well," *Social Work*, Vol. 21, No. 5 (September 1976). Ably states the case for an expanded role of private practice in social work.

Part III
Social Action, Planning, and Administration: Some Bridges from Policy

The first three of the four chapters in this unit introduce the fields of planning, social action, and social administration. These chapters are intended to serve as bridges from social welfare policy analysis and formulation to the implementation of policy. Each chapter is, of course, only a kind of primer, since these are complex subjects. We assume that students in schools of social work will take courses in these subjects after they have completed this course. Readers who are not in formal educational settings will find these chapters a general outline that will suggest further directions for independent study.

We have added a final speculative chapter to this unit in which we try to forecast the trends that we think will be followed in the next few years. The reader is encouraged to write his or her own final chapter, since to be able to do so is the major gain that we hope for from this book.

9 *Influencing Decision-Making in Public Policy*

The analysis and formulation of alternative social welfare policies remain academic exercises unless they lead to change in official public policy. This chapter deals, in broad outline, with the connections between policy formulation and the decision-making process.

How Are Policy Decisions Made?

It is oversimple to say that public policy is made by law, although that may be technically correct. We prefer to express it this way: Policy is made through a decision-making process. Enactment of law, the rendering of judicial decisions, and/or the issuance of administrative guidelines are outcomes of the policy process. Here we want to address some concerns about how those decisions are made.

It is only possible in one chapter to sketch the influence process. Our remarks will be general and will constitute a guide or outline, not a comprehensive picture.

The Nature of Power

We have the "gut feeling" that many social workers misunderstand the nature of power and its role in decision-making, so we want to begin with our understanding of the concept. Power is the ability to persuade.[1] The aim of using power is to get one decision made over another.

This is not the way that many people think of power. We have all heard people say, "You can make changes. You have the power to do it!" Persons making this statement apparently think that changes can be made if only the right person issues the orders or if the right body makes a decision. The exercise of power is simply not this easy. What actually happens is that people only accept new ideas when it is in their best interests to do so or when they have no other choice. They do not accept new ideas because it is in *someone else's* best interest and of no benefit to the decision maker. Franklin D. Roosevelt could not have inspired the changes in the United States in the 1930s if the American people had not believed that there was something in it for them and found themselves in fundamental agreement with his policies. What is often regarded as charisma is, in fact, the ability of a leader to ascertain the direction of the general will.

Force is not enough to get people to do something over time. While it may work over the short run, force is resented and tends to breed resistance. Persuasion, on the other hand, is something other than mere force. Richard Neustadt in his highly regarded study of presidential power argues that persuasion is contingent upon bargaining and reciprocity.[2] A can persuade B if A controls some important part of B's future. Both have something to trade. In Neustadt's words, "Influence derives from bargaining advantages; power is a give-and-take." [3]

This view of power may take some getting used to. Neustadt quotes President Harry Truman: "I sit here all day trying to persuade people to do the things they ought to have sense enough to do without my persuading them. . . . That's all the powers of the President amount to." [4] Mr. Truman's frustration captures the problem. The exercise of power is not just issuing orders, not just the perquisite of a position, not just a legal responsibility, and not just charisma, although each of these things enters into the picture. Persuasion is also more than just simple arm-twisting. It is a matter of convincing people that what they are asked to do is in their best interests and should be done.

The Decision-Making Process

With the above argument in mind, consider some common models of decision-making that have been identified. Lawrence D. Mann has provided a useful summary which we have followed.[5] The reader should study Mann's article in order to get the full discussion.

THE "TRADITIONAL" MODEL

- *A group of citizens, motivated by public interest, form a planning group. They engage a planner, make decisions by logic and rationality, and submit a benevolent plan that is untainted by politics.*

Mann suggests that such plans "gather more dust than sentiment." He argues that this is an incredibly naive view of the decision-making process. In the real world citizens are seldom benevolently disinterested, and plans are not made on the basis of nonpolitical rationality.

THE "POWER PYRAMID" MODEL

- *A few industrialists and businessmen, aided by tame politicians, make all decisions and enforce them on those lower down in the social structure.*

This model is easily recognizable as being rooted in the work of Floyd Hunter.[6] Many social workers readily accept this view. Political scientists have been highly critical of the model's simplicity. Mann, following the critique of Herbert Kaufman and Victor Jones, agrees that Hunter assumed that there was a power elite before he looked for it and that the model is "just too pat to have occurred in the real world."

THE YALE POLYARCHIC POWER MODEL

This approach is based on the work of Robert Dahl and his associates at Yale.

- *The fundamental idea is that different issues each have a "distinct leadership pattern with very little overlap between issue areas." Or, to put it simply, every issue has a different set of decision makers.*

THE QUALIFIED "DIFFUSED INFLUENCE" MODEL

This is similar to the "Yale" model described above. The difference is that in this model, influence is even more diffuse. Following the ideas of William L. C. Wheaton, Mann says:

- *Influence is spread among a multiplicity of interest groups that change in size and importance over time. Coalitions or constellations of these* groups constantly form and reform, depending upon the issue. Since communication is not constant, the effectiveness of the decision-making process is varied.

This model has a great deal of appeal when one looks at reality (which is after all the acid test of an explanatory model). Unless one has become a true believer in an alternative model (and hence a zealot), there is a certain appeal in the notion of a pluralist decision-making process that is open to inputs from various interest groups and coalitions. The model suggests that decisions are not just "locked up" by elites but can be affected by consumers and their advocates.

THE "DECISION PROCESS" MODEL

Based upon the work of Roscoe Martin and Frank Munger, Peter Rossi, and others, this model suggests:

- Decision-making should not be viewed in structural or pattern terms at all, but as a process. This is a systems approach which sees decision-making as a flow in which the final decision is a product of a series of interactions between or among various systems that have an interest in the decision.

Social workers should not have trouble understanding this view of decision-making, because it is akin to the notion of visualizing social casework, group work, or community organization as processes. The client (or group, neighborhood, community) and the social worker start at one point, move through phases of interactional change, and emerge at some future point which is different from the initial one. In other words, decisions are not all of a piece, but are outcomes of prior decisions which are related to still prior decisions.

It is this view that has influenced our approach to social policy analysis and formulation. Obviously, one's view of decision-making is crucial to how one operates in the social action arena. If, for example, one believes that decisions are made by a static power elite, then strategy is pretty much limited to either "lick 'em or join 'em." That is, one either beats the power structure in some kind of contest situation or infiltrates them and takes over the decision-making process. The danger of this view, of course, is that it rests on the deceptive notion that power is a *possession* and can be used at will—a notion that we have rejected earlier in our argument.

Acting on the notion that decision-making is a flow or process, we will discuss some tactical issues and then return to some observations about when these tactics can be used to influence decision-making.

The Tactics of Influence

The social worker who is interested in influencing the adoption of one policy over another has a considerable number of approaches from which to choose. We are following Arnold Panitch's lead in this discussion, but have departed from him somewhat.[7] He should not be held accountable for our digressions.

We have arranged these tactics in a rough order of the intensity of involvement and risk. That is, the further down the list one goes, the more time and energy will be expended and the greater the risk to one's safety. This does not mean that any of these tactics is safe, because there is always the possibility that danger can escalate out of proportion to one's activities in any change-oriented process.

THE CASE CONFERENCE It is possible for policy issues to be addressed as an outgrowth of a single case. An individual (or a group or neighborhood association) may not be receiving adequate service. The place to try to get policy change is through a conference that includes the agencies that logically should be offering the service. Even in large federal programs, changes have been made as the result of recognizing that what is dysfunctional for one client may be dysfunctional for many.

FACT-GATHERING Here again, this does not sound like a tactic at first hearing. However, the social worker interested in social policy change should maximize his or her role as a source of information at stages in the decision-making process. Although facts by themselves seldom persuade anybody, they are useful in ordering priorities, supporting points of view, and defending against opposing viewpoints. Very simply, having the right information in a form that can be used properly gives one leverage and influence for change. Knowledge can be persuasive when it is used by the right people at the appropriate time and place.

POSITION-TAKING When a group wishing to make a change takes a position by issuing a statement or a report, they have gone on public record as a participant (at some level at least) in a change process. Taking a position draws the lines for the contest. It clarifies one's own objectives and provides a point of identification. The influence generated from taking a position depends upon the importance of the one taking the position. While it is sometimes possible to influence change by issuing a position statement, this act is usually not enough by itself. It is, however, an important step in gaining recognition and legitimacy on the issue.

COMMITTEE WORK At some point in the policy change process, those committed to an alternative have the opportunity to make inputs to study and planning committees. The knowledgeable social worker probably has, by this stage, some direct experience with the policy problem, has made some kind of study of the problem, and has a position on the alternative that represents a change toward more effective policy. Committees, whether they be local, state, or national in scope, are a step in the decision-making process. We do not think that many important decisions are made in formal committee meetings. However, by providing a forum for the public discussion of ideas, committees of various kinds serve to publicize potential alternatives and get them into the decision-making process. Social workers can serve on such committees or act as consultants to committees on which they are not eligible to serve as regular members.

PETITIONS Many organizations committed to social change and/or policy change engage in petitioning. This process serves to proclaim public support (if the petitioners are perceived as important or threatening) for a policy alternative. It informs decision makers that there are people "out there" who have a stake in the decision. Occasionally a petition is effective, but it is usually not enough by itself. Petitioning must be seen as just one step in the influence process.

MEDIA CAMPAIGNS The use of radio, television, and newspapers can be an important part of the policy change process. Again, publicity, stories, and pictures bring issues to public attention. They help create a climate in which change is possible through the mobilization of public opinion. Although "public opinion" is a vague and often elusive concept, it is quite clear that on key issues, public support (or at least public acquiescence) has been of great value. The passage of Medicare legislation in the 1960s certainly owed something to the presidential use of the television medium.

EXPERT TESTIMONY When a policy alternative has been around long enough to be "seasoned" (and we cannot give a definite time limit for this seasoning process) and if it is deemed by decision makers to have merit, it will move into a formal consideration process. Legislative bodies (boards, city or community councils, and legislative committees) will conduct hearings. Social workers are often in a position to give expert testimony on the feasibility and desirability of the alternative. While no legislative body would adopt a policy simply because a social worker said it was good, inputs from social workers and their allies may be quite valuable.

LOBBYING More is required than having a good proposal that has received wide public support for policy to be changed. As we have repeatedly said in this context, there are a number of factors that bear upon policy decisions. Assuming that the policy is one that meets the tests that good policy should meet, it still needs to be sold. Here is where the going begins to get a bit rough. A determined group must be prepared to spend a lot of time selling their proposal to a decision-making body. Formally, this involves lobbying—but it may not mean lobbying with official public figures. It may involve direct selling to those to whom the public official will listen. This takes time, money, and work. Social workers may be in a position to do their own lobbying, but they often hire the services of a professional lobbyist.

Part of the lobbying process may involve the building of a coalition. Social workers have found it difficult to enter into cooperative influence efforts. In the past few years there has been a renewed interest in the coalition as a tactical entity.[8] Social workers can gain more leverage if they are able to find other groups with common concerns on an issue. A large enough coalition may be able to swing an election. It is most effective if an interest group can elect their own representative. Teachers' organizations have been especially adept in getting legislators elected from the ranks of teachers themselves. Since social workers are not as large a group as are teachers, it is unlikely that they will be able to elect people to decision-making bodies without a good deal of help. The coalition provides a base for a wider appeal, making possible the election of social workers or those who will support social workers' goals. The coalition has other uses too, particularly in bargaining.

BARGAINING A few years ago, Brager and Jorrin wrote what we believe to be a definitive discussion of bargaining.[9] There are some underlying assumptions to the bargaining process. First, it is assumed that the parties want to reach some accommodation. Both sides may not get exactly what they want, but there is the expectation that a resolution of differences is preferable to continued discomfort. A second assumption is that both sides have something to trade.

Initially, it is clear that those who are maintaining the current state of affairs have the superior bargaining position. They are in office and consequently are better organized and command more resources. However, as Brager and Jorrin point out, there are points of leverage that can be turned to the advantage of a change-oriented group. Most establishments do not want their public images tarnished. They do not want to be involved in lawsuits and "fair hearings" procedures. They do not want to be seen as ogres or to be personally embarrassed. In short, those who support the current policy—whatever it is—are vulnerable, particularly when the policy could be unfair, unfeeling, or embarrassing in its application.

A change-oriented group has something to trade. They can offer peace and quiet along with other social rewards that appeal to the public and private image of those who make decisions. However, the relatively lesser amount of influence possessed by those who want to see changes means that they have to be highly committed and willing to take risks.

The challengers will be in the position of making demands. There are three important points made by Brager and Jorrin about the process:

1. Making extreme demands seems to lessen the disadvantage of the more powerless group in initiating action. The initial demands may be unrealistic that the real beginning is made by the establishment that replies. In effect, the opponents appear to be the real initiators of change.

2. Making extreme demands allows some testing and some give and take to occur. One can always reduce demands, but can seldom expand them.

3. Demands define the limits of trading. They are maximum positions that cannot be exceeded.

Some community groups (and some national movements) produce a whole "laundry list" of demands. Brager and Jorrin suggest that it might be more effective to keep to one or two basic demands with some embellishments for trading purposes.

Should pressure groups focus on the problem to which policy changes are to be addressed? Or should they present their own proposal? We are assuming that most groups entering into bargaining have a policy alternative. On the other hand, Brager and Jorrin point out that there are strategic advantages in forcing the opponent to make all the moves. We acknowledge this, but would prefer to suggest a firm proposal. Brager and Jorrin suggest that offering a proposal demonstrates commitment and seriousness of purpose.

In any case, the willingness and the ability to negotiate with establishments of various kinds is an important tool of those who would change social policy. Consumers may have more power than they suppose, particularly if they have built an effective coalition.

DEMONSTRATIONS The mass demonstration is still a technique to be considered even though it has suffered from overuse in the past ten years. Obviously, there is considerable risk involved in this strategy. There is the danger of violence and of reprisals on the job. However, if the issue is important enough and a change-oriented group believes that the resulting publicity will enhance their ability to influence decision-making, they may want to organize a public demonstration. We have some reservations about organizing client groups for mass demonstrations. It seems very important to us that any clients who participate in a public demonstration know that they are taking a risk. It should be obvious that a professional who mounts a campaign of policy change should not use clients to further personal ambition.

CLASS-ACTION SUITS Policy changes can be initiated by legal action. In recent years we have seen the desegregation of southern schools and changes in women's rights begun as the result of judicial decisions. The class-action suit, in which a suit may be brought on behalf of a group of people who have similar situations, has recently become a powerful legal weapon. The limitation on pursuing policy change through legal action is that the issue must ultimately rest on a constitutional ground. Suits are expensive and time consuming. Persons entering the legal arena must be prepared for considerable struggle and a certain amount of adversity. Nevertheless, *where grounds exist*, judicial decisions are a fairly certain way of changing inequitable or unjust policy.

DISRUPTIVE TACTICS The most dangerous tactic that can be used by a change-oriented group involves disrupting the operation of an organization or political body. By disruptive, we refer to something more active than a demonstration or vigil. Harry Specht, who has written on this topic, includes these milder forms of protest.[10] We are using the term to mean actual disruption: strikes, boycotts, sit-ins, and civil disobedience. The object of these tactics is to shut down the operation so that it can no longer function as it normally would. The danger, as Specht points out, is that disruption may allow one's opponents to change the issue from the policy under consideration to that of the "rabble" in the streets. Obviously, those who are really promoting a policy (rather than taking an "ego trip") should not use this strategy if there is any danger of the issue becoming lost. The strike and the boycott would seem to be the effective choices (where they are applicable) simply because they hit pocketbooks quicker.

We have not included insurrection in our list of tactics. There are two reasons. First, we are talking about change rather than destruction. Second, and we believe Specht would agree with us, insurrection is uncertain and can lead to fascism. We continue to believe in the fundamental health of this society, although we recognize the need for change. We do not think that insurrection is a viable strategy for bringing about the ends that we consider desirable.

Centers of Decision-Making

In some countries it appears that policy-making is the responsibility of a very few people. As we have argued above, we think that it is more practical to think of decision-making in the United States as a diffuse, multilateral process. In policy-making there are a number of decision makers on a given issue and the nature of the decision-making group changes over time. Business, labor, agriculture, veterans' groups, religious bodies, consumer groups, and others all have their own agendas. Each group tends to equate its own agenda with the public interest.

Broadly speaking, because of the political structure of the United States, there are three arenas in which these groups seek to make their influence felt: legislatures, courts, and administrative structures. Although these centers of decision-making exist on several levels, we are going to treat them as if this were not so; that is, for discussion purposes we are going to talk as if one court is very much like any other court and that the city council is comparable to the Congress. While there are differences, the similarities are close enough for our purposes.

The Legislative Arena

Legislative decision-making tends to be done through consensus and compromise. Both are lengthy processes. The slowness with which decisions are made allows time for influence. Because legislators want to stay in office, they will listen to significant voices. It is important for those who are pursuing policy change to have one of the significant voices. Our legislative system is most responsive when interest groups intervene with timely concerns. The system fails when interest groups miss their opportunities and fail to mobilize themselves. Traditionally, we think of the American Medical Association and the National Association of Manufacturers as the most skilled in influencing legislative decisions. Recently, we have seen women's groups engage in successful policy change.

Of the tactics that we have discussed, some are more appropriate for influencing legislative decisions than others. Fact-gathering is important, at least for the purpose of presenting a case for a policy change. Position-taking raises the visibility of the issue. Media campaigns, expert testimony, and the formation of coalitions for lobbying are primary methods in working with legislative bodies.

Judicial Intervention

Most of us were not taught to think of judges as policy decision makers. We were taught that the legislature enacts laws, and the courts enforce them. Courts do, in fact, make policy decisions by the way they interpret laws and apply them. This is most obvious in those instances where there is an absence of clear-cut legislative intent or where legislative or executive policy violates constitutional protections.

Although the interpretation of the law tends to follow precedent, historical events and political pressures do enter in. The judges of today are not the same people who addressed civil rights questions in the 1880s.

Clearly, the Supreme Court under Chief Justice Earl Warren was a different court from that of his predecessor.

It would be deceptive to assume that judges have the ability to act arbitrarily. They can only deal with cases brought before the court that fit into their jurisdiction. Their decisions (except for the Supreme Court) are subject to appeal. Judges keep one eye on the appellate courts when they rule, since the prestige and status of a judge is related to the frequency with which his or her decisions are upheld on appeal. But the judge's other eye is on the public. Judges value the respect they believe that the public has for them and they are reluctant to make decisions that will be the subject of public ridicule.

Fact-gathering and expert testimony are two cooperative ways of assisting the judicial decision-making process. The class-action suit obviously is an important means of social change through judicial intervention. To be successful, the suit must be based on a violation of rights. A group wishing to press a class-action suit must find a compatible attorney and work within the constraints of the legal system. If the policy change that is contemplated clearly relates to a violation of due process or of legal rights, there is a good chance that the policy can be changed by legal action.

Administrative Structures

The power of the executive—regardless of the level of government—has fluctuated a good deal in the United States. We have seen variations in the "weak mayor" and "strong mayor" systems in city government. Although the presidency is neither "weak" nor "strong" in the same sense, it is clear that the leadership that can be expected from the president varies with the times and the occupant of the office. Franklin D. Roosevelt (whom most living Americans do not remember, since the median age of Americans is around 26 years!) probably exerted more influence in the office of president than any other occupant. Of course, the Great Depression and World War II were cataclysmic events. Strong administrative leadership was both required by Americans and allowed by Americans. Truman continued the tradition of strong leadership. Since Nixon's administration, Americans seem less trusting of administrative leadership and more inclined to seek policy change in the courts or in a legislative body. Nevertheless, administrators at various levels do have discretionary authority in certain aspects of policy; and these administrators are susceptible to influence procedures.

The literature on policy change in large bureaucratic structures clearly suggests certain directions. Awareness and use of the informal channels for communications and decision-making is very important. Mobilization of support behind the scenes before formal ratification of a new policy in a staff meeting or by an administrator is often vital. Planting ideas with administrators and seeing to it that they get the credit is an ancient strategy that still works. The use of pressure from outside may be helpful but is extremely dangerous to the career of the initiator.

A wide range of tactics can be used in dealing with administrative structures. The case conference is often effective in securing exceptions to general policies. These exceptions often constitute precedents for future policy change. Petitions may have some effect as part of an overall policy change campaign. Very often, administrative structures use study or advisory committees as sounding boards or screens for ideas. Sometimes social workers can be included on such committees and can make significant contributions to change. If a group attempting to change administrative rules or policies engages in bargaining, the media campaign may help build public support. Lobbying is also an effective tactic, provided it is done in such a way that allows the administrative structure to save face. In all-out contests, demonstrations and disruptive tactics probably are more effective in embarrassing administrative structures than they are with legislative bodies or the judiciary.

A Final Word on Tactics

Every group interested in policy change has to decide on its general strategy. A few years ago most change-oriented groups seemed to leap at the chance to take an adversary position and enter into either contest or conflict with decision-making bodies that they were trying to influence. There are times when contest or conflict gets some mileage. At least, the more dramatic tactics certainly get attention. Care must be taken, however, that dramatic approaches are really thought out. In the 1960s it was clear that some activists were interested in their own agenda: making a name for themselves, meeting members of the other sex, taking an ego trip. It is our opinion that the issues in social welfare policy are so vital that one engaged in policy change ought to look for the satisfaction of personal needs at another time and in another place. Hunger, illness, powerlessness, and discrimination are serious problems, and their control requires more dedication than one who is interested in meeting new people is able to give.

We also want to point out that contest and conflict are not the only strategies that are effective. A number of the items that we listed as strategies can be carried out as cooperative enterprises. Perhaps decision makers, like the mule, have to have something dramatic done in order to get their attention. At some point, however, conflict must be resolved and a cooperative basis must be found in order to get on with the job.

Alan Filley, whose field is management, has written of the need to re-solve conflicts in order to move organizations along in some consistent direction.[11] It is his belief that decisions are best made through consensus and integrative decision-making. Filley trains business managers in an ap-proach to conflict resolution that he has borrowed from transactional analysis. He believes that "win-lose" strategies, in which one party beats the other, are inefficient in the long run. Losers in such contests become resentful and ineffectual. He also believes that "lose-lose" strategies should be avoided. These are strategies that result in both sides losing because they have to give up too much and neither emerges feeling intact. A "win-win" strategy pursues its goals of consensus and integrative decision-making by keeping the discussion on the "adult-adult" level.

Although we see the need for contests and understand that conflict can arise over social welfare policy issues, we also recognize that at some point the two sides will have to reach some kind of agreement in order to work out what comes next. "What comes next" is planning for the implementation of policy decisions. A simple model of the planning process is addressed in the next chapter.

REFERENCES

1. Richard E. Neustadt, *Presidential Power* (New York: Science Editions, John Wiley, 1960), p. 10.
2. *Ibid.*
3. *Ibid.*, p. 39.
4. *Ibid.*, pp. 9–10.
5. Lawrence D. Mann, "Studies in Community Decision-Making," *Journal of the American Institute of Planners*, Vol. XXX, No. 1 (February 1964), pp. 58–65. This article has been reprinted in Ralph Kramer and Harry Specht, *Readings in Community Organization Practice*, 2nd ed. (Englewood Cliffs, N.J.: Prentice-Hall, 1975).
6. See Floyd Hunter, *Community Power Structure* (Chapel Hill, N.C.: University of North Carolina Press, 1953).
7. Arnold Panitch, "Advocacy in Practice," *Social Work*, Vol. 19, No. 3 (May 1974), pp. 326–332.
8. Charles S. Prigmore, "Use of the Coalition in Legislative Action," *Social Work*, Vol. 19, No. 1 (January 1974), pp. 96–102.
9. George A. Brager and Valerie Jorrin, "Bargaining: A Method in Community Change," *Social Work*, Vol. 14, No. 4 (October 1969), pp. 73–83.
10. Harry Specht, "Disruptive Tactics," *Social Work*, Vol. 14, No. 2 (April 1969), pp. 5–15.
11. Alan C. Filley, *Interpersonal Conflict Resolution* (Glenview, Ill.: Scott, Foresman, 1975).

QUESTIONS FOR DISCUSSION

1. Criticize the concept of power used in this chapter. Suggest an alternative explanation that has usefulness.
2. Which interest groups do you think will rise to importance in the United States in the next five to ten years? Which will decline?
3. Do you think that it might be possible for social workers to join forces with the National Association of Manufacturers or the Chamber of Commerce in a social policy change effort? Can you think of an issue?
4. Do you think that it would be practical for social workers to be directly involved in protests, boycotts, and other confrontation strategies?
5. Can you think of ways to bring opponents over to your side?
6. Can you think of examples of class-action suits that might be pressed to bring about social welfare policy change?

SUGGESTED PROJECTS

1. Talk with community leaders, editors, or politicians to determine which individuals or groups would be most effective in helping to implement a specific policy change, such as a better way of handling counseling needs.
2. Meet with a state senator or state representative to discuss social policy issues in the state. Ask specifically about mental health, public health, corrections, or Medicaid.
3. Talk with an attorney about the procedures, and costs involved in a class-action suit.
4. Talk to a U.S. senator or representative to get his or her thinking on the comparative strength of business, labor, agriculture, blacks, women, and other national power groups.

FOR FURTHER READING

Wilbur J. Cohen. "What Every Social Worker Should Know about Political Action," *Social Work,* Vol. 2, No. 3 (July 1966). A brief review of the steps in the legislative process by a former secretary of HEW. Cohen includes a section on administration of programs after a bill is passed. The examples are dated, but the article is still useful on the process.

Malcolm E. Jewell and Samuel C. Patterson. *The Legislative Process in the United States,* 2nd ed. New York: Random House, 1973. A scholarly presentation of the legislative system at federal and state levels, with attention to organization, procedures, and functions. Discusses the role of lobbyists, constituents, and the executive. Legislative norms and role orientations are discussed. A thorough work with extensive documentation.

Maryann Mahaffey. "Lobbying and Social Work," *Social Work*, Vol. 17, No. 1 (January 1972). A valuable review of the problem-solving aspects of the political process. Covers the use of cooperation, allies, and knowledge in lobbying. The major tasks of the lobbyist are discussed, and a model for legislative action is presented.

William T. Murphy, Jr. and Edward Schneier. *Vote Power*. New York: Anchor Books, 1974. A simply written but well-researched discussion of how Congress works and how political campaigns can be developed and carried out. The stress throughout is on getting a candidate elected and is aimed at the average citizen.

Rino J. Patti and Ronald B. Dear. "Legislative Advocacy: One Path to Social Change," *Social Work*, Vol. 20, No. 2 (March 1975). An up-to-date and realistic view of the role of social workers in the development of legislative policy, stressing compromise, the value of providing timely and balanced information to legislators and their staffs, and the sensitive use of tactics.

Charles S. Prigmore. "Use of the Coalition in Legislative Action," *Social Work*, Vol. 19, No. 1 (January 1974). A discussion, with examples, of the use of coalitions in policy implementation. The use of a wide range of organizations is stressed.

Alan D. Wade. "The Social Worker in the Political Process," *The Social Welfare Forum*, 1966. Wade discusses the resistances social workers have had to political action, the relevance of political action to policy implementation, and various roles for social workers. An early article in the movement of social workers into political action, but still valuable and pertinent.

Franklin M. Zweig. "The Social Worker as Legislative Ombudsman," *Social Work*, Vol. 14, No. 1 (January 1969). A practical discussion of the work and experiences of four graduate fieldwork students in the offices of federal and state legislators. The use of a wide range of skills is stressed, including conflict strategies.

10 *Connecting Policy to Planning*

What is the relationship of social welfare policy development to social welfare planning? How do social welfare policies become the basis for social programs and welfare services? The answer to the first question can be understood as one explores a series of stages that include the development of a social policy. Social planning usually follows the development of policy, and is the means through which a policy takes on meaning in the form of organized responses to human problems. The first part of this chapter develops that basic idea in more detail. The second part of the chapter examines the tasks that are performed by social welfare planners as they work to translate social policies into human service programs.

This chapter was written by Jerry Griffin, who is on the faculty of the School of Social Work at the University of Alabama. Prior to this appointment he did program development and planning.

Planning: One of Many Stages in Service Provision

In order to understand our society's response to social problems, it is necessary to view the context in which these problems develop and are treated. Every problem has a history, and most policies evolve over a long period of time as new approaches are taken. Each new policy, however, must be implemented according to some scheme that can reasonably be expected to produce the intended results. Social welfare planning, then, concerns itself primarily with the means through which social policies are actualized.

Planning, generally, is the process whereby one determines where one is going and how to get there. Planning leads to a selection of goals, a timetable for achieving them, and how the goals will be attained. It is possible to utilize the planning process to develop social policy; it is most often used, however, to determine ways to implement social policy. The process of social development and change is represented schematically in Figure 10–1.

Distinguishing Social Problems

At any one time there are many social conditions in our society, most of which are not necessarily viewed as social problems. Under certain circumstances, however, a social condition that had been viewed neutrally in an earlier time may be recognized as a problem that society feels compelled to address in some way. For an essentially neutral condition to become a problem, two factors are usually present. First, the condition must produce acute discomfort for an identifiable group of people. Someone, usually quite a few people, suffer in some way. A second factor often present in a condition's

FIGURE 10–1
Social Planning in Context

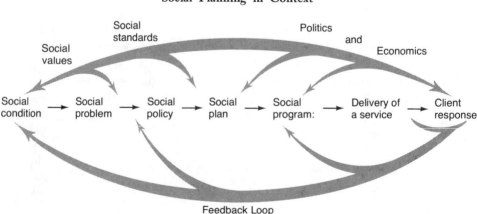

Source: Adapted from an unpublished schematic by Raymond Koleski, School of Applied Social Sciences, Case-Western Reserve University.

transition to problem status is a belief or conviction that something can be done to alleviate the problem.

Social values and standards provide guidance in distinguishing those situations that are on the way to becoming problems. The existence of outdoor toilets, for example, was not viewed as a problem when our population was widely scattered and when we knew nothing about bacteria. As people crowded their homes closer together, however, it became more difficult to maintain sanitary standards; disease was likely to be associated with too many outdoor toilets, too close together. The social value of maintaining privacy was difficult under such close living conditions. Value was also attached to living near one's work, and as cities developed out of the rural wilderness, it became more valued to live on small land space than to retain space for one's outhouse. What happened? Eventually, people came to recognize that something that had formerly been seen as a *condition* had shifted to the status of problem. The two requirements for this shift had been met. A large number of people were affected, and modern sanitary engineering had made advances that offered a way of dealing with the situation.

A wise local government had to recognize that the problem would only become worse over time. The solution would be a sewer system. First, a timetable would be set for construction in various parts of the city. The policy would have to be refined to take into account sectors outside the city that would be annexed later. As is the case with most social policies, this one had to be concerned with society's responsibility. In this example, government planned and operationalized a sanitary system.

Merely formulating a new policy did not resolve the problem. It was necessary for the city to compute the cost of installing sewer lines. Hills and valleys had to be taken into account; distances had to be measured, and the size of pipes needed had to be calculated. An acceptable collection point for the wastes had to be located, and means of disposing of the wastes had to be determined. The city also had to find a way to finance construction. This usually involved extra taxation or special fees. Since the city officials were elected, they were careful to "sell" the tax in such a way as to avoid getting themselves voted out of office at the next election. In sum, a total plan had to be developed, including ways to cope with both the politics and the economics of the situation.

The expected responses of clients (in this case, residents of the city) were satisfaction with the elimination of offensive odors and reduction in the spread of disease, but annoyance over the cost of connecting to the sewer. Eventually, however, the cost of an indoor bathroom became a moot consideration in the purchase or construction of a home; it was an inevitable part of the home and no longer considered a matter of choice. A new standard was thus set, and a new social value born. In areas where the rich had indoor toilets and lived inside the city, the poor were likely to live outside the city and continue to use outdoor toilets. Whether one had an indoor toilet became a factor of social status differential in the early development of American cities. The new social condition, as a result of the lengthy process, was one wherein all residents of high-density areas have indoor toilets.

The example should make obvious the many stages and factors that are present in a policy to program to evaluation to reformulation cycle. Planning is one of the very important stages and requires considerable skill. In fact, two basic types of skills are widely recognized as being absolutely necessary for social planners: *analytical* skill, which refers to the intellectual work of the planner, and *interactional* skill, which involves the person-to-person work of getting people organized and working together.[1] Education for social planning roles must include learning opportunities in which students can develop both kinds of skills to a considerable extent.

One of the most appealing aspects of social planning as a career in social work is its complexity. One never knows all about the systems within which social planning is practiced. New factors continually arise as problems change and times move ahead. The analytical tasks always present new challenges. Planners learn to think systematically and to take into account all important elements and factors in a given situation. A very special contribution the social work profession has made to modern concepts of planning is its history of concern for total communities. The more recent development of systems theory provides a modern rationale for total-community concern, as opposed to small-sector planning.

Social work's values are intricately linked with the highest ideal values of democratic society. It would be considered wrong, for example, to develop services for one group in a community at the undue expense of another. This concern for a total community development perspective is one that guided professional practice long before general systems theory was popularized and suggested a similar approach. The neckbone is, indeed, connected to the anklebone, and it is up to the astute planner to find the important connections and take them properly into account in any planning venture.

The Use of Planning Theory

Students of social planning have the benefit of experiences and perceptions of many planners who have written accounts of their experiences and their research on planning. There are several widely recognized and accepted models of the planning process, each produced by a different author or group of authors. No two writers see the planning process exactly alike;

each has special contributions to make to an interpretation of the process.

Planning theory typically consists of statements about how planning is or should be done. The statements represent a careful distillation of many planning experiences set forth in conceptual terms of what the student of planning should know in order to engage in planning activities. Models of the planning process serve as guides to planners as they decide what must be done at each stage of the process.

Practitioner Tasks

Without stating a comprehensive theory of social planning, it is possible to identify major clusters of tasks that must be performed by the professional planner. The tasks parallel theory, of course, but translate conceptual stages into the specific analytical and interactional behaviors that planners must perform. Let us examine the tasks as a way of understanding what a planner actually does. Of course, there will be variations in specific experiences, but the following ten tasks will be fairly typical of many planning experiences.

Identification and Understanding of the Problem

This first task is usually more difficult than it might seem. Planning usually flows from some recognition that a problem exists (see Figure 10–1), but different people will have different views on the problem. The planner must sort them out and determine who suffers and how many are affected. What are the consequences to persons affected by the problem? What are the consequences to society? The planner will also attempt to determine who recognizes that a problem exists and why, and who does not recognize the problem and why they do not.

Problems are usually thought to be rooted either in individual personality, an organization, the social structure, or some social institution or in a combination of these. The planner seeks the best possible interpretation of how the problem has developed and why it continues to exist. Possible solutions may become apparent as one searches for the antecedents of the problem. It is important to be clear about the possible consequences if no action is taken at all.

Selection of Participants

Most planning ventures involve many persons in addition to the professional planner. Although the planner does not always identify and select all of the important participants in a planning process, there is likely to be some opportunity to influence participant selection. Certain individuals can contribute useful knowledge; others will have influence that will be needed to bring about corrective action. For any given problem it is likely that several persons will have an important stake in either seeing it resolved or left undisturbed. The planner can identify persons and groups who have a stake in a particular problem and make an assessment of their potential helpfulness in finding and enacting a solution.

The planner has a major role in actually establishing a planning group to address the problem. In our society it is safe to assume that, with respect to any issue, there are one or more key persons whose influence must be reckoned with if action is to be taken on a particular issue. It is the planner's task to identify the influential people who are important to the particular issue being considered and to help develop ways to deal effectively with them.

Individuals and groups that are powerful are most frequently sought for allies to planning ventures. In some cases, however, a program, service, or change that is known to have powerful opponents may be in the planning stage. In either case, whether the center of power is an ally or an opposition force, the wise planner should have access to the thinking and actions of the power centers in order to keep the planning group working along lines that are likely to be productive. Access to the power centers needs to be established. This is most frequently achieved through persons close to the individuals or groups with power. Such people are often referred to as "gatekeepers." Gatekeepers serve as communication links between influential groups and individuals and a wide array of people.

It is often possible to develop a planning group that is made up of a fairly compatible combination of representatives from all important sectors, including some gatekeepers to appropriate power centers. The group will continue to be assisted by the professional planner, but will take on a character all its own as it proceeds to deal with the planning issues that are involved.

Determination of Goals

What is to be achieved by planning? What are the most desirable outcomes; what outcomes will actually be sought, giving consideration to both obstacles and opportunities? The professional planner has a strong responsibility to learn about and also inform the planning group about programs, services, or organizations in other places that are equivalent to those being planned. The success and failure of others' attempts to deal with a given problem serve as guides for local planning efforts. Although it is doubtful that successes elsewhere can be totally imported to a local situation, much can be gained from continual adaptation and improvement of good workable examples.

Much like the architect, the planner develops a wide array of working models or program examples through years of study and experience. These then serve as a storehouse of alternative possibilities that can be applied as needed in a local situation. There is ample room for creative development of new approaches to resolving problems also, since there are not, as yet, any standard formulas for dealing with some problems. The planner has a professional obligation to evaluate continually the plans that are developed, so that contributions can be made to the literature on workable solutions to the many social welfare problems.

The goals that are eventually sought may be considerably modified from the original statement. Most planning ventures, limited by financial and other constraints, rarely achieve what is seen as the ideal. Beginning with an idealized set of goals, however, enables the planner and the supporting group to select those features that are simultaneously most affordable and most workable.

Scientific knowledge for social welfare planning and policy development is in a state of early development. Politicians, elected to serve the majority, have long been reluctant to risk paying too much attention to the needy. Their major attention must be given to the majority of their constituents who can reelect them. In framing policies and financing social welfare programs, the elected have increasingly attempted to utilize scientific knowledge about the likely benefits of certain policies and programs. When certain bills are being considered by Congress or a state legislature, appropriate committees of those bodies hold legislative hearings on the proposed bills in order to get the testimony or opinions of interested persons. Increasingly, legislators attempt to include the testimony of expert professionals. Often such testimony appears to have some genuine impact on the decisions of law makers. Ultimately, however, most major decisions of legislative bodies are necessarily framed by a combination of social values and political and economic considerations.

One of the principal reasons frequently cited by professional planners for the lack of scientific certainty about ways to achieve desirable outcomes is the lack of investment in research. It was pointed out several years ago that "social work functions with the lowest investment in research and development of any major enterprise in the United States—perhaps less than .003 percent of the sums being planned for." [2]

Planners complain that without proper investment in alternative approaches to the solution of social welfare problems it is impossible to say with certainty which goals and means are most likely to succeed. Each planning effort will, therefore, continue to be handled individually, utilizing existing policies, available resources, and the best solutions that can be found which are acceptable to those whose points of view must be taken into consideration.

Determination of Action Needed

Several alternative types of action are possible when considering most social welfare problems, and it is usually important for the planner to be clear about the particular type or combination to be used. The types of action most frequently attempted are *prevention, alleviation, control,* or *correction.*

It would appear desirable to prevent problems from ever occurring. Some social welfare problems are thought to have their roots in places that are inaccessible, however, and are not to be tampered with by either policy makers or planners. A good example of such problems are those that are thought to be rooted in faulty early parent-child relationships. It is possible that a parent may unknowingly contribute to a child's later neurotic or psychotic mental conditions. Although society has established laws concerning both neglect and abuse of children, the laws are not sufficiently sensitive, and science is not sufficiently developed, to detect just which parental behaviors will produce problems for their offspring in later life. Early childhood parenting is usually considered to be a domain that official society does not tamper with in any mandatory way unless actual legal abuse or neglect are detected. Public social programs that are closest to that stage of life are health clinics and day care, neither of which involves mandatory participation. Prevention of other problems may not be possible because of the lack of scientific knowledge about where to direct preventive efforts and what those efforts should be.

Some problems can be *alleviated,* lessening their impact and severity. Poverty, when defined as the lack of sufficient funds to purchase the necessities of life, can be, and is, alleviated by providing funds for individuals and families. Without supplementary activities and services, however, poverty is neither prevented nor cured by providing money for basic needs. Families can receive minimal public welfare funds for years and, unless other special measures are also taken, the families will be just as poor as ever when the financial support is terminated. Alleviation is often the preferred action when other alternatives are either impossible to take or when they are too costly.

Control of certain kinds of problems appears to be the best approach. Health departments utilize a variety of measures to attempt to control to a reasonable level the spread of diseases that cannot be totally prevented.

Some problems can be *corrected,* on a person-to-person basis. Poor vision that is caused by certain correctible eye diseases in children has long been a concern of the Lions Clubs of America. Their sight conservation program, providing properly fitted eyeglasses to young children whose parents cannot afford them, can be said to have cured many vision problems. The best examples of corrected problems come from the health field, and include the almost total elimination of tuberculosis, polio, smallpox, and certain other communicable diseases.

Sometimes, whether or not a problem is solved depends upon how it is defined. Public begging, or mendicancy, as it was formerly called, has long been considered a nuisance. Public laws were passed in sixteenth-century England to prevent, control, or license begging, yet it persisted until societies found other ways to meet people's basic needs. Nevertheless, panhandlers can still be seen in large cities. Few social problems have been totally corrected, although many have been reduced in their severity, through a variety of means.

Determination of Targets for Intervention

The planner usually thinks simultaneously about desirable types of action and target systems. Target systems are individuals or societal systems upon whom some kind of action is to be taken in order to deal with the problem. Typical kinds of target systems are individuals, families, neighborhoods, subcultures, geographic or functional communities, specific organizations, and large institutions. Although some problems may be widespread throughout our society, one cannot usually target the entire society to bring about change. In the case of racial discrimination, attempts to correct its ill effects do focus on widespread changes in our social institutions and specific organizations. Individuals and corporate bodies can be and are directed by law to end certain practices that are thought to be discriminatory.

In the case of deteriorating housing, the geographic neighborhood is often the target of intervention, through slum clearance or rehabilitation. Planners must be careful, however, to be certain that their solutions do not create additional problems that may be worse than the ones being attacked. This is sometimes encountered when poor neighborhoods are broken up by urban renewal. Informal networks of mutual assistance and support that sustained residents of a dilapidated neighborhood may be broken up by the forced moving to new locations. Multitudes of new social problems have been generated as a result of forced relocation.

Ultimately, all target systems are people systems. It is new behavior that is sought, and the planner must assess whether the necessary resources can be organized and applied to the appropriate target systems to either prevent, alleviate, control, or correct the problem under consideration. This particular activity, usually a matter of judgment, is often called "feasibility testing." Goals and plans that are not feasible will need to be revised or adjusted in order to achieve expected feasibility before proceeding farther.[3]

Evaluation of Available Resources

To take action on many social welfare problems requires a vast outlay of funds. It is not often that planners and planning groups tackle large problems and plan large solutions without assurance of strong and stable financial assistance from a governmental source. Although the planning process may be utilized to develop a recommended policy and budget to deal with a problem, it is most often engaged after policies have already been determined and budgets fixed, at least for a period of time.

Money is not, by far, the only needed resource in dealing with problems. Although each situation will generate its own list of needed resources, some of those typically in high demand (other than money) are leadership capabilities, professional staff, social climate of willingness to take action, and supportive services and programs that may be needed in providing a continuity of care. Hospital expansions sometimes fail because of an insufficient supply of qualified nurses; entire service programs do not develop within some communities where there is insufficient leadership to bring them into the communities. Whatever the need, all required resources should be identified and plans for their procurement should be made.

The planner is actively involved in all aspects of the developing program. The planner's approach is systematic, requiring consideration of all essential relationships to assure that the planning process will result in effective treatment of the problem. Plans that are simply written notations of a particular individual's ideas about what ought to be done are often doomed to be shelved without even being considered for implementation. The effective planner, however, develops the resources to get the job done along with the intellectual work of planning.

Determination of Strategies

Significant program development through planning usually requires a variety of strategies to bring about the desired changes. Strategies are the short-range actions which, when considered altogether, move an effort forward toward realization of its larger goals. Examples include news media campaigns, organization of agency coalitions, writing financial proposals, retraining staff through continuing education, and a host of other efforts that contribute toward goal achievement in a larger sense. Each strategic effort is not considered to be an end in itself, but it is contributory toward a more important achievement.

Competent and effective planners rarely proceed very far into a planning venture without developing a general overall map of the entire planning process with respect to the issue at hand. The danger in beginning without thinking far ahead can readily be seen. An analogy can be drawn to an automobile trip that is begun on a particular highway, either because it is beautiful or familiar, without regard to whether it eventually connects with a destination. Some social planners are now utilizing a highly effective approach to develop overall maps of their thinking and to communicate that thinking to others. The approach involves the use of flow charts, a practice that has been highly developed in manufacturing and in computer technology.

Flow-charting in social planning can be used to reflect either simple or very complex machinations of the planning process, or any degree in between. It attempts to depict graphically activities and operations that must be performed within a given span of time. It identifies the individuals or groups that will perform the various operations and key decisions that must be made in the sequence in which they are most likely to occur. A flow chart of a particular planning process will generally represent the successive stages of a theory of planning that is appropriate to the situation.

Flow charts can be developed to reflect a wide variety of features the planners find desirable. It is possible to emphasize the efficient deployment of staff in planning or the intermittent decision role of a board of directors or any combination of those and other dynamics that will occur in the planning process. Flow charts provide a visual representation of what is to be done, when, and by whom; these can be used in working with planning groups and other decision-making bodies. Through prior agreement on a work plan it is possible to control the timing and substantive input of various interested parties. To provide important persons and groups access to plan development may be crucial; to show them where and when their contributions can be received is to regulate the process efficiently.

Setting of Priorities

Although proper attention to strategies causes the planner also to think about priorities, special attention should be given to this task. There always seems to be fierce competition for scarce resources. As the entire effort is reviewed, those matters that must be given certain attention should be identified and organized into a priority system. New information and increasingly understood external and internal factors may cause priority realignment just before final actions are to occur. A deliberate pause to reassess readiness to act and to identify key things to be done at this stage is well worth the planner's attention.

Implementation of Solutions

Because action to implement solutions is usually continuous with previous steps, it is not always possible to say just when it begins. Typically, action overlaps parts of prior stages and becomes continuous with evaluation and replanning. A new set of participants may be brought into the scene as plans are implemented. They are not necessarily planners and people movers; they are more likely to be the service personnel, managers, and others who will establish and maintain that which has been planned. In essence, the implementation stage is the allocation and deployment of resources: money, people, and power.

The professional planner may or may not be intimately involved in implementation of plans that he or she has helped to create. Ideally, the planner should be, just as the architect who designs a building should be available to consult with the contractor who is hired to construct it. Last-minute changes will be necessary. That which can go wrong will, and must be reprogrammed at the last minute. Unanticipated resistance will appear in some instances and will need to be handled.

The art and science of program administration comes strongly into play at this point; an entire later chapter will deal with implementation. The close interrelationship of planning and administration can be seen as one traces the path of a social policy's development, the planning that it generates, and the service administration that usually follows. Planning again appears as an essential function of program management, reflecting a continuous cycle of program redevelopment.

Evaluation and Replanning

As indicated earlier, planners need to be involved in evaluating the outcomes of their efforts. Feedback from what we do is one of the most effective instructors. Too often planning and administration become unjoined and a program is later evaluated by persons who had little or nothing to do with its creation. Without involvement in the evaluation process, the planner cannot learn what the mistakes were and how they could be avoided in the future. It may be difficult to determine who was responsible for certain problems; for example, was it faulty planning or faulty administration?

One practice that is not sufficiently utilized in social welfare planning is the development of detailed written specifications for programs that are being developed. The planning team should commit plans to paper in sufficient detail so that it is possible for an administrative team to be clear about what was intended.

Several relatively new approaches in program administration hold promise for assisting with program evaluation, the most notable of which is *management by objectives*. Theoretically, it should be possible to state program objectives clearly and in sufficient detail to control the program they serve. The specific characteristics of the program are therefore designed to achieve the stated objectives. They are periodically evaluated to determine whether that, in fact, is happening. When objectives are not being achieved sufficiently, replanning should produce necessary changes. Constant evaluation is essential for the continual improvement of programs and services.

REFERENCES

1. Robert Perlman and Arnold Gurin, *Community Organization and Social Planning* (New York: John Wiley and the Council on Social Work Education, 1972), p. 61.
2. Robert Morris, "Social Planning," in Henry S. Mass, ed., *Five Fields of Social Service: Reviews of Research* (New York: National Association of Social Workers, 1966), p. 186.
3. Robert Morris and Robert H. Binstock, *Feasible Planning for Social Change* (New York: Columbia University Press, 1966), p. 80.

QUESTIONS FOR DISCUSSION

1. How can planners anticipate future problems?
2. When does a social condition become a social problem?
3. Can a planner use rationality as the sole basis for planning?
4. Why is it necessary to involve people other than professionals in the planning task?
5. Why do planners not have scientific information available for planning purposes?
6. When does one know whether or not a given plan has succeeded?
7. What kinds of resources are needed in order for planning to be successful?
8. How do flow charts help the planner?
9. What is the role of evaluation in the planning process?

SUGGESTED PROJECTS

1. Contact the United Way office or community council in your city and make arrangements to attend a meeting of one of their planning task forces. You may be able to review the minutes of previous meetings to get background material on the matter that is being planned. Look for information that provides contextual understanding of the planning endeavor. At what stage of development is the project? What kinds of help is the professional planner giving the planning group?

2. Contact your local welfare department and request a copy of the Title
   XX (Social Security Act) plans that have been developed for your area
   for the current year. Inquire about any forthcoming public hearings on
   next year's plans that you might attend. Visit their offices and interview
   one of their planners to develop a written report on their annual planning cycle for Title XX funds.

FOR FURTHER READING

Edgar S. Cahn and Barry A. Passett, eds. *Citizen Participation*. Trenton, N.J.:
   Community Action Institute, 1970. An interestingly written book, especially
   useful to the student of social policy and social planning. The first section
   examines the conflict between government and citizens over the issue of
   individual and community self-determination. The second section presents
   an excellent discussion of issues in citizen participation in planning. The
   third section is a collection of planning cases in which selected issues are
   treated.

Fred M. Cox et al., eds., *Strategies of Community Organization*, 2nd ed. Itasca,
   Ill.: F. E. Peacock, 1974. A collection of excellent readings that serves as
   a good textbook on community organization. Although only one chapter
   specifically addresses social planning, the entire book helps to frame the
   practice of social planning in social work.

Joan Levin Ecklein and Armand A. Lauffer. *Community Organizers and Social
   Planners*. New York: John Wiley, 1972. A variety of cases in both community organization and social planning. The wide range of relatively brief cases
   is exceptional. Cases include planning for government policy implementation,
   grant proposal development, direct services development, and many more.
   This is a companion volume to the basic text by Perlman and Gurin (see
   below).

Ralph M. Kramer and Harry Specht, eds. *Readings in Community Organization Practice*. Englewood Cliffs, N.J.: Prentice-Hall, 1969. One section
   covers various topics related to social planning. The remainder of this book
   is a collection of outstanding contributions to community organization theory
   over the last two decades, written by many different authors.

Robert Perlman and Arnold Gurin. *Community Organization and Social Planning*. New York: John Wiley and the Council on Social Work Education,
   1972. A basic textbook that focuses on the relationship of community
   organization to social planning. It is built upon a careful study of the actual
   practices of planning and organizing in the United States. Its treatment of
   social planning theory is outstanding.

I I *Connecting Policy to Administration*

The opening chapters discussed the environmental influences on the formulation of social welfare policy. From the criteria for analysis of policy developed in Chapter 3, it is clear that a social welfare policy is to be considered as an input into a system designed to eliminate some adverse human condition; that is, a social policy is not an "end" but rather an element of the "means" to reduction of unemployment, crime, and so forth. The discussion in this chapter is based on the thesis that administration is the link between "the policy" and the "desired social change."

This chapter was written by Richard Crow and Charles Odewahn. Both are at the University of Alabama. Crow has a joint appointment with the School of Social Work and the College of Commerce and Business Administration, and Odewahn, whose field is management, is chairman of interdisciplinary programs in the College of Commerce and Business Administration.

221

Figure 11–1 depicts the relationships that make up the administrative system.

Several elements of this system are critical to the successful fulfillment of any social policy. First, those in the administrative process must recognize the role of social, political, economic, and cultural values. The diagram clearly demonstrates that the values which influence policy formulation also affect the implementation of programs to fulfill the policy. Second, policy creates the need for resource allocation, thus stipulating the primary function of the administration's allocation and coordination of resources. Third, the administrative system is oriented toward a purpose. The process receives its direction from, and is organized around, the purpose or mission declared by the policy. Fourth, the administrative system involves the performance of a series of functions (planning, organizing, leading, evaluating) which transform resources into specific services designed to accomplish the mission declared by the policy. Finally, each element of the system is constantly feeding back information and results. For example, feedback about the outcome of service delivery (desired social change) impacts on both the inputs (i.e., values, policy, and resources) and the administrative process (i.e., plans, organization, etc.).

The discussion which follows will clarify and build upon these relationships to increase the reader's understanding of the role of administration. Specifically, the plan for the remainder of the chapter is to sharpen definitions of administration and to look at the functions of an administrator and the activities involved in each of these functions.

What Is Administration?

Definitions of administration or management (for purposes of this chapter these terms are interchangeable) are as numerous as those who write about the subject. Massie, for example, defines management as "the process by which a cooperative group directs actions toward common goals." [1] Peter Drucker defines it as three tasks "equally important but essentially different, which management has to perform to enable the institution in its charge to function and to make its contribution: the specific purpose and mission of the institution, whether business enterprise, hospital, or university; making work productive and the worker achieving; managing social impacts and social responsibilities." [2] Sisk, on the other hand, adopts a more technocratic approach with his definition: "Management is the coordination of all resources through the process of plannning, organizing, leading, and controlling in order to attain stated objectives." [3]

These definitions may seem very different, even contradictory. Upon closer examination, however, several common elements appear. First, the

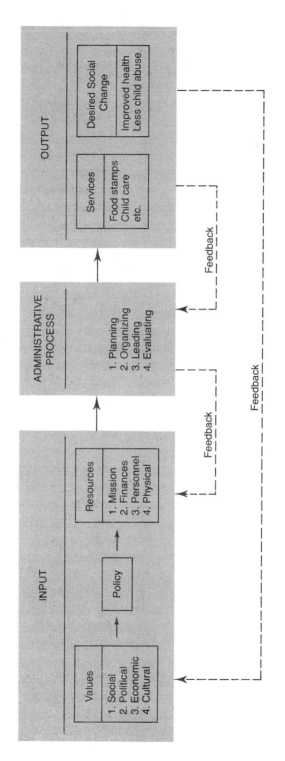

FIGURE 11–1
The Administrative System

stated or implied activity described by each of these definitions is universally applicable. All organizations attempting to achieve a common purpose, whether large or small, require administration. Second, administration is goal oriented. Administration has no life-cycle separate from the goals for which the agency is established. This principle constantly must be kept in mind, since the temptation is ever present to "administer an organization for the sake of administration." When this happens both the organization and its clients or customers are poorly served.

A third way of looking at administration is that it is a cooperative venture. The organization achieves its goals primarily through the efforts of people. A successful administrative process must cause a convergence of organizational goals and personal goals that will motivate individuals to join in a cooperative partnership. Finally, administration is task directed. The administrator engages in a number of activities related to the establishment of a plan; the development of an organization; providing leadership; and direction and the evaluation and control of performance.

The foregoing discussion has described administration as a cooperative action system. By this we mean that administration includes all activities necessary to transform social policy into the desired social changes. These activities are carried on by administrators, the next topic to be considered.

What Do Administrators Do?

The administrator's primary responsibility is to coordinate the work of others, not to personally perform tasks. On some occasions the administrator will perform tasks, but his or her success does not depend upon knowledge or skills in the field being administered. Rather the administrator is concerned with the functioning of the organization. The administrator is responsible for creating an environment that will enable subordinates to achieve agency goals efficiently and in a personally rewarding manner. How well this environment is designed and maintained will determine the ultimate success or failure of an agency. This environment, at minimum, must provide each individual within the organization with (1) an understanding of agency objectives and (2) an understanding of how they and their jobs contribute to the accomplishment of these objectives. In addition, the environment must contain a system to motivate individuals to maintain a high level of performance.

The statement of mission or objectives found in public policy pronouncements is customarily a list of broad statements of purpose with which the majority can agree. For example, a public policy may have the purpose of providing superior health care to every citizen. This objective statement, while laudable, is not very operational. With this as your only guidance you could not be expected to move very far toward the accomplishment of the objective. It is up to the administrator to clarify and develop objectives toward which everyone can work. Further, the administrator must ensure that these statements of objectives are clearly understood by all individuals involved in the pursuit of these objectives.

The administrator must ensure that each individual and unit within the agency understands the overall goals and objectives of the organization. Also, they must be made aware of how they as individual units fit into the master scheme. This requires that a set of subgoals be established that, when taken together, will result in the accomplishment of the larger agency mission. Each person in the system should be provided with a set of clear and verifiable goals against which his or her performance will be measured. Similarly, the administrator must ensure that each individual has the necessary information and a scope of authority to perform the tasks assigned.

The administrative environment should create a setting in which individuals strive to achieve organizational goals because they have accepted them as their own. In short, the administrator must be a facilitator who can focus an individual's knowledge, skills, talents, and aspirations toward the accomplishment of the organizational mission.

How does the administrator accomplish these goals? To answer this question we will have to look at the roles an administrator fulfills, the activities that occupy the workday, and the administrative functions to be directed.

The Roles of the Administrator

The administrator-manager is an individual of many identities and is called upon to perform in various administrative roles. Henry Mintzberg has identified ten separate roles that an administrator is likely to be called upon to perform.[4] He has delineated three interpersonal roles, three informational roles, and four decisional roles.

Interpersonal Roles

1. *The figurehead role*—As the head of an organization or organizational unit, an administrator is obliged to perform specific symbolic duties.

   • The executive director of the Family Service Association presents certificates of appreciation to foster home parents.

   • The commissioner of public welfare receives a call from an angry recipient and he in turn calls the county welfare director of the county involved to advise him of the call.

- The executive director of the United Way presents certificates of recognition to the key people in business who assisted in the annual United Way campaign.

2. *The leader role*—In this role the administrator is responsible for ensuring that the people assigned to the unit perform in a satisfactory manner. As leader, the administrator must motivate and encourage subordinates to achieve organizational goals.

- The director of a community mental health center congratulates the social worker who devised a new and quicker method for summarizing social histories.
- The director of the local community action program encourages the staff to continue with their regular daily responsibilities in spite of adverse public reaction and the threat of financial cutbacks.
- The bureau chief meets with supervisory personnel in an agency and advises them that too much time is being wasted in processing clients' requests for service and that the delay can no longer be tolerated.

3. *The liaison role*—In this role the administrator is concerned with establishing an external information and mutual assistance system.

- The superintendent of the boys' training school maintains contact with the local ministerial association and seeks their advice and counsel on programs in the school.
- The director of a regional program for retarded citizens contacts the executive secretary of the Chamber of Commerce and advises him that they will soon have graduates from a special training program.
- The director of a home for emotionally disturbed children calls the Junior League and seeks their assistance in recruiting volunteers.

Informational Roles

4. *The monitor role*—Here the administrator receives and filters information useful to his or her organization. This information flows both from the formal organizational communication network and the external information system developed in the liaison role.

- A memorandum is received from the central office of the mental health department which advises the regional director of changes in the definition of the developmentally disabled.
- The director of a private voluntary adoption agency receives a letter from the executive director of the United Fund outlining new

guidelines for program budgeting to be required of all funded agencies.

- A letter is received by the commissioner of the department of corrections from a private consulting firm seeking permission to interview prisoners.

5. *The disseminator role*—In this role important information that has been gathered is transferred to subordinates who would not otherwise have access to this information.

- An announcement of a workshop on transactional analysis is circulated among the professional staff of a mental health center.
- A request to the superintendent of the state school for the mentally retarded from the Civitan club for information on the guidelines for volunteers is forwarded to the supervisor of community services.
- A report from a schoolteacher in a residential treatment center is sent to the casework supervisor.

6. *The spokesman role*—The administrator, in this role, speaks on behalf of the organization to the external environment.

- The director of a halfway house for delinquent boys delivers a speech to the League of Women Voters describing the purpose of community-based programs.
- The director of a program for unwed mothers is invited to discuss the program on a television talk show.
- The executive director of the Children's Aid Society delivers a report to the board of directors on the developments within the agency during the past quarter.

Decisional Roles

7. *The entrepreneur role*—Through decisions to implement new programs or to change existing procedures the administrator acts as an entrepreneur.

- The superintendent of the state school for girls lobbies with key legislators to influence their consideration of a bill which would eliminate the commitment of pregnant delinquent girls to the state school.
- The director of a manpower center submits a proposal to the Department of Labor for a federal grant designed to provide training for the hard-core unemployed.
- The director of the planning and development commission holds a quarterly "brainstorming" session with the staff for the purpose of

coming up with new ideas for dealing with the human service needs
in the region.

8. *The disturbance handler role*—In any organization some situations
have the potential of becoming a crisis. The administrator must respond to such a situation.

- The director of social services in a large state mental hospital is
confronted with a serious conflict developing between the social
workers and the psychiatric residents which must be resolved.

- A county welfare director seeks a new approach to handling the
conflict between the typists and the professional staff.

- The director of a community action program schedules a meeting
between local residents and the social work staff to deal with com-
plaints of ineffective service to the community.

9. *The resource allocator role*—The administrator must decide within the
organization how resources will be allocated among the various unit
functions.

- The director of a senior citizen center decides to concentrate on the
development of new programs and hiring additional professional
staff rather than continuing the drive for larger physical facilities.

- The administrator of a regional mental health center issues a directive requiring all decisions regarding program development and purchase of equipment to be approved by his office.

- The commissioner of the state department of public welfare submits
an annual budget request which asks for appropriations to cover an
additional 100 social workers in the child support division of the
department and a cutback of 50 social workers in adult services.

10. *The negotiator role*—No organization or organizational unit is self-
sustaining or "an island unto itself." Every unit must interface with
other parts of the organization as well as with outside forces. The administrator is responsible for the negotiations which maintain the
proper environment with those other units.

- The chief probation officer of the family court and the regional
director of the division of family and children services negotiate
which children will be supervised by the court and which will be
supervised by the division of family and children services.

- The director of a program for inner-city youth confers with the
neighborhood school board to negotiate the use of the schools for
recreational programs in the evenings and on weekends.

- The director of a large multiservice center meets with the union representatives of the Federation of Social Workers to negotiate acceptable standards for the size of caseloads.

It is obvious that, while these ten roles must be performed by any administrator, they cannot be separated and neatly placed in a logbook. The administrator may perform several of these functions simultaneously. For example, when a bureau chief is having lunch with a group of peers, and the topic of next year's budget comes up: Is the bureau chief acting as the liaison, monitor, resource allocator, or negotiator?

It is quite likely that the chief is performing in all of these roles. This suggests yet another approach for understanding the task of administration —to look at the activities engaged in by administrators.

Activities of Administrators

A second avenue leading to an increased understanding of administrators is to view how they spend their time. How a "typical" administrator spends time provides insight into the specific tasks which compose the job of administration. Rino J. Patti has reported on the activities of ninety social welfare managers in the state of Washington.[5] Table 11.1 lists his thirteen functional groupings of administrative activities and the average number of hours spent per week on each activity.

TABLE 11.1
Time Spent in Each Activity by Managers

Activity	Mean Hours
Planning	3.9
Information Processing	6.2
Controlling	5.4
Coordinating	3.8
Evaluating	1.5
Negotiating	.7
Representing	1.8
Staffing	.9
Supervising	6.7
Supplying	.3
Extracurricular	1.9
Direct Service	4.1
Budgeting	1.0

Source: Rino J. Patti, "Patterns of Management Activity in Social Welfare Agencies," *Administration in Social Work* (Spring 1977), p. 7. Reprinted by permission.

In addition to asking the respondents how they spent their time, Patti asked each manager to rank the activities in order of importance to the

TABLE 11.2
Description of Management Activities

Planning	Determining goals, policies, and courses of action. For example: strategy-setting, staff work-scheduling, grant development.
Information Processing	Time spent in communicating information (reading, writing, compiling, telephoning) where the manager or interviewer was unable to specify the specific function these activities filled.
Controlling	Collecting and analyzing information as to how the total operation or major segments of it are going.
Coordinating	Exchanging information with persons within or outside the agency other than subordinates or superiors in order to relate and adjust programs.
Evaluating	The assessment and appraisal of proposals and reported or observed performance.
Negotiating	Conferring, bargaining, or discussing with a view to reaching an agreement with another party.
Representing	Advancing the interests of the agency through contacts with individuals, groups, or constituencies outside the organization.
Staffing	Recruiting, interviewing, hiring, and promoting staff.
Supervising	Leading, directing, training, and reviewing the work of subordinates.
Supplying	Obtaining space, equipment, supplies, and other nonfinancial resources required for the work of the agency.
Extracurricular	Activities done during the work week that would not be part of a job description such as partisan political activity or attending classes.
Direct Service	Giving counseling, treatment, or advice directly to a client.
Budgeting	Planning expenditures and allocating resources among items in the budget.

Source: Rino J. Patti et al., *Educating for Management in Social Welfare*, unpublished report, The University of Washington (July 1976), Vol. II, p. 17. Mimeographed. Reprinted by permission.

effective performance of the manager's job. He reported several findings as particularly significant. For example, "Over two-thirds of the managers in this sample judged activities subsumed under controlling, supervising, and planning as the most important ones they had performed during the prior week. Somewhat less than one-half of the respondents ranked coordinating as significant, while one-quarter or less of the managers felt that activities associated with representing, information processing, direct practice, and evaluating were important to effective job performance." [6] It can be seen from Table 11.1 that the three activities ranked most significant, planning, controlling, and supervising, occupied approximately 40 percent of these managers' time each week. This statistic, however, masks the fact that each manager engaged in a wide variety of tasks and activities throughout the survey week. In fact, most studies of this nature, as well as this one, have found a chief characteristic of the job of manager to be rapid change from one task or activity to another.[7] To provide insight into the breadth of activity subsumed under the categorial headings, Table 11.2 presents a summary of the specific activities engaged in by a typical manager in performance of the major functions.

This and the foregoing section have approached the topic of administration from the perspective of administrator characteristics and activities. The intent was to provide the reader an overview of the nature of the management process without describing the process itself. Now that you have some understanding of the administrative role it is time to turn our attention to the processes which constitute administration—planning, organizing, leading, and controlling.

Administrative Processes

Planning

In a very real sense, planning may be considered the essence of administration. Earlier in this discussion, we described management as the link between social policy and desired social changes. Planning is the backbone of that linkage, in that it is the initial step or function performed by an administrator.

Plans are the means by which administrators extend and operationalize the mission stated in a social welfare policy. This planning function may be separated into the broad categories of strategic and operational planning. Strategic planning is customarily carried out at the highest administrative level within an agency. It begins with the determination of the major objectives of the organization. In this context, an objective is the specific target or need that an agency must achieve in order to continue to exist. Examples of subjects included in strategic plans are matters such as the types of service to be provided, type and number of personnel necessary to perform these services, capital expenditures, and costs associated with each of these activities. Strategic plans tend to be long range and are mainly concerned with broad statements to provide coordination of the various elements composing the organization. The output of strategic planning efforts are statements of principles which constitute guides for movement toward the accomplishment of agency objectives. We call these statements of principles "policies." Policies act as guideposts for decision-making throughout the organization.

Operational planning, on the other hand, involves the translation of objective statements and policy guidelines into action statements. This type of planning has a much shorter time frame than strategic planning, usually one year or less, and is conducted by middle and lower level managers. Operational plans are derived from the objectives or strategic plans originating from the upper levels of administration. They are concerned with definite actions which must be taken in order to accomplish the goals established for the unit by the strategic plan.

Operational plans, then, provide the specific program direction necessary to carry out policy statements. Examples of these types of plans are to be found in documents such as procedure manuals, rules, and the unit's budget.

Whether one is attempting to develop an agency-wide strategy or a plan of action for next week, the rudiments of the planning process remain the same. The rational planner, it has been said, undertakes five interrelated steps:

1. Identify the problems to be solved and the opportunities to be seized upon.

2. Design alternative solutions or courses of action (i.e., policies, plans, and programs) to solve the problems or seize upon the opportunities and forecast the consequences and effectiveness of each alternative.

3. Compare and evaluate the alternatives with each other and with the forecasted consequences of unplanned development and choose the alternative whose probable consequences would be preferable.

4. Develop a plan of action for implementing the alternative selected, including budgets, project schedules, regulatory measures and the like.

5. Maintain the plan on a current basis through feedback and review of information.[8]

This sequence describes a process not too unlike what you and your family face when attempting to decide upon a vacation trip. Initial consideration must be given to individual family members' preferences—the beach or the mountains. Second, you must choose the goals to be accomplished by the trip—rest and relaxation or sightseeing and activity. Third, basic premises affecting the final decision must be considered—length of vacation possible, money available. Fourth, vacation alternatives that will satisfy the goals set must be identified and compared to determine the best choice—which vacation plan will satisfy the greatest number of family members. After you decide upon the actual trip to be taken, supporting plans must be formulated—development of an itinerary, purchase of needed materials, making reservations. Finally, during and after the vacation, the plan will be evaluated by all members of the family for future vacation planning.

Organizing

The plans discussed in the previous section result in a "road map" leading the agency toward the objectives established by a social welfare policy. If this is the case, then, the organization structure is the vehicle which transports the agency to the objective. The formal organizational structure allocates responsibility, authority, and accountability to individuals within the agency. Through the organization structure each individual is made responsible for a group of tasks which constitute a job. The structure also extends to each individual and the authority to make decisions within the assigned area of responsibility. Finally, the structure makes each individual accountable to a higher authority for the results achieved in the performance of the job.

From this, it may be concluded that the initial task of organizing consists of determining what activities will constitute a basic job. Once again, it should be noted that the activities to be performed must flow from the basic objectives set out for the agency. The collection of activities or tasks that we describe as a job then becomes the foundation for organizing.

Following the grouping of activities or tasks into jobs, a framework must be constructed to specify the relationships between these elements. That is, jobs must be grouped so that the performance of each of the specialized activities fits together into a "chain of command," in which responsibility, authority, and accountability are understood.

Organizationally, the agency will have a wide choice of patterns that will accomplish this goal. For example, a functional pattern may be chosen which logically reflects occupational specialization. Under this pattern all jobs containing like activities are placed in the same department—for example, all fiscal activities. A second structural pattern may group all jobs related to the same service program into the same department. For example, all personnel related to providing day care for children of working mothers may be grouped into one department. Another possibility is to base the pattern of organization on the location of a given set of activities, for example, a county welfare department. Another form of structure might be to organize the agency by client group. All child-care activities, for example, may be placed in a single department.

These structural patterns, while not constituting all the available organizational forms, are representative examples of useful bases for developing effective and efficient work structures. In practice, you are likely to find
a mixture of the patterns within any given agency. You may find functional
grouping at the statewide level and client grouping at the local level. In
short, the form of organizational structure will depend, in the final analysis,
on pragmatic considerations.

Whatever the pattern of structure selected, is must clearly establish for
each individual within the organization the flow of authority and responsibility, while ensuring accountability of each person for their performance of
organizational tasks.

Leading and Directing

The last two sections have shown us that the plan provides the organization with a map of its objectives, and the structure provides the transportation to the objective. In this section, we will see that it is leadership which
provides the energy to obtain the organization's goals.

The difference between simply "minding the store" and actively striving
to achieve goals is the level of motivation found among the personnel in the
organization. The administrator through his or her abilities as a manager-
leader has the responsibility of motivating employees to strive for high performance. Thus, the manager-leader must understand the factors that influence human work behavior.

Managers must think about the people within their organization, yet
they must also think of the goals to be attained. Managerial leadership then
may be defined "as the process of influencing the activities of a group in
efforts towards goal attainment in a given situation. The key elements in
this definition are leader, followers, and situation." [9] These three variables
interact to affect leader behavior and may result in a variety of styles. Figure
11–2 depicts a leadership style continuum that varies from a task-oriented,
highly autocratic style to a people-oriented, highly participative style. The
factors of leader, follower, and situation will indicate where on this continuum an individual manager is likely to fall.

The leader's actions at any given time are influenced by his or her own
personality and the environment. Since the manager constantly deals with
ambiguous situations with a high level of uncertainty, the manager's own
feelings of security about his or her position will influence leadership style.
The leader's feelings of security, in turn, influence the level of confidence
placed in subordinates. The higher this level of confidence, the higher the
degree of freedom granted subordinates. Similarly, the leader's own value
system and philosophy of leadership will affect the type of leadership. The
leader, for example, who believes subordinates to be naturally lazy will likely

FIGURE 11–2
Leadership Style

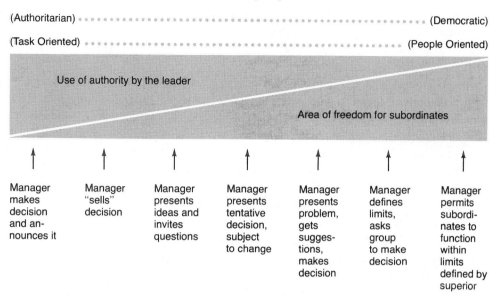

(Authoritarian) ·· (Democratic)

(Task Oriented) ·· (People Oriented)

| Manager makes decision and announces it | Manager "sells" decision | Manager presents ideas and invites questions | Manager presents tentative decision, subject to change | Manager presents problem, gets suggestions, makes decision | Manager defines limits, asks group to make decision | Manager permits subordinates to function within limits defined by superior |

Source: Robert Tannenbaum *et al.*, *Leadership and Organization: A Behavioral Approach* (New York: McGraw-Hill, 1961), p. 69. Reprinted by permission.

be much more authoritarian and directive in leadership style than the leader who believes that subordinates have a high degree of commitment and a natural inclination to achieve work goals. This latter manager is more likely to permit subordinates a greater area of freedom and be more participative in leadership style.

The follower also is influenced by personality and environment. Each of us responds to direction in a different way. Some subordinates have a relatively high need for structure and do not wish to take responsibility for making decisions, but would prefer to remain dependent upon the leader. Others, however, feel a high degree of identification with the organization and feel they possess the ability to deal with most situations. This latter type of subordinate is likely to be very receptive to a democratic leadership style and would reject the highly authoritarian style.

Situational factors are an influential element in leader behavior. The number of individuals involved in a problem requiring action will affect the degree of participation possible. For example, it is unlikely that even the most democratic leader could consult with two hundred field staff about a new program. The pressure of time is also likely to increase the degree of authoritarianism in leadership style. In a crisis situation it is more difficult to involve others. Geographic proximity and the ease with which people can interact also are situational variables that affect the style of leadership. Widely dispersed units or highly mechanized kinds of operations make interaction difficult and thereby reduce the chance for participative decision-making.

Evaluating and Controlling

Throughout the discussion of administration we have placed great emphasis upon ensuring that each activity is consistent with the objectives and goals of the agency. How are we to ascertain the extent to which these objectives are being obtained? How are we to determine if an alternative program might improve overall service delivery? How are we to provide flexibility in service delivery to meet the changing needs of clients? How are we to respond to the legislative call for accountability? The answer to each of these questions is—through an evaluation and control system.

A primary problem facing all administrators is the determination of the extent to which their unit is accomplishing what it was established to do. A good program evaluation system, coupled with adequate managerial control, is an essential element of the administrative system. Such a system contains four critical elements: establishing standards for performance; information-gathering; information analysis; and deviation correction.

Establishing standards for performance involves translating the goal or goals of a program into measurable indicators of success. Care must be exercised to ensure that indicators are developed for all outcomes, both those intended and those not intended. For example, the goal of increasing client purchasing power by 50 percent may have the unintended consequence of increasing price levels, thereby negating the higher income. Unless both of these indicators are considered in evaluating the program, incorrect conclusions will result. A second major factor to be considered is that the goals of many social programs tend to be ambiguous and, therefore, create difficulties in establishing measurable standards. The temptation is great in these cases to substitute hunches and unsupported claims for more objective criteria. This temptation must be resisted if we are to improve the operation of social welfare delivery systems.

The compilation, analysis, and comparison of information necessary to evaluation incorporates most of the commonly used research methods. Information for analysis may be collected from a wide variety of sources, including budgets, published statistics, client records, and interviews. Similarly, there is a wide variety of experimental designs and statistical techniques available for the purposes of evaluation. A word of caution is necessary. Many times the evaluator is faced with "information overkill" and must pause to evaluate the contribution of given bits of information. For example, a great deal of time and effort can go into the accumulation of very precise financial data related to supplies purchased for a program, only to discover that total funds expended on supplies accounts for less than one percent of total costs. In such a situation, the costs of supplies contribute little to our evaluation of the program. Similarly, the sophistication of the statistical tests performed in evaluation should be comparable to the level of sophistication of the information being measured. Again, much time and expensive effort can be spent in performing intricate and complex statistical comparisons that add little to our basic understanding of the program being evaluated.

The final and perhaps the key element in the evaluation process is that of correction. It must be remembered that evaluation is a tool of management control and, as such, should result in improved program administration. Finding out what is wrong with a unit or program is meaningless unless such knowledge is used to correct the problem and improve the service. It is in this way that evaluation is a means of control. It controls the movement of the organization toward the objective by providing the information to correct the course when there is deviation from the planned progress toward the objective.

Importance of Good Communications

All organizations must ultimately depend upon people to meet their objectives. To perform effectively, these individuals must depend upon the exchange of information and the directions they receive about functions to perform, methods to be used, and progress of the various units within the organization toward goals. In this context the manager is responsible for establishing the type of multidimensional communications network that will ensure unambiguous directions for subordinates as well as maintaining contact with superiors and with other units within the organization. Any communication involves four elements: the person sending the message; the thoughts to be transmitted; the person who is to receive the thoughts; and the feedback system. The communicator must decide who is to receive the message, then must plan carefully what is to be communicated, and how it is to be communicated. The message itself must be free from semantic barriers, such as jargon and technical language, and should be construed with the receiver in mind. The receiver, of course, must be aware of the message, its purpose, and be free of biases that will obstruct reception. Without some form of feedback, it is impossible to determine whether the message has been understood. Some form of feedback should accompany or be an integral part of any message, since without this feedback we are not certain whether there has been any actual communicating.

There are many barriers to communications, both organizational and human. One need only look at the organizational communications chart of the large organization to see how someone may be omitted from a communications chain and how difficult it would be to develop a truly one-way communication process. Similarly, differences in education, background, and environment of individuals can act to preclude understanding of any communication on personal relationship problems. It is essential for the successful manager to understand the basic principles of communication and to apply these principles in such a way as to stress the removal of these barriers.

Importance of the Administrator

Throughout our discussion of the administrative process we assumed an important element—implementation. A plan must be placed in operation; organization structure requires decision; leadership implies direction; and evaluation must lead to action. Thus, the ability of an administrator-manager to make the correct decision weighs most heavily on the ultimate success of the manager, program, and organization.

Managerial decision-making, like any situation requiring problem-solving, contains four basic elements. First, the manager must assess the situation and find the element that needs action. This requires an investigation into the causes of unsatisfactory performance to determine what outcome is necessary to a satisfactory solution. Second, the manager must formulate alternative solutions that may yield the desired outcome. The third step in the decision-making process is the analysis of the alternatives. This analysis may range from a simple listing of advantages and disadvantages associated with each alternative to highly sophisticated mathematical formulations. The final critical element in decision-making is the choice and implementation of a solution. This involves putting together a definite plan of attack and communicating this decision to all those with a role in the implementation.

REFERENCES

1. Joseph L. Massie, *Essentials of Management* (Englewood Cliffs, N.J.: Prentice-Hall, 1971), p. 4.
2. Peter F. Drucker, *Management: Tasks, Responsibilities, Practices* (New York: Harper & Row, 1974), p. 40.
3. Henry L. Sisk, *Management and Organization*, 3rd ed. (Cincinnati, Ohio: Southwestern, 1977), p. 9.
4. Henry Mintzberg, *The Nature of Managerial Work* (New York: Harper & Row, 1973), pp. 92–93.

5. Rino J. Patti, "Patterns of Management Activity in Social Welfare Agencies," *Administration in Social Work* (Spring 1977), pp. 5–17.

6. *Ibid.*, p. 8.

7. For examples of other studies see: Sune Carlson, *Executive Behavior* (Stockholm: Strombergs, 1951); Rosemary Stewart, *Managers and Their Jobs* (London: Macmillan, 1968).

8. Grover Starling, *Managing the Public Sector* (Homewood, Ill.: The Dorsey Press, 1977), p. 128.

9. *Ibid.*, p. 346.

QUESTIONS FOR DISCUSSION

1. Why should administrators be concerned with social, political, economic, and cultural values? Is it not likely that these things have already received enough attention in the policy formulation and planning process?

2. The authors state that administration is a cooperative venture with staff. In your experience, is this statement a fair description of the true state of affairs?

3. Do you agree that administrators should generally not provide direct services to clients? Would it not make sense for administrators to "get their hands dirty" with some of the work of the agency?

4. Evaluate Mintzberg's ten administrative roles. Can you add to the list?

5. React to Patti's finding that 40 percent of the manager's time is spent in planning, controlling, and supervising. Does this use of time seem appropriate?

6. Of the styles discussed, what kind of leadership seems most appropriate in social agencies? Why?

7. Discuss the implications of the authors' idea that evaluation is a means of improving program administration. What are the positive aspects of evaluation? In what ways can evaluation be misused?

8. Could health and welfare agencies operate without administrators? What kind of an organizational structure would be possible if there were no administrators or managers?

SUGGESTED PROJECTS

1. Visit a social service agency and interview the administrator. Using the Patti model ask the administrator to rank in order of priority the thir-

teen managerial activities. Discuss each managerial activity with the administrator and then assess the significance of each activity relative to the overall administration of the agency.

2. Using the Mintzberg model of roles, discuss and analyze the managerial functions of a selected administrator in a social service agency.

3. Propose and discuss an administrative system for a county department of public welfare.

FOR FURTHER READING

Walter H. Ehlers et al. *Administration for the Human Services: An Introductory Programmed Text.* New York: Harper & Row, 1976. Extremely useful for students at any level. The book is quite thorough in its treatment of the scope of administration but requires supplemental support to augment the material. It deals with administration from a traditional perspective and identifies the functions performed by the administrator: planning, organizing, staffing, coordinating, reporting, budgeting, and evaluating.

Justin G. Longenecker. *Principles of Management and Organizational Behavior,* 4th ed. (Columbus, Ohio: Charles E. Merrill, 1977). An introduction to the process of management that expands upon the concepts presented in this chapter. Like this chapter, the text focuses upon the manager's job and the behavior of people in an organizational setting.

Grover Starling. *Managing the Public Sector.* Homewood, Ill.: The Dorsey Press, 1977. Provides a basic understanding of the socio-politico-economic environment of public administration. Introduces the primary management tools in a readable and interesting fashion. The illustrations used throughout the book increase the readers' ability to understand and utilize the basic principles of management in the public sector.

Harleigh B. Trecker. *Social Work Administration: Principles and Practices.* New York: Association Press, 1971. An overall perspective of the process and function of administration in social work. Useful for the student who has little understanding of administration in social work. There is specific attention given to agency-community relations as well as client participation and cooperation in agency decision-making. The inclusion of illustrative cases allows the student to assess and apply the concepts and principles presented throughout the book.

Harold H. Weissman. *Overcoming Mismanagement in the Human Services Professions.* San Francisco: Jossey-Bass, 1974. A unique perspective on the management of the delivery service. It attacks the traditional response of the entrenched bureaucratic orientation and suggests new approaches that have the potential for success. Through the use of case studies from a variety of human service contexts, the student is given the opportunity to learn how to employ effective action.

12 *Prospects for the Future*

It is time to sum up where we are and to look down the road. In this concluding chapter, we want to make some comments on the present state of social welfare policy and to speculate on what may be before us. It is, of course, far easier to discuss where we are than it is to sort out the future. But, from our present vantage point, we think that we can discern some of these areas that will have an impact upon future social welfare policies.

In earlier chapters we were careful to point out that the policies that we used as alternatives were illustrative and not to be regarded as recommendations. We must now confess that we would not be surprised to see some of them come to pass in an altered, but still recognizable form. We think that these policies have promise—not because we stated them, but because it appears that others, far more influential than we, are also thinking about these alternatives. Further, some of the proposals do satisfy our criteria better than existing policy.

Let us return to our original premise of Chapter 1 and follow it through the succeeding chapters. We began by noting that social services are a given in the modern world and that they have deep roots. Although not everyone would agree with our belief that they are a natural outgrowth of the need for mutual aid, most would surely agree that throughout history there has been evidence of concern for other human beings. Whether one calls it mutual aid or prefers to call it humanism, a type of formalized social welfare is firmly entrenched in today's technological societies. The key question is not, "Should we have social welfare?" but rather, "What form should it take?" In Chapter 2 we argued that this question was influenced by societal values. Every society has its own prevailing definitions of the nature of social problems and works out solutions (or at least responses of some sort) based on those values. Even though societies differ on the nature of social problems, they all institutionalize ways of dealing with their problems. Sometimes societies' values lead to constructive and successful ways of dealing with problems, and the society and its members survive as a unit and grow as human beings. Sometimes, solutions are punitive and dehumanizing and the society and its individual members are brutalized, both persecutors and victims alike. The society does not survive, at least in the original form. It is only when a society's way of dealing with its social problems works for the benefit of everybody (or at least most people) that both institutions and individuals survive and grow.

In the United States we have a number of contradictory societal values. Therefore, it is not surprising that our social welfare system marches to an awkward drumbeat. We are all mixtures of rugged pioneer individualism (even if we do not come from pioneer stock) and a portion of caring concern for others. At one minute we rail against welfare cheaters and the next donate to a fund for sending poor children to summer camp. We oppose governmental intervention in our lives, but we expect the government to "do something" about a whole host of things. Our biggest stumbling block is our self-righteousness toward the poor while we accept that the rich may be hedonistic. Our second biggest problem is our lip service to rationality while we behave in irrational ways.

In Chapter 3 we presented a fledgling model for social welfare policy analysis and formulation that tries to take into account the various factors that bear on social welfare decision-making. We think it is a rational approach to a problem that has irrational elements involving politics, economics, and personal values. With this model, we examined five key areas in Chapters 4 through 8. Based upon our discussions of these key areas, we offer our conjectures of what the future holds.

Income Maintenance and Social Welfare Policy in the Future

The major issues that we raised in Chapter 4 regarding current policies were:

1. The mix of auspices for income maintenance programs: state, federal-state partnership, and federal.

2. The mix of aims and purposes.

3. The intent to make employers the primary source of financing for income maintenance programs.

4. The stress on work-connected benefits.

5. The preference for minimum benefits.

Will the mix of auspices continue? Will the diverse purposes of the income maintenance programs be simplified into one clear goal of income maintenance? Will the financial support base broaden to include employees or, as an alternative, all taxpayers? Will work-connectedness still be required for the payment of benefits? Will benefits continue to be minimal?

We think that the mix of auspices will continue for a while; however, we believe that the differences in benefits from unemployment insurance and workmen's compensation for each state may result in a challenge to their legality under the "equal protection" clause of the Constitution. If and when such a suit is pressed, change will occur. We suggest that the outcome will be a federal workmen's compensation program and a federally operated unemployment insurance system. *Then*, it will be obvious that one agency is better than three, and workmen's compensation and unemployment insurance will be integrated with RSDHI.

The mix of aims and purposes clearly can no longer continue. The inefficiency of this situation will be resolved along with the federalization of the programs.

The financial support bases will broaden. Taxes on employers have increased the cost of doing business to a critical degree. The Carter administration has proposed raising the employer's portion of RSDHI taxes to increase benefits. The idea of using money from general revenues to support RSDHI may be an idea that will be increasingly popular as the cost increases. Employers may agitate to shift the burden of workmen's compensation to the general revenue even in the absence of an "equal protection" suit. This will spread the tax burden more evenly.

Work-connectedness will, we think, persist the longest. This requirement's hardiness depends heavily on the work patterns of the future. Unless there is a tremendous displacement of workers due to technology (which we do not think will happen soon), we think that work will continue to be the major criterion for eligibility for income maintenance benefits, although we would prefer to see it deemphasized.

The preference for minimum benefits is already slipping. Social insurance benefits, at least in the case of RSDHI, are moving in the direction of adequacy. This movement is slow and there is a very long way to go, but the direction seems to be there.

Poverty

In Chapter 5 we said that the major policy that guided the approach to poverty in the United States was coerced work or stigmatized discomfort. We argued that the policy was heavily based on a self-righteous value position that equated poverty with moral or personal failure, rather than putting the blame on forces in the social system. It is true that individual cases can be found which appear to result from personal inadequacies, but poverty as a social problem is something more than just the sum total of "shiftlessness" in the population. The major obstacle to more effective policy is clearly our moral "hang-up" toward the poor. This prevents a more rationalistic view of the problem.

We suggested that it makes sense to us to redefine divorce, desertion, and unmarried parenthood as social risks, and to shift the programs that are now aimed at those enmeshed in these contingencies to a social insurance approach. We would encourage the federal government to raise the benefits from minimum levels to some semblance of adequacy, given the cost of living in the United States. We would not require work, but would make it available and provide the training necessary to make work rewarding. We think that CETA could provide the necessary prototype for a permanent structure of governmental employment. We would like to see certain services available—counseling services, family planning, legal services, and low-cost housing—on a voluntary basis, totally separated from financial services.

As of this writing, President Carter is recommending an approach that is not too far from where we think things should go—but there are important differences. The president's plan (as it has been currently reported) would guarantee an income above the poverty line, but would require work. There is no provision for training to equip people for jobs in private industry. Public service jobs, which the poor would be required to take, would pay at the minimum wage. This is based on the notion, apparently, that private employers who do not now pay the minimum wage would be forced to follow suit.

As we see it, the major problems with the president's plan are the following: (1) a lack of expanded opportunities for the mother or father with young children; (2) the lack of any means of training for private jobs; and (3) the work requirement, again. Basically, the Carter plan only changes structures. It does not represent a shift in policy, but continues the notion of coerced work with the alternative being stigmatized discomfort.

At the risk of boredom, we repeat that we think that any policy directed toward the problem of poverty that uses work as a moral activity, and forces it on people, is going to fail. Sound policy should make work attractive, offer training that can lead somewhere, and provide a permanent and meaningful job structure that can take up the slack in the private sector.

At least the Carter plan seeks to raise benefits in the direction of adequacy and recognizes the need to provide jobs. If the work requirement were eliminated and extended training opportunities provided, we think that the proposals would reflect a policy shift.

Some union leaders have opposed Carter's plan on the grounds that local governments might use any public service jobs created to displace persons already in the work force. Clearly, it is important that any jobs created by the Carter plan (if it comes to pass), or any alternative plan, be in areas that do not displace the present work force. We think that there are enough things that need doing that the problem need not arise. For example, there are enough tasks connected with cleaning up the environment, that are not now being done, to employ millions. We are not talking about the technical or engineering aspects, but simply tasks that can be done by people with few skills. There is time to build skilled positions in such a program—and managerial opportunities too—for those who have an interest in advancement but do not want to shift to private sector employment.

In a sense, the Carter proposals might be a step backward. His plan to reunite SSI with AFDC and food stamps may turn out to be a return to the public assistance approach. It is too soon to tell, however, and we prefer to think that the president's program moves in a more liberal direction.

It is too much, perhaps, to hope for the elimination of all poverty. The social mechanism of any society seems to continue creating new poor as old poor move out of poverty. However, we do hope that poverty can be reduced to a small and temporary problem for most people. It seems important to note that socialist countries have not solved all the problems of poverty, so it is still fair to say that poverty is a problem common to all societies.

Health and Mental Health

Clearly, the area of health and mental health care is an emergency situation. Health care costs have risen dramatically. The old system of "sick care" is no longer beneficial—and the concept of "preventive medicine" is not yet realized. It seems clear that the next step will be a national health insurance scheme of some sort with a co-payment feature. Some attempt will be made to keep costs to a relatively low level of increase. The incremental nature of policy change in the health care field probably means slow progress, but those managing the campaign have made a number of gains whose effect is cumulative. The increasingly heavy burdens of Medicaid on state budgets is a spur to a national health scheme. In an ironic sense, the persons most opposed to a national health plan may be the ones who provide the occasion for bringing it off. Doctors' fees, drug costs, and hospital bills have created powerful resentment and a climate in which action is all but inevitable. The health care establishment has not been as prudent or as cost conscious as it might have been.

For the immediate future, the community-based approach to mental health seems to be firmly entrenched. The days of the large state hospital are slowly, but surely, drawing to a close. Some states have already closed some hospitals in favor of smaller treatment centers closer to patients' home communities. It is harder to commit people to institutions in today's mental health system, and there is a new stress on patient rights. The suit *Wyatt* v. *Stuckney* has established a legal basis for the patient's right to treatment in humane and nonpunitive ways. We expect that the stress on patients' rights will continue.

As it was pointed out in Chapter 6, the community mental health concept may well have implications for health care delivery in general. There is some similarity between the two systems now. In Alabama, for instance, we have a fairly extensive community-based mental health service which combines outpatient service and the regional inpatient treatment center. Alongside the public system is, of course, the private psychiatrist and the private hospital. We also have a public health clinic system which treats people for many diseases and conditions that have been deemed public health problems. There is also a private health care system. How far away is the time when the publicly provided and private proprietary systems are options to traditional private care? They are options, to an extent, for the poor at this time. While it is not possible to foresee the exact resolution of the health care problem, it is conceivable that the United States may emerge with a physical health care system that closely resembles the mental health care system. It does appear unlikely, however, that a strictly socialized medical system in which physicians become governmental employees will come to pass. We think that the national health insurance scheme which leaves patients and doctors free to contract with each other is much more palatable to Americans.

Speculators will want to keep their eyes on the health maintenance organization concept. This appears to be a vehicle for the incorporation of virtues acceptable to both physicians and patients without the alleged faults of "government medicine."

Problems in Living Space

It seems to us that public housing, as we have known it, is dead. We doubt that any more public housing will be built—at least as mass produced high-rises. The cost of housing (as is true of the cost of medical care) will, however, prompt government to act. It is fairly clear that government will continue its successful policies in the support of home ownership. It is extremely unlikely that the mechanisms for insuring home mortgages and providing for the availability of capital will be dismembered. It is likely, however, that government will increase its subsidies for using the existing housing stock. It is also likely that American homes will get smaller, and more people will opt for apartment living; the ostentatious will, of course, continue to build monuments to themselves. Subsidies, coupled with strict enforcement of building codes, fire codes, and sensible zoning restrictions, would go a long way toward solution of America's housing problems. Restoration of sound structures is much cheaper than mass destruction of neighborhoods, and this movement is gaining strength.

While all of this is somewhat short term and only buys time, time is on the side of improved housing. If the population continues toward zero growth, there will not be a need for an unrestrained explosion of homes in the future. While it is true that there is a population shift to the so-called "sun belt," this phenomenon will probably be limited by the availability of land and water sources. Besides, the South can see what has happened as a result of unrestrained growth in the Northeast and act in the light of that knowledge. Some shift in the population can be helpful, provided that wholesale destruction of homes that have been left behind does not occur.

In short, we think that a judicious use of subsidies to the consumer is an idea whose time has come. This will give the poor more leverage as consumers. The growth of community organizations that can act for the poor will help to keep the landlord honest.

Service Delivery

We want to repeat the point we made in Chapter 8. We think that the policy aspects of service delivery need a good shaking up. Service delivery is largely as it was in the nineteenth century. Even medicine, which is certainly the most hoary conservative field around, has changed from the image of the old country doctor carrying his nostrums from house to house in his little black bag. The modern physician, if one can afford the services, can do a lot more for the patient—and can see more patients, in a modern group clinic. The rise of the new breed of emergency room physicians, while an expensive way to practice medicine, offers a dynamic mode of crisis intervention. The use of therapeutic groups, the crisis center, the hotline, are all innovations of which social workers can be proud. We would like to think that the constraints of the waiting list, the standard fifty-minute hour, and the interminable course of weekly interviews are anachronistic. Surely, some clients need only fifteen minutes, while others may need two hours a week; and some clients' problems can be handled on a group basis. A great deal of flexibility in service delivery is needed.

We think that the innovations that social workers have developed in the past ten years or so need no longer be regarded as unwanted stepchildren. Schools of social work have inadvertently maintained the model of the traditional practitioner and actually lag behind the field's practices. We think that the independent social work practitioner who has to compete with other practitioners is going to be more responsive to consumer need. Certainly, the increase in private practice is a healthy sign. Now that third-party insurance payments are possible, we see the ground being laid for the kind of group practice that we think would be much more in keeping with the twentieth century. One can picture a facility to which one would turn for help, staffed with specialists in specific problem areas that could offer services at individual, group, and community levels. Such a firm could also contract planning services.

This is not so wild as it may sound at first hearing. There are agencies in existence now that work very much like our suggested approach. One agency in the Midwest will contract with any group or individual for a number of social services. A planning agency in the South has moved out from under United Fund control and now, in effect, is a planning and consulting firm. We think that so-called private practice has another advantage—it gives people the right to determine when and how they shall have counseling.

Conclusion

If there is a key to the future, it is perhaps best expressed in the old social work value of self-determination. Probably the most critical thing that one can say of the welfare policy of the United States is that over it all lingers the ghost of a more paternalistic era.

We think that the consumer's turn has finally come in social welfare. Social workers and other social welfare personnel are under a great deal of pressure to be accountable—and accountability increasingly involves client wishes. We believe that the whole institutional network of social service is moving toward a more appropriate balance between service providers and service users. It is no longer possible to plan services for people. Service providers must learn to plan with the consumer.

It is clear that the social insurances as they presently exist do not suit their beneficiaries. It is also clear that the poor are not willing to be passive recipients of social and economic leftovers. Medical care, housing, and social services all have their own consumer-critics.

We believe that the only salvation lies in a reaffirmation of the basic human value of mutuality. This is not a time for power struggles, since the social welfare complex is surely less powerful than its opponents. We think that the social welfare enterprise is naturally inclined toward mutuality, anyway, because of its commitment to human values.

There are a number of social forces that are interested in rational new social welfare policy decisions. Further, these forces have learned to participate in the formulation of policy and the creation of programs. Some of the gains in RSDHI coverage are the result of lobbying efforts and media campaigns of older citizens. The poor too have found strength by organizing and have become allies. Even though most American poor are white, it has been the black organizations that have taken the lead in forcing policy makers to program for the poor. In short, the consumer has learned to organize, to confront, and to use the media for an airing of grievances. The class-action suit has become a powerful weapon for the redress of grievances. Legislative action, exemplified by Title XX of the Social Security Act, has caused what may become an important policy shift.

Consumers are moving from a state of powerlessness into a position of equality with those who deliver the services. Blacks, women, the old, mental patients, the handicapped—citizens in general—have had their consciousness raised and will no longer settle for less. It is vital to note that none of these groups has demanded a position superior to others. Their demands are for equal treatment, decency, and justice. The social welfare enterprise must not take refuge in a narrow concept of professionalism, but must continue to think and act boldly. As new policies are needed, social workers and other social welfare personnel must be ready with useful strategies for policy analysis and formulation, sound planning, equitable administrative techniques, and effective implementation of mutually beneficial social welfare policy.

QUESTIONS FOR DISCUSSION

1. Is it really practical to move toward a unified social insurance scheme? Won't states continue to want to exercise their prerogatives of planning for local needs?
2. Is the mix of aims of the individual social insurances necessarily bad? Build a case for *not* making the changes recommended in this book.

3. Sweden supposedly has no poverty. Has the Swedish approach really achieved this end? Are there lessons in the Swedish experience for American social welfare policy?

4. Is there a practical, workable way to totally end the work requirement in public assistance plans?

5. England has a health care system largely supported by general taxation, although neither doctors nor patients are compelled to be part of it. Do you think that American plans for national health care will parallel the British system?

6. Do you think that the swing toward patient rights has gone too far?

7. Is consumer subsidy a viable plan for the provision of housing? Do you think the future will bring a radical change in housing patterns in the United States?

8. Do you look for much real change in the way services are delivered in the immediate future? Will the innovations that have been developed really become widespread, or will they remain only infrequently encountered options?

9. Can American professionals, including social workers, live with consumer militancy? Are we not heading for a crisis situation in which experts and consumers engage in behavior harmful to both groups?

SUGGESTED PROJECTS

1. Having read this book, evaluate the use of "welfare as mutual aid" as the underlying theme of social welfare policy.

2. Invite a person to class who is involved with social welfare policy. Ask him or her to discuss the probable changes in social welfare policy within the next ten years.

3. Do your own forecasting. Organize a panel discussion using students who have experience in each of the five fields of policy covered in this book. What does the future hold from the students' point of view?

FOR FURTHER READING

Daniel Bell. *The Coming of Post-Industrial Society.* New York: Basic Books, 1973. A look at the year 2000 by one of the country's most respected social thinkers. This book has greatly influenced our belief in the triumph of pluralism and mutuality in the future.

Harleigh Trecker, ed., *Goals for Social Welfare 1973–1993*. New York: Association Press, 1973. A look at the future from the vantage point of 1973 by a number of social work educators who really deserve the adjective "distinguished." They, too, talk of opening up society, including social work, to increasing citizen participation.

Social Work, Vol. 22, No. 5 (September 1977). An entire issue devoted to the question of conceptual frameworks for social work practice. While not precisely a future-oriented series of articles, these papers are important for their insight into social work's continual self-assessment process.

Index